The Just Shall Live by Faith Series

Principles for Life

USING BIBLICAL PRINCIPLES TO BRING DYNAMIC PSYCHOLOGICAL HEALING

Dr. Troy Reiner

Reiner **Publishing**

Unless otherwise noted, Scripture quotations in this book are taken from the King James Version of the Bible.

Scripture references marked AMP are taken from The "Amplified" trademark is registered in the United States Patent and Trademark Office by The Lockman Foundation. Use of this trademark requires the permission of The Lockman Foundation.

Scripture references marked NLT are taken from Holy Bible. New Living Translation copyright © 1996 by Tyndale Charitable Trust. Used by permission of Tyndale House Publishers.

Scripture references marked NIV are taken from the Holy Bible, New International Version, Copyright © 1973, 1978, 1984 by the International Bible Society. Used by permission of Zondervan Publishing House. The "NIV" and "New International Version" trademarks are registered in the United States Patent and Trademark Office by International Bible Society.

Scripture references marked WEY are taken from Weymouth: The Modern Speech New Testament by Richard F. Weymouth, 3rd Edition (1912), Revised & edited by E. Hampden-Cooke.

Cover Photograph by Micah Goulart

ISBN 978-0-9903856-2-2
Library of Congress Catalog Card Number: 2005905979

Table of Contents

Introduction

Our world is full of hurting people. The Word of God is the answer but somehow attempts to apply biblical principles to bring psychological healing have fallen short of the deeper needs of many of these hurting people. This has been true for several reasons.

First, most classical models of biblical change have been limited to either confronting and demanding change, or acting and practicing new biblical ways of doing things. These methods do not deal with the entire person: will, spirit, mind, perceptions, needs, motivation, actions, experiences, and emotions. They do not adequately take into account the complexity of the human heart and the interactions between its members. Applying simplistic solutions to complex problems cannot provide the deep healing so desperately needed.

Second, even though I and others have developed biblical counseling models for treating many of the more complex problems faced in the church today (see my books *Faith Therapy, Transformation! and Revelations That Will Set You Free*), there are still many other types of problems not specifically addressed in the Bible. This is especially true concerning the more-difficult types of mental illness listed in the Diagnostic and Statistical Manual of Mental Disorders (DSM IV). Therefore, it is essential that we develop a comprehensive plan for resolving problems using biblical principles for which we do not yet have a counseling model. This method must use biblical principles in such a way as to bring dynamic healing to the whole person: will, mind, emotions and spirit.

Third, many who attempt to apply biblical principles to help other people do not really have an in-depth understanding of these principles or specific proven techniques for applying them to difficult psychological problems. They may have studied their Bible, gone to seminars, and listened to anointed preaching for most of their lives but still do not understand them as an integrated whole. In order to effectively address the many types of difficult problems facing the church today, it is critical that Christian counselors more adequately understand the basic principles of the Bible and that they have more effective methods and techniques for applying them to complex problems in order to help their clients.

In order to address all three of these problems, this book has been designed to provide a fundamental understanding of many of the most important principles in the Bible as an integrated whole, present methods and techniques for applying these principles to effect lasting change, and develop a detailed process for building complex counseling plans using biblical principles. It addresses the complexities of the human heart through the use of the "Train of Psychological Wholeness," a concept derived from Proverbs Chapter 3. The overall goal of this book is to provide the tools necessary for more effectively applying biblical principles to a wide range of psychological problems in such a way as to bring about dynamic spiritual and psychological healing of the entire person.

The reader should understand the nature of principles. They are general laws that apply to most situations. They are usually presented in somewhat absolute terms with the expectation that they must be applied with wisdom. They are useful because they give us an overall picture concerning how things generally are. However, that does not mean that there are no exceptions, especially under extreme circumstances, to the application of a particular principle. For example, the Sermon on the Mount (Matthew Chapters 5-7) expounds the principles of the Kingdom of God. However, in Matthew 7:6 it warns us not to apply these principles to depraved individuals (dogs and swine) "lest they trample them under their feet, and turn again and rend you."

This book is part of a complete system for implementing salvation-based therapy within the church. The remaining three books in the series – *Faith Therapy, Transformation!, and Revelations That Set You Free* – provide an in-depth understanding of the process of salvation by faith, tools for applying faith in counseling, a detailed plan for the conduct of counseling, biblical models for addressing the most complex and difficult problems, and a comprehensive roadmap for psychological and spiritual growth.

I want specifically to thank all of my clients and students, my wife, Nancy, my mother, Hildegard, my daughter, Sarah, and our assistant administrator, Loretta Goetting for their contributions in preparing this manuscript for publication. My gratitude also goes to Athena Dean and all the other wonderful people at Pleasant Word Publishing for their patience and assistance in publishing this book.

All Bible references are from the Authorized Version (AV) of the King James Bible, The New Living Translation (NLT), or the Weymouth New Testament (WEY). These versions of the Bible are quoted as originally written and therefore spelling, grammar and capitalization may not agree with modern usage. For example, in my writing I have chosen to capitalize all references to God. This is not done in the King James Version of the Bible. Greek, Hebrew, most Bible translations and biblical dictionary references are obtained and quoted directly from The Online Bible Millennium Edition (2000) by Larry Pierce.

It is my hope that this book will provide the information, tools, and detailed understanding required for more effectively using biblical principles within our churches in order to provide the help for emotionally and psychologically hurting people that our Lord promised when He said "You shall know the truth and the truth shall make you free." (John 8:32)

PART I

Principles of Biblical Change

Chapter 1

Biblical Principles

Change is possibly the one absolute in life. Nothing stays the same for long. This is especially true concerning our circumstances and our lives. Still, there are forces, especially in humans, that resist positive change as well as forces that precipitate change in a negative direction. In fact, without intervention of any sort, nature moves in the direction of disorganization and deterioration, rather than toward wholeness. It is God who develops, improves and creates; and it is Satan who attempts to steal, kill and destroy. (John 10:10) However, we must understand that it is not the forces outside of us, but those on the inside that have the greatest influence on us and provide the greatest potential for change.

In the Bible, God provides the truth, the basic principles for life and the counseling models. The truth is just a statement of how things actually are. The direct application of a specific truth many times is sufficient to effect change in simple problems of limited scope and complexity. Principles are combinations of truth. Many of the more moderate problems can be resolved through the application of these basic principles if they are applied to influence the whole person using a number of interventions or techniques. The more complex and difficult problems require a more in-depth understanding of the problem and specific guidance on how to resolve them. These require counseling models or plans that tell us how to approach and apply a specific number of principles to resolve these complex problems. As an analogy, statements of truth are the street signs, principles are the written instructions; and counseling models and plans are the maps to life.

Through God's Word, we are given an understanding of the world in which we live, the spirit world that we cannot see, and a glimpse into the future world that is to come. The process of change toward wholeness is brought about primarily through our knowledge of God and His process of salvation by faith. However, it is through the application of the truth, principles, and models (or plans) embodied in God's Word that we are able to remove the roadblocks that hinder this process. However, whether we act, change our viewpoint or transform our heart is dependent on whether we believe the truth that we have been taught. Without faith, change will not happen. Without an understanding of the Bible's truth, the basic biblical principles, and the more complex biblical models, we are lost and at the mercy of the world's system without any direction, without tools to effect change, and adrift in the sea of life. (For more on these issues see my books *Faith Therapy* and *Revelations That Will Set You Free.*)

Types of Biblical Principles

Biblical principles are combinations of biblical truths focused on a particular area of interest and designed for application in that area. In order to understand clearly how to employ specific biblical principles, we must ask the question, "principles of what?" Biblical principles fall into several categories: 1. Those that give us information about the physical and spiritual world (worldview). 2. Those that tell us what to do or not do (the law). 3. Those that tell us how to do it (application). 4. Those that tell us how to transform our lives (change). Each particular type of principle is designed to assist us in different ways.

1. <u>Principles Related to Worldview.</u> These principles, that tell us about the physical and spiritual world in which we live, help us to change our perceptions of our world and can result in a paradigm shift. They run counter to what we have learned from the world and challenge us to change how we perceive our world. This is the place of narrative therapy and the teaching of biblical stories and parables. If we believe the metanarrative (an overall explanation of the meaning of life in our world) of the Bible and become saved, our life will change forever because we will perceive life through a biblical worldview. Bible principles also have the same effect to the extent that we believe them. If, when we learn these Bible principles, we change how we perceive our world and ourselves, we will act, think, or feel according to these new perceptions.

2. <u>Principles of the Law.</u> Those principles, that tell us what to do and what not to do, provide boundaries for our thoughts, attitudes and actions. These eventually affect our emotions. They are useful to help us to identify our areas of dysfunction, change our ways and purify our lives. Sin is the symptom that tells us that we have a problem. When we break a law, we usually learn by our consequences that we need to change; but we do not necessarily understand how to change. Even if we are able to change our actions, the underlying problem may still exist and may resurface at another time or in another way. Historically, the identification of what is wrong and changing how a person acts has been the major focus of "biblical counseling."

3. <u>Principles for Application.</u> Those principles, that tell us how to do something, give us a plan of how to accomplish what we have been commanded to do in our lives. These principles give us the capability to know how to do things, but that does not necessarily make us want to do them. Without these principles, we might know that we should pray and that our prayerlessness is an indication that we have a problem, but we would not know how to pray.

4. <u>Principles of Change.</u> Those principles, that tell us how to change, give us a more in-depth understanding of how we function so that we can permanently make changes in our lives. Even if we know that we should do something and we know how to do it, we may not yet understand why we still do not do it, or why we are still motivated to sin. These principles delve into the complexities of the human heart.

The Principles of Change

1. <u>God desires right actions, right motivation, and right thinking.</u> Even when we act right, God sees our right actions as filthy rags if they are motivated by selfishness. If we think evil thoughts, to God it is the same as if we actually did them because we really wanted to do evil in our hearts.

Mt 25:34 Then shall the King say unto them on his right hand, Come, ye blessed of my Father, inherit the kingdom prepared for you from the foundation of the world:

35 For I was an hungred, and ye gave me meat: I was thirsty, and ye gave me drink: I was a stranger, and ye took me in:

36 Naked, and ye clothed me: I was sick, and ye visited me: I was in prison, and ye came unto me.

37 Then shall the righteous answer him, saying, Lord, when saw we thee an hungred, and fed [thee]? or thirsty, and gave [thee] drink?

38 When saw we thee a stranger, and took [thee] in? or naked, and clothed [thee]?

39 Or when saw we thee sick, or in prison, and came unto thee?

40 And the King shall answer and say unto them, Verily I say unto you, Inasmuch as ye have done [it] unto one of the least of these my brethren, ye have done [it] unto me.

Isa 64:6 But we are all as an unclean thing, and all our righteousnesses are as filthy rags; and we all do fade as a leaf; and our iniquities, like the wind, have taken us away.

Mt 5:28 But I say unto you, That whosoever looketh on a woman to lust after her hath committed adultery with her already in his heart.

2. Righteousness results from sowing right deeds. However, it is important for us to understand that to God deeds include thoughts, words and actions. Entertaining wrong thoughts can be just as much of a sin as speaking or doing something evil. We can sow good or bad seed through our thoughts, words or actions.

    Ga 6:7 Be not deceived; God is not mocked: for whatsoever a man soweth, that shall he also reap.

    8 For he that soweth to his flesh shall of the flesh reap corruption; but he that soweth to the Spirit shall of the Spirit reap life everlasting.

3. Wholeness requires a pure heart. Because our heart determines what we think, say, and do, we cannot hope to become whole or healthy without purifying our heart from evil. We can only truly love (or have the best interests of others in mind) if we have a pure heart devoid of selfishness.

    1 Ti 1:5 Now the end of the commandment is charity out of a pure heart, and *of* a good conscience, and *of* faith unfeigned:

4. Understanding the heart is difficult but necessary. If we do not understand our own hearts, we cannot purify them or have any control over our thoughts, words or actions.

    Jer 17:9 The heart [is] deceitful above all [things], and desperately wicked: who can know it?

    10 I the LORD search the heart, [I] try the reins, even to give every man according to his ways, [and] according to the fruit of his doings.

    Pr 4:23 Keep thy heart with all diligence; for out of it are the issues of life.

5. The heart consists of our mind, emotions, will, and spirit. This is clear from the definition of the Greek word *kardia* which denotes "the center of all physical and spiritual life." We can also prove this to ourselves by examining the verses listed below when we realize that we understand with our mind, we love with our emotion, we intend with our will, and we are condemned by our conscience, which is part of our spirit.

    a. Mind: Mt 13:15 For this people's heart is waxed gross, and [their] ears are dull of hearing, and their eyes they have closed; lest at any time they should see with [their] eyes, and hear with [their] ears, and should understand with [their] heart, and should be converted, and I should heal them.
    b. Emotions: Mr 12:33 And to love him with all the heart, and with all the understanding, and with all the soul, and with all the strength, and to love [his] neighbour as himself, is more than all whole burnt offerings and sacrifices.
    c. Will: Heb 4:12 For the word of God [is] quick, and powerful, and sharper than any twoedged sword, piercing even to the dividing asunder of soul and spirit, and of the joints and marrow, and [is] a discerner of the thoughts and intents of the heart.
    d. Spirit: 1 Jo 3:20 For if our heart condemn us, God is greater than our heart, and knoweth all things.

6. <u>We are changed at the deepest level by what we believe.</u> In my book, *Faith Therapy,* I explain how the process of salvation changes us from the inside out at the need or root cause level through faith. As we believe that God has and always will meet all our needs (including our psychological needs for security, love, worth, and significance), we are set free from our selfishness (bias toward the self) to truly love others for the first time. Through faith, we can feel secure in every situation, experience so much love from God that all we want to do is give it away, feel completely worthwhile, and see ourselves as so significant that we cannot possibly ever become more significant.

    Ro 10:9 That if thou shalt confess with thy mouth the Lord Jesus, and shalt believe in thine heart that God hath raised him from the dead, thou shalt be saved.

    3:22 Even the righteousness of God which is by faith of Jesus Christ unto all and upon all them that believe: for there is no difference:

    Jo 20:31 But these are written, that ye might believe that Jesus is the Christ, the Son of God; and that believing ye might have life through his name.

Over the years, since the time of Christ, a number of specific methods of change based on the Bible have been developed which provide the basis for what is today called biblical counseling. These methods can be categorized into several basic approaches. Unfortunately, all are somewhat limited in scope and application. Each can be effective in its own area of application and each can teach us something about how we, as people, function psychologically.

The Methods of Change

1. <u>Acting on the Word of God.</u> At its most fundamental level, change comes simply by choosing to act according to the Word of God. If we simply obey what we are told, we will be blessed in what we do.

    Jas 1:22 But be ye doers of the word, and not hearers only, deceiving your own selves.

    25 But whoso looketh into the perfect law of liberty, and continueth [therein], he being not a forgetful hearer, but a doer of the work, this man shall be blessed in his deed.

    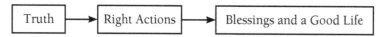

2. <u>Replacing the lies we believe in our minds with the truth.</u> This method is based on the renewing of our mind. It is clearly presented in *Search for Significance* (1990). When we recognize an ungodly emotion, motivation or desire, it indicates that we have believed a lie in our mind that has resulted in this feeling. If we do nothing about the lie, it will eventually result in wrong actions. We need to search our hearts to discover the lie and then replace it with the truth. When we do, the truth will result in Godly emotions (which will replace the original ungodly ones) and we will then be predisposed to take Godly actions.

    Ro 12:2 And be not conformed to this world: but be ye transformed by the renewing of your mind, that ye may prove what is that good, and acceptable, and perfect, will of God.

    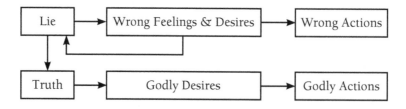

3. <u>Replace old behaviors with new ones.</u> This is called the "put off, put on" method of biblical counseling. This method recognizes that there is a void to be filled when we stop doing evil and that this void needs to be filled with positive action if the change is to be long lasting.

    Eph 4:25 Wherefore putting away lying, speak every man truth with his neighbour: for we are members one of another.

    28 Let him that stole steal no more: but rather let him labour, working with his hands the thing which is good, that he may have to give to him that needeth.

    29 Let no corrupt communication proceed out of your mouth, but that which is good to the use of edifying, that it may minister grace unto the hearers.

4. <u>We are changed by the way we perceive things.</u> This is what has been called a paradigm shift. The underlying principle is that we will act according to the way we see ourselves and our circumstances. In marriage counseling, this has been called "reframing." Valid perceptions bring valid actions.

    Lu 11:34 The light of the body is the eye: therefore when thine eye is single, thy whole body also is full of light; but when thine eye is evil, thy body also is full of darkness.

    35 Take heed therefore that the light which is in thee be not darkness.

    36 If thy whole body therefore be full of light, having no part dark, the whole shall be full of light, as when the bright shining of a candle doth give thee light.

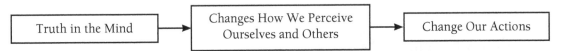

5. <u>Accountability can motivate us to change.</u> Accountability partners, support groups and other people who love us, can motivate us to face our faults and change. Adding caring prayer can be very effective. This is a type of external motivation.

    Jas 5:16 Confess [your] faults one to another, and pray one for another, that ye may be healed. The effectual fervent prayer of a righteous man availeth much.

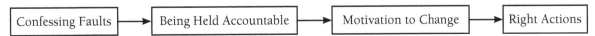

6. <u>Temptations can be overcome if we will submit to God and resist the devil.</u> Many times we have made the mistake of trying to resist without first submitting ourselves to God and trusting Him to help us.

    Jas 4:7 Submit yourselves therefore to God. Resist the devil, and he will flee from you.

7. <u>We can change the consequences in our life by changing the actions that we sow.</u> This is what has been called sowing and reaping. It has been particularly applied to giving to God and to the conflict between the flesh and spirit. Your crop will be determined by what you have planted.

Ga 6:7 Be not deceived; God is not mocked: for whatsoever a man soweth, that shall he also reap.

8 For he that soweth to his flesh shall of the flesh reap corruption; but he that soweth to the Spirit shall of the Spirit reap life everlasting.

8. <u>Recognize our fallen state, repent, and act correctly.</u> These are the methods suggested by Jay Adams (1973), who is probably one of the best known authors concerning classical biblical counseling. His method of biblical change called *noutheteo* counseling is to confront what the person is doing as sin and demand that they repent. If they do repent, their life is changed. It provides a very direct approach to counseling.

Re 2:4 Nevertheless I have [somewhat] against thee, because thou hast left thy first love.

5 Remember therefore from whence thou art fallen, and repent, and do the first works; or else I will come unto thee quickly, and will remove thy candlestick out of his place, except thou repent.

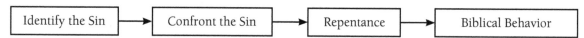

9. <u>Teaching, confronting, correcting, and instructing in God's principles.</u> The Biblical Counseling Foundation suggests a four step change process: 1. See it as God does. 2. Build Biblical hope. 3. Put off the wrong behavior and put on the new behavior. 4. Practice the new behavior. (*Biblical Principles for Discipleship/Counseling*, 1998, p. 13)

2 Ti 3:16 All scripture [is] given by inspiration of God, and [is] profitable for doctrine, for reproof, for correction, for instruction in righteousness:

17 That the man of God may be perfect, thoroughly furnished unto all good works.

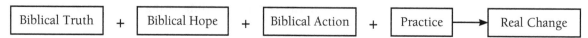

10. <u>Spiritual hindrances can be removed by casting out evil spirits.</u> Because Christ has given us power over all the power of the enemy, we have a right to cast them out in Jesus name. Although this has sometimes been excessively applied by some Christian groups, it still has application in biblical counseling.

Lu 10:19 Behold, I give unto you power to tread on serpents and scorpions, and over all the power of the enemy: and nothing shall by any means hurt you.

11. <u>We can find the promised way of escape to overcome temptation.</u> This method helps the client overcome temptation when he feels overwhelmed. Since God has promised that there would always be a way of escape in every circumstance, the counselor encourages the client and assists him in finding the way of escape.

1 Co 10:13 There hath no temptation taken you but such as is common to man: but God is faithful, who will not suffer you to be tempted above that ye are able; but will with the temptation also make a way to escape, that ye may be able to bear it.

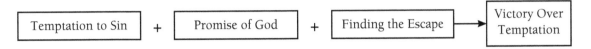

12. <u>The spiritual armor of God protects us from attack.</u> Some of us have even gone so far as to "put on the armor of God" each morning when we arose to make this promise more real to ourselves. Of course, the real emphasis here is that God has given us His truth to resist the lies or "fiery darts" of the devil so that they will not harm us. We do not have to accept the devil's ideas or the thoughts that he attempts to plant in our minds.

Eph 6:13 Wherefore take unto you the whole armour of God, that ye may be able to withstand in the evil day, and having done all, to stand.

14 Stand therefore, having your loins girt about with truth, and having on the breastplate of righteousness;

15 And your feet shod with the preparation of the gospel of peace;

16 Above all, taking the shield of faith, wherewith ye shall be able to quench all the fiery darts of the wicked.

17 And take the helmet of salvation, and the sword of the Spirit, which is the word of God:

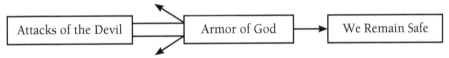

13. <u>Past and present experiences can be healed through changing our perceptions of them and releasing them to God through forgiveness.</u> Although we cannot change a past experience, we can change how it affects us by how we perceive it and process our feelings concerning it. One of these methods is Theophostic ministry (Smith, 1996) which invites the Holy Spirit to reveal God's truth about the event in order to change our perception of that event. Through forgiveness, we give up our rights to take vengeance for the offense to God; and, therefore, release ourselves from the responsibly to personally resolve it.

Jo 16:13 Howbeit when he, the Spirit of truth, is come, he will guide you into all truth: for he shall not speak of himself; but whatsoever he shall hear, that shall he speak: and he will shew you things to come.

Col 3:13 Forbearing one another, and forgiving one another, if any man have a quarrel against any: even as Christ forgave you, so also do ye.

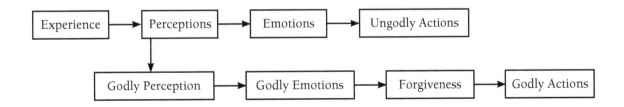

Chapter 2

The Train of
Psychological Wholeness

A Biblical Model for Psychological Wholeness

Although each of the methods presented in the last chapter are clearly biblical and valid in their areas of application, they unfortunately do little to address much of the complexity of the human heart. In fact, even the idea that the heart consists of the will, mind, emotions, and spirit is too simplistic for actual application. Many of these parts have multiple functions and interact with each other. For example, we use our mind to store information concerning what we believe is true, logically process that information, and use it to evaluate our experiences. How we evaluate our experiences determines our emotions. Our emotions motivate us to act, and our actions result in new experiences that strongly affect what we believe is true.

If we are to use biblical truth more effectively to bring dynamic change, we are going to have to find a more comprehensive model for psychological functioning in order to know where and how to apply it. King Solomon, the wisest man who ever lived, and one who spent much of his time investigating the deeper issues of life wrote almost all of the Book of Proverbs. Therefore, it is not surprising that God would use him to provide us clear direction concerning what it takes to have a full and complete life. In Proverbs Chapter 3, he provided the information necessary to identify the components of the heart and to understand how they are to function.

Pr 3:5 Trust in the LORD with all thine heart; and lean not unto thine own understanding.

6 In all thy ways acknowledge him, and he shall direct thy paths.

7 Be not wise in thine own eyes: fear the LORD, and depart from evil.

8 It shall be health to thy navel, and marrow to thy bones.

The Train of Psychological Wholeness

Without being fully aware of its significance, for years I used a method for helping a client change his emotions and feelings that I called the "Emotional Train." I would explain that a person's emotions are primarily affected by his will, mind and actions. These form an emotional train in which the engine is his will, followed by his mind, followed by his actions, and finally followed by the caboose, his emotions. In order to change how a client feels, he needs to decide to go a different direction (repent), convince his mind to agree, act according to what he decides to do, and eventually his emotions will follow. Of course, a client may try to run his train backwards using his emotions to determine his actions, which affect his mind and his will. Attempting to run his emotional train backwards only leads downhill and into depression; since the caboose only has momentum, not an engine.

As I studied biblical principles and asked God to reveal a more comprehensive method for applying these principles, He led me back again and again to the very familiar verses of Proverbs 3:5-8. As I meditated on them, I realized that this was a much more elaborate description of the emotional train. It describes the principles for a healthy life. In addition, it addresses the areas of intervention that must be addressed in order to change the whole person. I now call it the "Train of Psychological Wholeness." (See the chart at the end of this chapter for a graphic rendition of this train.)

When we investigate the meaning of the words used in these verses in the Hebrew language we find that they provide specific direction for all aspects of our life:

Pr 3:5 Trust in the LORD with all thine heart (we are to have faith in mind, will, emotions, and spirit); and lean not unto thine own understanding (our spirit, not our mind is to control the train).

6 In all thy ways (actions) acknowledge (or know) him (we develop the truth in our spirit by knowing God), and he shall direct thy paths (our will should be run by the Spirit).

7 Be not wise in thine own eyes (do not trust in our own perceptions): fear the LORD (we should be motivated by God's truth), and depart from evil (our actions must resist evil).

8 It shall be health to thy navel (our emotional needs are met), and marrow (inner refreshing of the spirit) to thy bones (our experience will be inner health or wholeness).

My paraphrase of this verse goes like this: "Have faith in your heart, don't think you can direct your life, know God's truth in your spirit and allow it to direct your will. Don't trust your own perceptions, be motivated by the fact that God loves you and will do what is best for you, and in your actions avoid evil things. If you do these things you will experience emotional, physical, and psychological health and all your needs will be met."

We have now identified some biblical concepts for living a full and successful life and some of the factors involved. We must still integrate these concepts in order to understand how these components of the heart function together in order to produce a useable counseling model. As we continue to analyze these verses, we find that they list each component of the heart and offer suggestions for intervening to bring wholeness in the life of a person. These include:

- <u>Faith</u> in the entire heart.
- Direction of the <u>will</u> by the Spirit.
- Truth in the <u>spirit</u>.
- A <u>mind</u> yielded and open to the Spirit.
- Not trusting our <u>perceptions</u> but seeing God's viewpoint.
- Perceiving our <u>needs</u> as God does.
- Being <u>motivated</u> by our awe of and allegiance to God
- Not acting wrongly.
- Right <u>actions</u> bring wholeness and healing <u>experiences</u>.
- Right actions and experiences bring positive <u>emotions</u>.

Condensing this information, we find that to affect the whole man, we must address the issues of the will, spirit, mind, perceptions, needs, motivation, actions, experiences and emotions. We should note that perceptions are a function of the mind and that motivation is a function of the emotions. Our needs are a basic part of the self, and our experiences are the result of our actions that are directed by our will. Faith is a function of all of the members of our heart. Each of these affects the others in a rather complex way.

In the diagram on the following page, I have attempted to present a simplistic view of the human functioning and some of the dynamics involved. Note that the spirit has little influence in unbelievers because they have not been regenerated by the Spirit of God and their will does not yield to the Spirit. It is God's plan that we yield our will to the influence of our spirit, which, in the believer, is yielded to the Spirit of God. It is through the influence of the Spirit of God that we should interpret or perceive our lives. These perceptions, in turn, influence our will. This is what I have labeled the mental process.

Our emotional process begins with our perceptions of our needs. We are motivated to meet our needs, as we perceive them and we will act in ways that attempt to meet these perceived needs. Our actions will lead to our emotions and all of this will lead to new experiences that will again affect our mental process. From a biblical point of view, we will either be primarily influenced by our spirit and walk according to the Spirit or be primarily influenced by the perceived needs of our self and try to meet them by walking according to the flesh.

Using this model, let us take a more in-depth view of what Proverbs 3:5-8 is telling us. It says that the key to becoming psychologically whole is to have trust or faith in the whole heart (or the entire diagram). Particularly, if we trust God to meet all our needs and to direct our lives, we will yield our will to the direction of the Spirit. If we fill our spirit and mind with God's truth and refuse to trust our own perceptions of things, we will see life from God's point of view. If we believe that God loves us and will meet our needs, we will be motivated by appreciation to avoid evil and selfish actions. If we avoid these selfish actions, which result in negative experiences, we will also avoid the unpleasant emotions that they produce. Furthermore, our Godly motivation will result in Godly actions and Godly emotions. These emotions will produce Godly experiences that will result in positive emotions. These verses suggest that following these principles of interaction can only lead to emotional, physical, and psychological health.

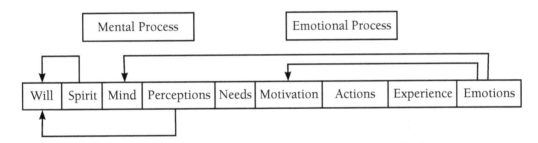

The challenge before us, then, is to understand these components of the human heart, to investigate what the Bible says about each one, and to determine how they can interact with each other to bring mental health and complete wholeness. Based on our understanding of the "Train of Psychological Wholeness," we can now learn to intervene to bring change in our will, spirit, mind (including perceptions), needs, actions, experiences and emotions (including motivation). Because this book emphasizes psychological and emotional healing using biblical principles; in Part II, I will discuss the most important biblical principles and counseling methods, which apply to each component of our heart. In Part III, I will present a detailed method for building counseling plans using biblical principles as well as a number of examples for counseling specific areas for which biblical models have not yet been developed.

The Train of Psychological Wholeness

Proverbs 3:5 Trust (have faith) in the LORD with all thine heart (innermost being); and lean not unto thine own understanding (but to God's Spirit).

6 In all thy ways acknowledge (have knowledge) of him, and he shall direct thy paths (will).

7 Be not wise in thine own eyes (perceptions): fear (be motivated to serve) the LORD, and depart from evil (actions).

8 It shall be health (met needs) to thy navel (innermost emotions), and marrow (life) to thy bones (experience).

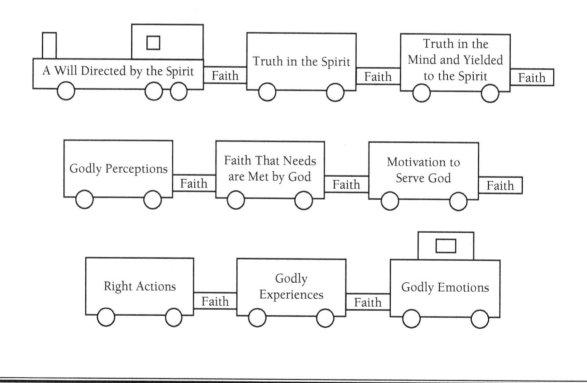

Chapter 3

The Principles of Faith

Faith is the critical factor in the Train of Psychological Wholeness. It applies to every function of the heart, and is the coupling that keeps the cars together. If we do not believe, we will not take action or be able to receive from God. We will most likely experience life as meaningless, refuse to accept the truth, perceive life cynically, try to meet our own needs through the flesh, lack motivation to do good, refuse to face our fears, and live a depressed life. Without faith, our life becomes a lot of unused rusting train cars sitting around a freight yard because they have no purpose, or worse yet, an out of control train with a huge amount of destructive power.

Because numerous books have been written on the subject of faith, in this section I will only discuss those principles applicable to resolving spiritual and psychological problems, and present the counseling methods and techniques most often needed in Christian counseling. (For a more detailed listing of the principles of faith, see my book *Faith Therapy* (2005))

The Principles of Faith

1. Faith is the inner conviction that something will happen. For it to be effective we must know it in our spirit and it must pervade our entire heart. If it does not, all we have is mental ascent (faith only in our mind), presumption (faith only in our will) or feeling faith (faith only in our emotions). None of these are able to produce supernatural results.

    Heb 11:1 Now faith is the substance of things hoped for, the evidence of things not seen.

2. Natural evidence can lead us to believe after the fact, but God desires for us to have faith just based on His Word. Everyone has some level of natural faith. If you are sitting in a chair reading this book, this fact shows that you at least have faith that the chair you are sitting in will support your weight. If you did not have faith in the chair you are sitting on, you would have been afraid to sit on it. You believed that the chair would hold you because it or similar chairs have held your weight in the past. God wants us to go beyond natural faith and trust Him to do supernatural things for us that we have not experienced before.

    Jo 20:27 Then saith he to Thomas, Reach hither thy finger, and behold my hands; and reach hither thy hand, and thrust it into my side: and be not faithless, but believing.

    28 And Thomas answered and said unto him, My Lord and my God.

    29 Jesus saith unto him, Thomas, because thou hast seen me, thou hast believed: blessed are they that have not seen, and yet have believed.

3. <u>Supernatural faith in God's Word allows us to act before we see things, trusting in God for the outcome.</u> Supernatural faith is based on the Word of God or supernatural revelation and believes that it is possible to accomplish things that supercede natural laws. This verse refers to the *rhema* or spoken Word of God. If we trust God and know in our spirit that God has spoken something to us, we can believe what He says is true even before we see it manifested. Thus, we can act according to what He has told us.

    Ro 10:17 So then faith [cometh] by hearing, and hearing by the word of God.

4. <u>Faith is the means of receiving salvation.</u> Through faith, we invite the Spirit of God into our lives. The Holy Spirit motivates us to want to become holy. When we believe that God loves us and will meet all of our needs, we are delivered from our selfishness, which is the root of our dysfunctional and sinful lives.

    Eph 2:8 For by grace are ye saved through faith; and that not of yourselves: [it is] the gift of God:

5. <u>Faith is the key to supernatural manifestations and answered prayer.</u> The entire spiritual realm operates on faith. Without supernatural faith, we are limited in what we can do by the laws of nature.

    Mt 21:21 Jesus answered and said unto them, Verily I say unto you, If ye have faith, and doubt not, ye shall not only do this [which is done] to the fig tree, but also if ye shall say unto this mountain, Be thou removed, and be thou cast into the sea; it shall be done.
    22 And all things, whatsoever ye shall ask in prayer, believing, ye shall receive.

6. <u>Righteousness or wholeness comes through faith.</u> We cannot do anything truly righteous without trusting and relying on Christ. This is because we must believe that God will meet all of our needs in order to be delivered from our selfish motivation. Without faith, all of us come short of what God expects of us: right actions motivated by love.

    Ro 3:22 Even the righteousness of God [which is] by faith of Jesus Christ unto all and upon all them that believe: for there is no difference:
    23 For all have sinned, and come short of the glory of God;

7. <u>Victory over our problems comes through faith.</u> Without the power of God working in our lives by faith, we do not have the resources to overcome the world. Relying on the flesh can never be sufficient to achieve victory in our lives because the flesh must be overcome. The flesh cannot and will not overcome the problems of the flesh.

    1 Jo 5:4 For whatsoever is born of God overcometh the world: and this is the victory that overcometh the world, [even] our faith.

8. <u>The promises of God come through faith and patience.</u> It is only through persevering faith that we can see the promises of God manifested in our lives. If we do not press in and believe those promises until they are manifested in the natural realm, we will miss out on what God has promised to provide for us.

    Heb 6:12 That ye be not slothful, but followers of them who through faith and patience inherit the promises.

9. <u>We must accept what is spoken and believe it or it will do us no good.</u> God may speak to us in many ways but we must know that He has spoken a particular word to us so that we have a foundation on which to base our faith. It is not good enough to simply read a promise in the Bible (*logos*) and decide we want it. We must be convinced that this particular promise from God applies to us in particular. When we know that God has spoken this word to us and it applies to our situation, it becomes *rhema* (a word spoken directly from God) to us.

   Heb 4:2 For unto us was the gospel preached, as well as unto them: but the word preached did not profit them, not being mixed with faith in them that heard [it].

10. <u>We need to act according to the faith we have.</u> If we truly believe something, we will act according to what we believe. If we do not, our lack of action is proof that we really did not believe it with our whole heart.

    Jas 1:22 But be ye doers of the word, and not hearers only, deceiving your own selves.
    2:17 Even so faith, if it hath not works, is dead, being alone.

11. <u>We only need enough faith to overcome our unbelief.</u> It does not necessarily take great faith to move a mountain but just enough faith to overcome our unbelief.

    Mt 17:20 And Jesus said unto them, Because of your unbelief: for verily I say unto you, If ye have faith as a grain of mustard seed, ye shall say unto this mountain, Remove hence to yonder place; and it shall remove; and nothing shall be impossible unto you.

12. <u>When we lack faith, fear will overwhelm us and we will be unable to carry out the directions of God.</u> Because the children of Israel did not believe they could conquer the Promised Land, they were not able to enter it. In the same way, without faith we cannot enter our own land of blessing that the promises of God offer to us.

    Nu 13:31 But the men that went up with him said, We be not able to go up against the people; for they [are] stronger than we.

13. <u>We must believe and trust God like a little child, humbly relying on Him to meet all our needs in order to receive all that God has for us.</u> True peace and contentment come only when we yield fully to His will and completely trust in Him for everything, knowing that He will work everything for our good.

    Lu 18:17 Verily I say unto you, Whosoever shall not receive the kingdom of God as a little child shall in no wise enter therein.

Counseling Methods and Techniques

1. <u>We need to build a faith foundation based on God's Word.</u> Clients need something more than opinions on which to base their faith. For developing faith in the truth of the Bible, I rely heavily on the writings of Josh McDowell, especially *Evidence That Demands a Verdict, Volumes I and II* (1972, 1975). The direct physical evidence presented in these books helps the client realize that he is dealing with reality, not just some unsupported myth, and that he can believe what he reads in the Word of God.

2. <u>We must learn the principles of faith.</u> Faith is the evidence of things not yet seen. This evidence can take physical, experiential, written, verbal and spiritual forms, but all evidence must be based on something. The client must be led to understand that the most reliable form of evidence is what God Himself says, since He knows everything and cannot lie. God's Word is even more reliable than what a person sees, experiences, or is told. Without this foundation, changes in circumstances will overwhelm his faith; and it will be difficult to receive anything from God.

3. <u>We must do our part to increase our faith.</u> We must: 1. Make ourselves available to hear and receive additional revelation. 2. Gather evidence to support the faith that we have. 3. Act on the faith that we have, before we expect to receive the manifestation of it. 4. Stand on that faith, even in the face of adverse circumstances or physical evidence, until we receive the manifestation of our faith.

4. <u>We can use the building block approach to begin with limited faith.</u> We can see God accomplish great things in our lives by using our faith one step at a time and acting on it until that phase has been manifested. With a stronger faith, based on the recent victory, we can expand our vision and again act on our faith. One faith victory sets the stage and provides additional evidence to believe for the next victory.

5. <u>We can use the "Faith Ladder" to move from hope to true faith.</u> As a client's faith increases over time, he can believe that if he has been hoping for victory in 10 years, it will happen in two years, or even in six months. When he knows in his heart that it will happen now he has moved from hope to true faith. After victory has been achieved for 10 days, why can it not be maintained for one month, and if for one month, why not forever? (See my book *Faith Therapy* for a complete description of the "Faith Ladder.")

6. <u>We can increase faith through developing a close relationship with God.</u> Sometimes people think that developing a close relationship with God is a mysterious and difficult task when, in fact, it is extremely simple. Whatever works in developing relationships with people, works in our relationship with God and whatever works with God, works with people. In order to get closer to God, we must spend time with Him in the spiritual disciplines such as Bible study, meditating on God's Word, prayer, fasting, quiet time and worship.

PART II

Biblical Principles
for Application

Chapter 4

Principles of the Will

The will is our capability to choose; it is our volition. It is our will that eventually determines the entire outcome of our lives. We can choose what we will or will not do, what we will or will not accept and how we perceive things. Therefore, we can also determine how we feel, what we think, our attitudes, our identity, and whom we will serve. Our choices are also affected by all of the other members of the heart. What we think, what we believe, how we perceive our world and our needs, what we do, our experiences and how we feel all affect what we choose to do. God will not force us to do anything that we do not want to do. He will not even override our will in order to save us from hell. He does not want robots, but people with a free will who choose to serve Him. Consequently, it is not surprising that the Bible seems to address the choices of our will more than any other area of psychological intervention.

Our will has four dimensions: direction, allegiance, force and the ability to change direction. These are called choice, lordship, commitment and repentance. If we continue the analogy of the second chapter, our free choice determines which tracks we direct the train onto at each rail switch. We must decide if we will direct the train according to our own choices or make Jesus Lord of our lives and follow the directions of the railroad's chief executive, God. Our commitment will determine how hard we will work to get the train to its destination. It is through repentance that we are able to redirect the train when we realize that we are headed in the wrong direction.

The Principles of Free Choice

Making the right choice is not necessarily simple. It is true that God gives a man the ability to direct his own life and to choose what he will do with his life. Unfortunately, people usually choose to rebel against God and decide to meet their needs in their own strength through the flesh. This dominance of the flesh provides the opportunity for the influence of sin—especially selfishness, lust and addictions—to dominate the will. In turn, the flesh and sin provide the opportunity for evil spirits to affect the will and dominate it when a person yields to temptation. However, thanks to what Jesus did at Calvary, man can now be set free from sin. Through the power of Christ, he is again now free to choose what he will do with his life.

Counseling in the area of free choice requires considerable care. This is because there is a fine line between insuring that the client maintains responsibility for his own recovery and truly having the best interest of the client and others in mind from a biblical perspective. Many times, what the client may feel is in his best interest may not be best for those close to him or for the Kingdom of God. Sometimes the way the client would like to "solve" his problems violates the principles of the Bible.

On one extreme, according to secular counseling ethics the client should be allowed to make his own choices based on what he chooses to believe or do. No one is assumed to have absolute answers to the issues of life, and the client's beliefs are to be respected. The counselor is not supposed to declare that a certain behavior is sin or tell him that it is wrong, but help the client determine which decision will be in his best interest. In one case, a Christian counselor was sued for violating this secular counseling ethic, because he directly stated that abortion was wrong.

On the other hand, the Christian counselor has an obligation to declare what the Word of God says and explain how a particular decision will affect the client's spiritual well-being as well as how it will affect the client and others in the client's life. A clear case of this is explaining what the Bible says about divorce. Once the client understands that God hates divorce, that the only biblical grounds for divorce are adultery or abandonment by an unbeliever, that to remarry after a non-biblical divorce is to commit adultery, and that there are extreme negative effects on everyone involved, the client must still be allowed free choice. It is not the Christian counselor's job to force the client to make the right choice or manipulate him to do something since the counselor will not get the consequences of the decision. He must never violate the client's free choice or take responsibility for the client's recovery. It is never his job to "fix" the client. Each client must be allowed to "work out their own salvation" or wholeness. (Philippians 2:12b) God will not even force someone to make the choice to be saved even though the consequence is eternal damnation.

1. <u>Through Adam, we chose to serve sin.</u> Unfortunately, it was Adam's free choice to eat of the tree of the knowledge of good and evil that resulted in our bondage to the sin nature—our desire to be our own God and meet our own needs our way.

   Ro 5:14 Nevertheless death reigned from Adam to Moses, even over them that had not sinned after the similitude of Adam's transgression, who is the figure of him that was to come.

2. <u>Christ came to set us free and restore our free choice.</u> It is difficult for Westerners to understand what the Bible calls "our identification with Christ." This is because we are so time-conscious and God operates outside of time. When we were saved, we became part of the body of Christ; and therefore, when Christ died on the cross, we died with Him, and our sin nature also died. Therefore, we are no longer under the influence of the sin of Adam, but have now been set free.

   Ro 6:6 Knowing this, that our old man is crucified with him, that the body of sin might be destroyed, that henceforth we should not serve sin.

3. <u>Because of what Jesus did, we are again free to choose how we direct our lives.</u> If we believe that Christ has set us free, we are no longer under the power of our sin nature. Reckoning means to count something as true. Consequently, we no longer have to yield our members to sin or the flesh. Nonetheless, it is still our choice to yield ourselves to whom we choose—to God or to sin—and live in liberty or bondage.

   Ro 6:11 Likewise reckon ye also yourselves to be dead indeed unto sin, but alive unto God through Jesus Christ our Lord.

   12 Let not sin therefore reign in your mortal body, that ye should obey it in the lusts thereof.

   13 Neither yield ye your members as instruments of unrighteousness unto sin: but yield your-selves unto God, as those that are alive from the dead, and your members as instruments of righteousness unto God.

4. <u>Because of the power we have in Christ, we can now choose to do what is right and are able to carry it out as we rely on Him to help us.</u> If we try again to rely on ourselves (the flesh) to carry out what God requires (the law), we will still fail. The Bible tells us that the law is the strength of sin. (1 Corinthians 15:56b)

Ro 8:3 For what the law could not do, in that it was weak through the flesh, God sending his own Son in the likeness of sinful flesh, and for sin, condemned sin in the flesh:

4 That the righteousness of the law might be fulfilled in us, who walk not after the flesh, but after the Spirit.

5. <u>Even salvation does not take away our free choice.</u> Just because we now have the power to choose to do right, it does not necessarily force us to choose to do what is right. However, because we now have the ability to do right, it is our duty to choose to do it.

    Ro 6:19 I speak after the manner of men because of the infirmity of your flesh: for as ye have yielded your members servants to uncleanness and to iniquity unto iniquity; even so now yield your members servants to righteousness unto holiness.

6. <u>Our flesh and our spirit are in a battle for the control of our will.</u> Whichever controls our will, also will eventually gain control of our entire soul. Whichever controls our soul will control our actions and our future.

    Ga 5:17 For the flesh lusteth against the Spirit, and the Spirit against the flesh: and these are contrary the one to the other: so that ye cannot do the things that ye would.

7. <u>Our will can be taken captive by the flesh or other spirits if we yield to them.</u> Anyone who has ever counseled clients with addictions or wondered how "good Christians" could fall into such deep sin can attest to the fact that our will can become captive to a particular lust or spirit if we yield to it even just a little bit at a time. Ask any alcoholic how he got started drinking, and now, if he is still able to take just one drink?

    Ro 7:18 For I know that in me (that is, in my flesh,) dwelleth no good thing: for to will is present with me; but how to perform that which is good I find not.

8. <u>We choose whom we will serve.</u> The flesh and spirits have no power over us unless we choose to give it to them. Jesus took away all of Satan's power and the power of our sin nature at Calvary.

    Ro 6:16 Know ye not, that to whom ye yield yourselves servants to obey, his servants ye are to whom ye obey; whether of sin unto death, or of obedience unto righteousness?

9. <u>Although we may initially be free to choose in a particular area of our lives, we can forfeit our ability to choose and yield to bondage.</u> We ask, how could that man of God do such a terrible thing? It is simple. He chose to yield himself to sin a little at a time.

    Ro 6:12 Let not sin therefore reign in your mortal body, that ye should obey it in the lusts thereof.

10. <u>Many times, our choices are between short-term pleasure or long-term good.</u> Moses chose to follow the Hebrew God instead of partaking in the sins of the Egyptians.

    Heb 11:25 Choosing rather to suffer affliction with the people of God, than to enjoy the pleasures of sin for a season;

11. <u>The real issue is whether we will obey God, ourselves, or other people.</u> Every choice we make either is a choice for the best interests of the Kingdom of God or against it. If we truly believe that God has our best interests in mind, we will obey Him.

    Ac 5:29 Then Peter and the other apostles answered and said, We ought to obey God rather than men.

12. <u>Not obeying can nullify the promises of God.</u>

    Jos 5:6 For the children of Israel walked forty years in the wilderness, till all the people that were men of war, which came out of Egypt, were consumed, because they obeyed not the voice of the LORD: unto whom the LORD sware that he would not shew them the land, which the LORD sware unto their fathers that he would give us, a land that floweth with milk and honey.

13. <u>Obedience is learned through experience.</u> We learn by the consequences of our choices.

    Heb 5:8 Though he were a Son, yet learned he obedience by the things which he suffered;

14. <u>Doing God's will is more important than what we accomplish for Him.</u> A soldier is expected to obey orders, cooperate and do whatever his commanding officer thinks is best. If, instead, he does what he wants to do—even if it is successful—he will be reprimanded or court-martialed.

    Mt 7:21 Not every one that saith unto me, Lord, Lord, shall enter into the kingdom of heaven; but he that doeth the will of my Father which is in heaven.

    22 Many will say to me in that day, Lord, Lord, have we not prophesied in thy name? and in thy name have cast out devils? and in thy name done many wonderful works?

    23 And then will I profess unto them, I never knew you: depart from me, ye that work iniquity.

15. <u>Doing God's will is the solid foundation of the Christian life.</u>

    Mt 7:24 Therefore whosoever heareth these sayings of mine, and doeth them, I will liken him unto a wise man, which built his house upon a rock:

    25 And the rain descended, and the floods came, and the winds blew, and beat upon that house; and it fell not: for it was founded upon a rock.

    26 And every one that heareth these sayings of mine, and doeth them not, shall be likened unto a foolish man, which built his house upon the sand:

    27 And the rain descended, and the floods came, and the winds blew, and beat upon that house; and it fell: and great was the fall of it.

Counseling Methods and Techniques

1. <u>We can trust God to change our will.</u> This method of change is based on Philippians 2:13, "For it is God which worketh in you both to will and to do of his good pleasure." We must do our part and trust God to do His part. Although we might not have any understanding about how it takes place, God can and will change our will if we will trust Him to do it. The client should simply admit to God that he cannot change his will about something, and then trust God to do it.

2. <u>We can be willing to be willing for God to change our heart.</u> Sometimes I suggest that the client pray, "Lord, I am willing for you to make me willing to be willing to ...." If we give the Spirit of God the smallest opportunity to work in our life, He will do so. This is important because God will not force a person to change his will and because continually resisting the will of God can harden a person's heart.

3. <u>Make right choices by focusing on long-term consequences.</u> Ask the client what he thinks the long-term results will be when considering a choice. It is especially useful when dealing with addictions or violence to have clients add up how much that problem has already cost them and estimate what it will cost them in the future.

4. <u>We can influence our will by what we allow into our minds.</u> The client who chooses to go to adult bookstores or who watches certain movies is choosing to be dominated by lust. The one who concentrates on productive, loving, and good books, movies, or events is choosing to be influenced in his will in that direction. Wherever our mind and emotions go, our will usually follows.

5. <u>We will want to obey when we realize that if we do not do what we are told, God cannot help us.</u> Many times, I use two stories about the training of dogs from Bob Mumford's audio tape series, "The Nature and Spirit of Obedience." (not dated) In the first, he relates that in training police dogs, the goal is not to have the dog fetch a purse or attack, but to do what the handler directs, even if he commands "heel" after throwing out the purse. In the second, he relates watching how the well-trained dogs at a dog show were the happiest dogs of all. Of course, there are many verses in the Bible on the subject of obedience. I usually make the point clear that unless they choose to obey, clients are on their own, and God cannot help or protect them. Another illustration I use is this: "If you were running across the street and a semi truck was about to hit you and I yelled stop—but you kept on running—is there anything I could do to help you? Of course, the answer is no, unless I was close enough to push you out of the way. By disobedience, we greatly limit what God can do for us!

The Principles of Lordship

One of the very basic principles of Christianity is that if Jesus is not Lord of all of our life, He is not Lord at all. Our will declares allegiance and chooses to follow someone or something. In the analogy of the train, I must choose whom the engineer (my will) will follow: either Christ or myself and the desires of my flesh. Possibly the failure to follow this principle is responsible for most of the carnal Christians in our churches and is the reason why so many Christians have not been significantly changed or delivered. If Jesus is not in charge of all aspects of our lives, we are not much better off than non-believers who are trying to direct their own lives. Christians who insist on directing their own lives sometimes want God to bless everything that they want to do. He will not be their "genie." Either we yield to Him, or He will watch us flounder until we do.

1. <u>Salvation requires making Jesus Lord.</u>

   Ro 10:9 That if thou shalt confess with thy mouth the Lord Jesus, and shalt believe in thine heart that God hath raised him from the dead, thou shalt be saved.

   13 For whosoever shall call upon the name of the Lord shall be saved.

2. <u>God can only help us to the extent that we are willing to yield to Him.</u>

   1 Pe 3:12 For the eyes of the Lord are over the righteous, and his ears are open unto their prayers: but the face of the Lord is against them that do evil.

3. <u>Either God is in charge of our lives or we are.</u>

   Lu 16:13 No servant can serve two masters: for either he will hate the one, and love the other; or else he will hold to the one, and despise the other. Ye cannot serve God and mammon.

4. <u>We do not have enough information to direct our lives.</u>

   Pr 27:1 Boast not thyself of to morrow; for thou knowest not what a day may bring forth.

   Jas 4:14 Whereas ye know not what shall be on the morrow. For what is your life? It is even a vapour, that appeareth for a little time, and then vanisheth away.

5. <u>We must realize that His ways are better than our ways.</u>

   Isa 55:8 For my thoughts are not your thoughts, neither are your ways my ways, saith the LORD. For as the heavens are higher than the earth, so are my ways higher than your ways, and my thoughts than your thoughts.

6. <u>God has a specific mission for each of us.</u>

   Ac 9:6 And he trembling and astonished said, Lord, what wilt thou have me to do? And the Lord said unto him, Arise, and go into the city, and it shall be told thee what thou must do.

7. <u>We cannot be successful in our lives until we yield to His direction.</u> We tend to trust ourselves until we realize that we cannot be our own God and direct our own lives without receiving the consequences of sin. We usually have to fail in our own efforts or face an impossible situation before we will fully yield to God. As long as we think we can be our own God and direct our own lives successfully, we will attempt to do so.

   Ro 6:23 For the wages of sin is death; but the gift of God is eternal life through Jesus Christ our Lord.

8. <u>We will not trust or yield to God until we believe He has our best interests in mind.</u> Having another's best interest in mind is a rudimentary definition of love. If we feel loved, we will love God and want to follow His directions or commandments.

   1 Jo 4:19 We love him, because he first loved us.

   5:3 For this is the love of God, that we keep his commandments: and his commandments are not grievous.

9. <u>If we feel unloved by our parents, we will have a difficult time yielding our will to God.</u> Our first concept of God comes from our parents. We must realize that God is not like our parents. He always has our best interests in mind.

   Ps 27:10 When my father and my mother forsake me, then the LORD will take me up.

   Nu 23:19 God is not a man, that he should lie; neither the son of man, that he should repent: hath he said, and shall he not do it? or hath he spoken, and shall he not make it good?

10. <u>God blesses and honors those who yield to His will and serve Him.</u>

De 30:16 In that I command thee this day to love the LORD thy God, to walk in his ways, and to keep his commandments and his statutes and his judgments, that thou mayest live and multiply: and the LORD thy God shall bless thee in the land whither thou goest to possess it.

Jo 12:26 If any man serve me, let him follow me; and where I am, there shall also my servant be: if any man serve me, him will my Father honour.

11. <u>We will not have rest and peace until, through faith, we cease trying to control our own lives and quit relying on ourselves.</u>

Heb 4: 9 There remaineth therefore a rest to the people of God.

10 For he that is entered into his rest, he also hath ceased from his own works, as God did from his.

11 Let us labour therefore to enter into that rest, lest any man fall after the same example of unbelief.

12. <u>Eventually everyone will yield to God.</u>

Ro 14:11 For it is written, As I live, saith the Lord, every knee shall bow to me, and every tongue shall confess to God.

Counseling Methods and Techniques

1. <u>Convince ourselves that we do not have enough data to direct our lives.</u> Following a blind man (ourselves) does not make sense. Here, I usually use my testimony explaining how God brought me to the point of realizing that I could not direct my life through asking me three difficult questions: 1. What had I accomplished so far in life that will still exist 200 years from now? 2. What specifically will happen to me tomorrow? 3. What specifically has God designed me for and called me to do in this life?

2. <u>To convince ourselves that God loves us, we should ask ourselves if we love our own children and have their best interests in mind?</u> This is important because clients will not yield to God unless they feel loved. Of course, another way is to direct them to Jesus' sacrifice on the cross.

3. <u>Confront resistance to change with the "concrete wall."</u> If a client is not willing to make changes, I say to them that if they wish, they can just lower their head and take another run at the concrete wall. This method of confronting makes the point that what the client is doing will not work and all his efforts on his own are simply running into a concrete wall that he can never break. He can keep up his fruitless efforts or he can yield to God's direction for his life. Until he does, he will continue to experience the emotional pain that brought him to counseling in the first place.

The Principles of Commitment

Where Lordship deals with receiving and following directions for our lives, commitment determines how much effort will be invested in seeking to serve Christ or deal with the issues in our lives. This effort is reflected in our priorities. Just as in a marriage, where commitment is a large determiner of whether the marriage will succeed or fail under adverse circumstances, the committed Christian presses through in prayer and seeks God until he gets results.

In counseling, the client who is fully committed will eventually recover. Those who are not willing to face the emotional pain of honestly dealing with issues or who just want the pain to go away will only achieve limited results. In *Overcoming Chemical Dependency* (1990), McGee suggests that recovery primarily depends on two things—whether a client believes he will recover and if he is willing to do whatever it takes. Commitment is being willing to do whatever it takes. It is not unusual for a client to refuse to go to a needed support group, fail to attend counseling consistently or just "forget" to do homework assignments. One of the more difficult counseling challenges is helping an uncommitted client find the motivation necessary for recovery.

1. <u>We must be more committed to Christ than to our families.</u>

    Lu 14:26 If any man come to me, and hate not his father, and mother, and wife, and children, and brethren, and sisters, yea, and his own life also, he cannot be my disciple.

2. <u>We must be willing to deny ourselves and face hardships for Christ.</u>

    Mt 16:24 Then said Jesus unto his disciples, If any man will come after me, let him deny himself, and take up his cross, and follow me.

    Mr 8:34 And when he had called the people unto him with his disciples also, he said unto them, Whosoever will come after me, let him deny himself, and take up his cross, and follow me.

3. <u>We must search carefully for the Kingdom of God and do whatever is necessary not to get diverted.</u>

    Mt 7:13 Enter ye in at the strait gate: for wide is the gate, and broad is the way, that leadeth to destruction, and many there be which go in thereat:

    14 Because strait is the gate, and narrow is the way, which leadeth unto life, and few there be that find it.

4. <u>We must be willing to take whatever measures are necessary to eradicate sin from our lives.</u>

    Mt 5:29 And if thy right eye offend thee, pluck it out, and cast it from thee: for it is profitable for thee that one of thy members should perish, and not that thy whole body should be cast into hell.

    30 And if thy right hand offend thee, cut it off, and cast it from thee: for it is profitable for thee that one of thy members should perish, and not that thy whole body should be cast into hell.

5. <u>If necessary, we must be willing to give up everything we own for Christ.</u>

    Mr 10:21 Then Jesus beholding him loved him, and said unto him, One thing thou lackest: go thy way, sell whatsoever thou hast, and give to the poor, and thou shalt have treasure in heaven: and come, take up the cross, and follow me.

6. <u>We must treasure the Kingdom of God above everything else</u>

    Mt 13:44 Again, the kingdom of heaven is like unto treasure hid in a field; the which when a man hath found, he hideth, and for joy thereof goeth and selleth all that he hath, and buyeth that field.

    45 Again, the kingdom of heaven is like unto a merchant man, seeking goodly pearls:

    46 Who, when he had found one pearl of great price, went and sold all that he had, and bought it.

7. <u>We are to offer our bodies sacrificially unto God and not be like the world.</u>

   Ro 12:1 I beseech you therefore, brethren, by the mercies of God, that ye present your bodies a living sacrifice, holy, acceptable unto God, which is your reasonable service.

   2 And be not conformed to this world: but be ye transformed by the renewing of your mind, that ye may prove what is that good, and acceptable, and perfect, will of God.

8. <u>We belong to God and everything we do is to be done for God and not for men.</u>

   Ro 14:8 For whether we live, we live unto the Lord; and whether we die, we die unto the Lord: whether we live therefore, or die, we are the Lord's.

   Col 3:17 And whatsoever ye do in word or deed, do all in the name of the Lord Jesus, giving thanks to God and the Father by him.

   23 And whatsoever ye do, do it heartily, as to the Lord, and not unto men;

9. <u>We direct our hearts by what we choose to value in our lives.</u> Through a choice of our will, the rest of our heart—mind, emotions, and spirit—will be influenced to value the same things. This will influence the other decisions that we make.

   Mt 6:21 For where your treasure is, there will your heart be also.

10. <u>Making the world our priority shows that we do not love God.</u> What we gain in the world will not last for long.

    1 Jo 2:15 Love not the world, neither the things that are in the world. If any man love the world, the love of the Father is not in him.

    16 For all that is in the world, the lust of the flesh, and the lust of the eyes, and the pride of life, is not of the Father, but is of the world.

    17 And the world passeth away, and the lust thereof: but he that doeth the will of God abideth for ever.

11. <u>If we make God's kingdom our priority, God will meet our needs.</u>

    Mt 6:33 But seek ye first the kingdom of God, and his righteousness; and all these things shall be added unto you.

12. <u>We are to do whatever it takes to focus on and fulfill our mission here on earth.</u>

    Php 3:7 But what things were gain to me, those I counted loss for Christ.

    8 Yea doubtless, and I count all things but loss for the excellency of the knowledge of Christ Jesus my Lord: for whom I have suffered the loss of all things, and do count them but dung, that I may win Christ,

    13 Brethren, I count not myself to have apprehended: but this one thing I do, forgetting those things which are behind, and reaching forth unto those things which are before,

    14 I press toward the mark for the prize of the high calling of God in Christ Jesus.

13. <u>We must do all we can to resist the devil's temptations to do evil.</u>

    Jas 4:7 Submit yourselves therefore to God. Resist the devil, and he will flee from you.

    1 Pe 5:9 Whom resist stedfast in the faith, knowing that the same afflictions are accomplished in your brethren that are in the world.

14. <u>We should realize that God expects us to fervently follow Him.</u> He would rather have us cold so that we might repent than for us to become a mediocre, lukewarm follower of His.

    Re 3:16 So then because thou art lukewarm, and neither cold nor hot, I will spue thee out of my mouth.

Counseling Methods and Techniques

1. <u>We can change our will by changing our priorities.</u> Commitment is a matter of priorities. What we value we put first. If we place God first in all we do and if we choose to make the things of God our chief desire or treasure, the remainder of our heart, including our will, will follow.

2. <u>We can focus our will by finding and committing to God's call.</u> We are led by vision. The more we do for God, the more we will want to do. The Apostle Paul pressed on to accomplish his high calling. Without a vision, the people perish. (Proverbs 29:18) One of the tasks of the counselor is to help the client find God's specific call for their lives. When they find what God has called them to do and when they begin to find success in doing it, they will press forward to God's calling for them.

3. <u>We can decide to do God's will and not be sidetracked.</u> We have a part in resisting temptation and resisting the devil, since God will not override our decisions. Through sheer will power, we can decide to do the will of God and not be derailed by the diversions and tactics of the devil. Once we make up our mind; if we are fully committed to God and rely on Him, nothing can stop us.

The Principles of Repentance

Repentance is the method for turning the train of our life around when we realize that we are going in the wrong direction. The word in the Greek is *metanoe* which means "to change one's mind for the better or to heartily make amends with abhorrence of one's past sins." *Metamellomai* means "to care about something afterward or to regret." To regret is passive and does not necessarily imply action as in the case where Judas repented (regretted) what he had done. (Matthew 27:3) This is not true repentance!

1. <u>Repentance is turning from our way of doing things.</u>

    Jer 8:6 I hearkened and heard, but they spake not aright: no man repented him of his wickedness, saying, What have I done? every one turned to his course, as the horse rusheth into the battle.

2. <u>Repentance is the first step in asking for the remission of sins.</u>

    Isa 55:7 Let the wicked forsake his way, and the unrighteous man his thoughts: and let him return unto the LORD, and he will have mercy upon him; and to our God, for he will abundantly pardon.

    Mr 1:4 John did baptize in the wilderness, and preach the baptism of repentance for the remission of sins.

3. <u>God highly values repentance, because it is the first step in changing our lives.</u>

   Lu 15:7 I say unto you, that likewise joy shall be in heaven over one sinner that repenteth, more than over ninety and nine just persons, which need no repentance.

   10 Likewise, I say unto you, there is joy in the presence of the angels of God over one sinner that repenteth

4. <u>If we repent, God will not punish us for our sins.</u>

   Jer 18:8 If that nation, against whom I have pronounced, turn from their evil, I will repent of the evil that I thought to do unto them.

5. <u>God is close to and will help those who are broken and contrite in their repentance.</u>

   Ps 34:18 The LORD is nigh unto them that are of a broken heart; and saveth such as be of a contrite spirit.

6. <u>We must humble ourselves, pray, seek God's face, repent and turn from our wicked ways in order to be heard by God, receive the forgiveness of our sins, and the healing of our land.</u>

   2 Chr 7:14 If my people, which are called by my name, shall humble themselves, and pray, and seek my face, and turn from their wicked ways; then will I hear from heaven, and will forgive their sin, and will heal their land.

7. <u>If we change our minds and do evil, God will remove the blessings He intended for us.</u>

   Jer 18:10 If it do evil in my sight, that it obey not my voice, then I will repent of the good, wherewith I said I would benefit them.

8. <u>If we truly repent, others will know it is true through our actions.</u>

   Mt 3:8 Bring forth therefore fruits meet for repentance:

9. <u>Our actions that show our repentance must fit the sin for which we are repenting.</u>

   Lu 3:8 Bring forth therefore fruits worthy of repentance, and begin not to say within yourselves, We have Abraham to our father: for I say unto you, That God is able of these stones to raise up children unto Abraham.

10. <u>Failing and then repenting is better than agreeing to do something and not following through.</u>

    Mt 21:28 But what think ye? A certain man had two sons; and he came to the first, and said, Son, go work to day in my vineyard.

    29 He answered and said, I will not: but afterward he repented, and went.

    30 And he came to the second, and said likewise. And he answered and said, I go, sir: and went not.

31 Whether of them twain did the will of his father? They say unto him, The first. Jesus saith unto them, Verily I say unto you, That the publicans and the harlots go into the kingdom of God before you.

11. <u>Regretting is not sufficient.</u> True repentance includes going to the one whom you have offended, asking for forgiveness and making restitution. Judas simply regretted the consequences that resulted from what he had done and never went to Jesus and asked for forgiveness. If he had, Jesus would have forgiven him.

    Mt 27:3 Then Judas, which had betrayed him, when he saw that he was condemned, repented himself, and brought again the thirty pieces of silver to the chief priests and elders,

    2 Co 7:10 For godly sorrow worketh repentance to salvation not to be repented of: but the sorrow of the world worketh death.

12. <u>No amount of evidence can make us repent if we do not want to do so.</u>

    Lu 16:30 And he said, Nay, father Abraham: but if one went unto them from the dead, they will repent.

    31 And he said unto him, If they hear not Moses and the prophets, neither will they be persuaded, though one rose from the dead.

13. <u>It is the goodness of God that leads us to repentance.</u>

    Ro 2:4 Or despisest thou the riches of his goodness and forbearance and longsuffering; not knowing that the goodness of God leadeth thee to repentance?

14. <u>God, in His great mercy, allows even wicked people time to realize they are wrong and repent; because He wants everyone to be saved.</u>

    2 Pe 3:9 The Lord is not slack concerning his promise, as some men count slackness; but is longsuffering to us-ward, not willing that any should perish, but that all should come to repentance.

15. <u>All that do not repent, perish.</u>

    Lu 13:3 I tell you, Nay: but, except ye repent, ye shall all likewise perish.

Counseling Methods and Techniques

1. <u>True repentance requires change, not just regretting our consequences.</u> Regretting that we were caught or that our decisions have led to consequences in our lives or the lives of others should not be confused with true repentance which requires a turning around and a change in behavior. God looks at the heart. If we simply regret the consequences, we will only be motivated to avoid the consequences and not do that which is right.

2. <u>We should give people time to repent because God gives us time.</u> Many times, we want immediate judgment on others, but want grace and mercy for ourselves. We cannot have both.

3. <u>Repentance is better sought with patience, love, grace and mercy than through argument and reproof.</u> We should do what we can to stay on the same side rather than oppose those we are attempting to lead to repentance.

4. <u>We should repent of our part and correct it, rather than blame others.</u> The wisest strategy is to judge ourselves, admit our faults and repent so that we will not eventually be judged, receive correction or forfeit our blessings. In a situation where there are two wrongs, we are required to take responsibility for our part even if the other person refuses to do so. It is not our job to convict the other person. In the Christian movie based upon a true-life story, entitled "Fury to Freedom," Raul, after he was saved, went to his abusive father and simply asked forgiveness "for being such a rotten son." He did not accuse his father of all the maltreatment and physical abuse he and his mother had suffered. In this true story, Raul's father eventually accepted Christ.

5. <u>When we need to repent, we should remember the goodness of God.</u> When we realize He is on our side and gracious to forgive, it makes it easier for us to admit that we are wrong and repent.

6. <u>When repenting, we must ask for forgiveness and make restitution.</u> This is clear from the story of Jacob and Esau. When they met, Jacob, who had stolen Esau's birthright, presented Esau with gifts to show that he was sorry and had changed. (Genesis 32-33)

Chapter 5

Principles of the Spirit

Each of us has a spirit and we are affected by both good and evil spirits. Spirits attempt to influence our spirit, place deceptive thoughts into our mind and try to control our will. All spirits operate and are empowered by the faith or the trust that we place in them.

One of the hindrances that Christian counselors face today is the misunderstanding of spiritual reality known as dualism. Most Westerners—even Christians—tend to categorize problems as either spiritual or psychological. The Bible integrates the two and identifies both soul and spirit as the heart. Root problems are heart problems. The spirit affects the soul (mind, emotions, and will), and the soul affects the spirit. Almost every counseling problem will, therefore, have a spiritual and psychological aspect, although one of these may predominate. Some clients expect the counselor to deal with their problems solely from a spiritual direction, and others may be offended that the counselor is too spiritually minded. From a biblical point of view, the principles of the Spirit are critical to the entire process of salvation and wholeness. Watchman Nee, in *The Spiritual Man* (1968), suggests that our spirit includes our intuition (or ability to hear from God), our communion with God (our ability to experience Him), and our conscience (our ability to know what is right and wrong). In order to understand these functions we must learn the principles of the Spirit: How spirits function, Salvation, the baptism of the Holy Spirit, Prayer, Thanksgiving, Praise and Worship, Fasting, Revelation, Conscience, and Walking according to the Spirit.

Principles of How Spirits Function

1. <u>Receiving the Spirit of God is called spiritual re-birth and is required to experience and enter into a relationship with God.</u> The Holy Spirit tries to influence us to become holy like God so that we can have fellowship with Him. To be born again means to accept the Spirit of God into our hearts by faith. It is the beginning of the process of salvation and a mandatory requirement for salvation.

    Jo 3:3 Jesus answered and said unto him, Verily, verily, I say unto thee, Except a man be born again, he cannot see the kingdom of God.

    5 Jesus answered, Verily, verily, I say unto thee, Except a man be born of water and [of] the Spirit, he cannot enter into the kingdom of God.

2. <u>Because the flesh is weak, we cannot obey the law without the help of the Spirit of God.</u>

    Ro 8:2 For the law of the Spirit of life in Christ Jesus hath made me free from the law of sin and death.

    3 For what the law could not do, in that it was weak through the flesh, God sending his own Son in the likeness of sinful flesh, and for sin, condemned sin in the flesh:

4 That the righteousness of the law might be fulfilled in us, who walk not after the flesh, but after the Spirit

3. We cannot truly change without the help of the Spirit of God.

    Ga 3:2 This only would I learn of you, Received ye the Spirit by the works of the law, or by the hearing of faith?

    3 Are ye so foolish? having begun in the Spirit, are ye now made perfect by the flesh?

    5 He therefore that ministereth to you the Spirit, and worketh miracles among you, [doeth he it] by the works of the law, or by the hearing of faith?

4. Spirits affect us by influencing our will.

    Lu 1:17 And he shall go before him in the spirit and power of Elias, to turn the hearts (will) of the fathers to the children, and the disobedient to the wisdom of the just; to make ready a people prepared for the Lord.

5. Spirits, both good and evil, are received by faith. Unless we believe that they exist and want what they represent in our lives, they cannot continue to have influence over us.

    Ga 3:14 That the blessing of Abraham might come on the Gentiles through Jesus Christ; that we might receive the promise of the Spirit through faith.

    Eph 1:13 In whom ye also trusted, after that ye heard the word of truth, the gospel of your salvation: in whom also after that ye believed, ye were sealed with that holy Spirit of promise,

    1 Jo 4:1 Beloved, believe not every spirit, but try the spirits whether they are of God: because many false prophets are gone out into the world.

6. Spirits that are unwanted can be commanded and cast out. Because Jesus won the victory over all the power of the devil at the cross, spirits no longer possess any power that we do not give them. They attempt to deceive us into giving them power by convincing us that we need and can rely on them to help us or to meet our needs. As suggested by Neil Anderson (2000), today dealing with spirits is a truth encounter, not a power encounter.

    Mr 9:25 When Jesus saw that the people came running together, he rebuked the foul spirit, saying unto him, [Thou] dumb and deaf spirit, I charge thee, come out of him, and enter no more into him.

    Lu 10:19 Behold, I give unto you power to tread on serpents and scorpions, and over all the power of the enemy: and nothing shall by any means hurt you.

7. An evil spirit must be replaced or it may return. We accept spirits for what we believe they will do for us to meet our needs. Unless we learn to meet our needs in some other way, we will eventually desire to have them back. This is the spiritual application of the "put off-put on" method of change.

    Mt 12:43 When the unclean spirit is gone out of a man, he walketh through dry places, seeking rest, and findeth none.

    44 Then he saith, I will return into my house from whence I came out; and when he is come, he findeth [it] empty, swept, and garnished.

45 Then goeth he, and taketh with himself seven other spirits more wicked than himself, and they enter in and dwell there: and the last [state] of that man is worse than the first. Even so shall it be also unto this wicked generation.

8. <u>We must learn to rule our own spiritual nature.</u>

   Pr 25:28 He that [hath] no rule over his own spirit [is like] a city [that is] broken down, [and] without walls.

9. <u>Unsaved people cannot understand the spiritual things of God.</u>

   1 Co 2:14 But the natural man receiveth not the things of the Spirit of God: for they are foolishness unto him: neither can he know [them], because they are spiritually discerned.

Counseling Methods and Techniques

1. <u>Spirits only have as much power as we give them by yielding to them.</u> As we yield to and desire for the Holy Spirit to make us holy, He will. As long as we refuse to yield to Him, He can do nothing. This is also true of evil spirits. Satan lost all of his power that had been given to him by Adam, 2000 years ago at the cross, and today he only has whatever amount of power we choose to give him. Of course, he acquires most of this power through deception. Spirits control us by influencing our will.

2. <u>We open ourselves to spirits through desire, faith and psychological problems.</u> We invite spirits—good and evil—into us through our desire for them and our faith in them. Sometimes they attempt to gain entrance through generational sins or curses, but even in these cases, they cannot remain if we do not want them. When we are saved, through faith, we invite the Holy Spirit into us and yield control to Him. In the same way, evil spirits are invited in by witches and Satanists. Psychological problems provide openings in our spiritual armor for spirits to gain entrance into our lives and they will remain as long as we desire them or as long as we refuse to close these points of entrance by dealing with these psychological problems.

3. <u>We have authority over spirits through faith in Jesus' victory over them.</u> It is our relationship with Christ that gives us this power as long as we believe that we have it. The seven sons of Sceva are a good example of the need for faith in dealing with spirits.

   Ac 19:13 Then certain of the vagabond Jews, exorcists, took upon them to call over them which had evil spirits the name of the Lord Jesus, saying, We adjure you by Jesus whom Paul preacheth.

   14 And there were seven sons of one Sceva, a Jew, and chief of the priests, which did so.

   15 And the evil spirit answered and said, Jesus I know, and Paul I know; but who are ye?

   16 And the man in whom the evil spirit was leaped on them, and overcame them, and prevailed against them, so that they fled out of that house naked and wounded.

The Principles of Salvation

The Bible tells us that the salvation or wholeness that God provides through Christ is complete; spirit, soul, and body. When we believe and accept Christ, our spirit is regenerated or saved. When we are born of the Spirit we receive a new nature, are forgiven and Christ's Spirit comes to dwell within us so that we can have fellowship with Him. Through salvation, in this lifetime, our soul becomes progressively more whole as we yield to the Holy Spirit and renew our mind (which controls our emotions and will, and which, in turn, results in right actions). Healing is available for our bodies through faith, but our bodies will never fully "put off corruption" until they are renewed in the resurrection. Consequently, salvation includes complete wholeness in its fullest sense!

1. The requirements for salvation are most clearly described in Romans 10:9.

    Ro 10:9 That if thou shalt confess with thy mouth the Lord Jesus, and shalt believe in thine heart that God hath raised him from the dead, thou shalt be saved.

2. Salvation or wholeness comes only through believing in Jesus and acting on that faith.

    Ac 2:21 And it shall come to pass, that whosoever shall call on the name of the Lord shall be saved.

    4:12 Neither is there salvation in any other: for there is none other name under heaven given among men, whereby we must be saved.

3. Hearing the Word of God and believing what is preached is the first step in the process of salvation.

    1 Co 1:21 For after that in the wisdom of God the world by wisdom knew not God, it pleased God by the foolishness of preaching to save them that believe.

4. The Gospel or good news about Jesus is the life-changing message that we must believe, in order to be saved.

    Ro 1:16 For I am not ashamed of the gospel of Christ: for it is the power of God unto salvation to every one that believeth; to the Jew first, and also to the Greek.

5. Salvation is a gift of God that He gives to us based solely on His unmerited favor for us and not due to anything that we have done.

    Eph 2:8 For by grace are ye saved through faith; and that not of yourselves: it is the gift of God:

    2 Ti 1:9 Who hath saved us, and called us with an holy calling, not according to our works, but according to his own purpose and grace, which was given us in Christ Jesus before the world began,

6. Faith is the most important factor in the process of salvation and it results in the salvation or wholeness of our souls.

    1 Pe 1:9 Receiving the end of your faith, even the salvation of your souls.

7. It is necessary for us to repent or change the direction of our lives in order to be saved. Repentance is the action that clearly demonstrates that we have believed in our hearts.

    2 Co 7:10 For godly sorrow worketh repentance to salvation not to be repented of: but the sorrow of the world worketh death.

8. Our full salvation comes progressively over a period of time and is culminated in the transformation of our bodies when Christ returns for a second time.

   1 Jo 3:2 Beloved, now are we the sons of God, and it doth not yet appear what we shall be: but we know that, when he shall appear, we shall be like him; for we shall see him as he is.

9. There is no other way to escape from our selfish and sinful life, except through the process of salvation by faith.

   Heb 2:3 How shall we escape, if we neglect so great salvation; which at the first began to be spoken by the Lord, and was confirmed unto us by them that heard him;

10. When we accept Christ, we are justified by His blood and are reconciled to God.

    Ro 5:9 Much more then, being now justified by His blood, we shall be saved from wrath through him.

11. We have a part in the salvation process: yielding our will to God's directions and acting according to the Word of God. Without this yielding to the Spirit of God and acting on what we believe, the amount of change in our lives will be limited.

    Php 2:12 Wherefore, my beloved, as ye have always obeyed, not as in my presence only, but now much more in my absence, work out your own salvation with fear and trembling.

12. The Holy Scriptures help us understand and do our part in the process of salvation by faith.

    2 Ti 3:15 And that from a child thou hast known the holy scriptures, which are able to make thee wise unto salvation through faith which is in Christ Jesus.

13. It is God's will that everyone be saved and made completely whole.

    1 Ti 2:4 Who will have all men to be saved, and to come unto the knowledge of the truth.

14. Because salvation or wholeness is a process, we must continue in it until we are completely transformed and receive eternal life.

    Mt 10:22 And ye shall be hated of all men for my name's sake: but he that endureth to the end shall be saved.

Counseling Methods and Techniques

1. To be saved, we must believe with the heart, confess, and make Jesus Lord.

   a. Believe with the heart: In the Bible, the Greek word for heart is *kardia*. It means, "the center of all physical and spiritual life." Verses can be found where it refers to the mind, emotions, will, spirit or any combination of these. To be saved, we must believe in our hearts that God raised Jesus from the dead. We must have faith that Jesus was "to be the firstborn of many brethren" (Romans 8:29), and that God will also resurrect us, meet our needs, and make us completely whole. The Greek word here for believe is *pisteuo* which is defined as, "to think to be true, to be persuaded of, to credit, place confidence in, …to entrust a thing to one or to be entrusted with a thing." It is the same root word as the word translated as faith. Therefore, believing is a lot more than mental assent or agreeing that something is true. We must actually trust, place our confidence in and rely on God to aid us, obtain our desires or meet our needs.

b. <u>Confess with our mouth what we believe.</u> The Greek word for confess is *homologeo* which means "To say the same thing as another, i.e. to agree with, assent, to promise, not to deny, to declare openly, speak out freely, to profess one's self the worshipper of one, to praise, and celebrate." The meaning here is to openly and outwardly speak and act in accordance with what we believe—that God has and will meet our needs through Jesus' death and resurrection. In James Chapter 2, it is clear that faith without works or action is dead; and salvation will not work if we fail to act according to our trust in Him.

c. <u>Confess Jesus as Lord.</u> The Greek word for Lord here is *kurios* which means "He to whom a person or thing belongs, about which he has power of deciding; master, lord; the possessor and disposer of a thing; the owner; one who has control of the person." The issue here is submission and control. If we refuse to cooperate with God's day-by-day direction of our lives, God's plan for our transformation can be thwarted. The child who will not obey his parents makes the wonderful life they intend for him impossible or at least significantly more difficult. Either God is our boss, or we are our own boss. God will not be our genie and just bless whatever we selfishly want to do! When we seek His direction for our lives, to that extent salvation or the process of moving toward wholeness will be working in our lives.

2. <u>If we are saved, we will know it by our desires and actions.</u> Even a carnal Christian who is still controlled by the flesh will find that they want to do what is right and that they will make attempts to act according to their faith. This is because when we are saved the Holy Spirit comes into us and influences us to want to be holy and do the will of God. When a young girl was asked what difference Christ had made in her life she replied, "…before I was a Christian I ran after sin. Now I run from it though sometimes I am still overtaken." (Tan, 1979, p. 1230) The Bible says we become a new creature (2 Corinthians 5:17).

The Principles of the Baptism of the Holy Spirit

Although there is still controversy in some Christian denominations over the experience commonly referred to as the baptism of the Holy Spirit, this spiritual experience can provide a very significant spiritual catalyst in the life of the believer (just as it did on the day of Pentecost in Acts Chapter 2). Unfortunately, we, as people, generally defend what we have been taught instead of more openly examining the Scriptures to find out what they say. As discussed in my book *Transformation!,* two and one half of the tribes of Israel asked to be allowed to dwell on the other side of the Jordan River outside of the Land of Canaan. They were allowed by God to do so if they were willing to help their brothers take the land. I believe that the supernatural parting of the Jordan River stands for the baptism of the Holy Spirit just as the supernatural parting of the Red Sea stands for water baptism. If this is so, then God has clearly indicated that Christians should be given free choice to dwell on whichever side of this controversy they might choose.

However, because it is not unusual for clients to come to counseling looking to move forward in their spiritual walk, including receiving the baptism of the Holy Spirit or seeking the gifts of the Spirit, it is important for each counselor to at least become familiar with what the Scriptures say about this subject. Both the baptism of the Holy Spirit and the gifts of the Spirit can prove to be powerful change agents in the life of a client.

1. It was prophesied that the gift of the Holy Spirit was to take place after the death and resurrection of Jesus.

   Jo 7:39 (But this spake he of the Spirit, which they that believe on him should receive: for the Holy Ghost was not yet given; because that Jesus was not yet glorified.)

2. The disciples received the Holy Spirit into their hearts after Jesus' resurrection, but before His ascension.

   Jo 20:22 And when he had said this, he breathed on them, and saith unto them, Receive ye the Holy Ghost:

3. At that time, Jesus also promised that they would be baptized in the Holy Ghost.

   Ac 1:5 For John truly baptized with water; but ye shall be baptized with the Holy Ghost not many days hence.

   8 But ye shall receive power, after that the Holy Ghost is come upon you: and ye shall be witnesses unto me both in Jerusalem, and in all Judaea, and in Samaria, and unto the uttermost part of the earth.

   11:16 Then remembered I the word of the Lord, how that he said, John indeed baptized with water; but ye shall be baptized with the Holy Ghost.

4. This second promise was first fulfilled at Pentecost and was accompanied with the ability to speak with other languages that they had never learned.

   Ac 2:4 And they were all filled with the Holy Ghost, and began to speak with other tongues, as the Spirit gave them utterance.

   38 Then Peter said unto them, Repent, and be baptized every one of you in the name of Jesus Christ for the remission of sins, and ye shall receive the gift of the Holy Ghost.

5. Receiving the Spirit of God into our hearts and being baptized in water are distinctly different experiences from that of the baptism of the Holy Spirit. Although those in Samaria were clearly saved through the preaching of Philip and were baptized in water, they did not receive the baptism of the Holy Spirit until Peter and John came from Jerusalem and laid their hands on them.

   Ac 8:12 But when they believed Philip preaching the things concerning the kingdom of God, and the name of Jesus Christ, they were baptized, both men and women.

   14 Now when the apostles which were at Jerusalem heard that Samaria had received the word of God, they sent unto them Peter and John:

   15 Who, when they were come down, prayed for them, that they might receive the Holy Ghost:

   16 (For as yet he was fallen upon none of them: only they were baptized in the name of the Lord Jesus.)

   17 Then laid they their hands on them, and they received the Holy Ghost.

6. In most cases described in the Bible, the baptism of the Holy Spirit was received after accepting Christ and after water baptism. It was accompanied by speaking in tongues and the manifestation of spiritual gifts.

Ac 19:1 And it came to pass, that, while Apollos was at Corinth, Paul having passed through the upper coasts came to Ephesus: and finding certain disciples,

2 He said unto them, Have ye received the Holy Ghost since ye believed? And they said unto him, We have not so much as heard whether there be any Holy Ghost.

3 And he said unto them, Unto what then were ye baptized? And they said, Unto John's baptism.

4 Then said Paul, John verily baptized with the baptism of repentance, saying unto the people, that they should believe on him which should come after him, that is, on Christ Jesus.

5 When they heard this, they were baptized in the name of the Lord Jesus.

6 And when Paul had laid his hands upon them, the Holy Ghost came on them; and they spake with tongues, and prophesied.

7. <u>Still, it is possible to receive salvation and the baptism of the Holy Ghost at the same time.</u> This occurred when the Gentiles received both salvation and the baptism of the Holy Spirit at the house of Cornelius. Clearly, the disciples believed that the manifestation of the baptism of the Holy Spirit (speaking in other tongues and magnifying God) was a definite indication that the person had already been saved.

Ac 10:44 While Peter yet spake these words, the Holy Ghost fell on all them which heard the word.

45 And they of the circumcision which believed were astonished, as many as came with Peter, because that on the Gentiles also was poured out the gift of the Holy Ghost.

46 For they heard them speak with tongues, and magnify God. Then answered Peter,

47 Can any man forbid water, that these should not be baptized, which have received the Holy Ghost as well as we?

48 And he commanded them to be baptized in the name of the Lord. Then prayed they him to tarry certain days.

8. <u>The Spirit of God gives spiritual gifts to whom He desires.</u> For most, this occurs after the baptism of the Holy Spirit.

1 Co 12:4 Now there are diversities of gifts, but the same Spirit.

7 But the manifestation of the Spirit is given to every man to profit withal.

8 For to one is given by the Spirit the word of wisdom; to another the word of knowledge by the same Spirit;

9 To another faith by the same Spirit; to another the gifts of healing by the same Spirit;

10 To another the working of miracles; to another prophecy; to another discerning of spirits; to another divers kinds of tongues; to another the interpretation of tongues:

11 But all these worketh that one and the selfsame Spirit, dividing to every man severally as he will.

9. <u>Much of the confusion that exists over the use of tongues is due to the fact that the Bible refers to two different types of tongues:</u> One type, which is used to communicate and pray to God and edifies that person, requires no interpretation since God already understands it. The other, which is one of the nine supernatural gifts of the Spirit, brings a message from God to the church and, therefore, requires interpretation. Notice that in the first paragraph (verses 2 and 4), tongues are spoken unto

God and edify the person. In the second paragraph (verse 6 and 13), tongues are spoken unto other people for their profit and require interpretation.

1 Co 14:2 For <u>he that speaketh in an unknown tongue speaketh not unto men, but unto God:</u> for no man understandeth him; howbeit in the spirit he speaketh mysteries.

4 He that speaketh in an unknown tongue edifieth himself; but he that prophesieth edifieth the church.

6 Now, brethren, <u>if I come unto you speaking with tongues,</u> what shall I profit you, except I shall speak to you either by revelation, or by knowledge, or by prophesying, or by doctrine?

13 Wherefore let him that speaketh in an unknown tongue pray that he may interpret.

10. <u>After being saved and receiving the baptism of the Holy Spirit, we are to continue to be filled with the Spirit of God.</u>

Eph 5:18 And be not drunk with wine, wherein is excess; but be filled with the Spirit;

Ac 4:31 And when they had prayed, the place was shaken where they were assembled together; and they were all filled with the Holy Ghost, and they spake the word of God with boldness.

Counseling Methods and Techniques

1. <u>The baptism of the Holy Spirit is a separate experience from salvation.</u> It occurs when, through faith, we yield our spirit fully to the Spirit of God. One of the evidences of the baptism of the Holy Spirit is the ability to speak in other languages (human or spiritual) without learning them. It can be received at the moment of salvation (as Cornelius did) or at a future time (like at Samaria). Its purpose is to strengthen the believer to reach others for Christ and to usher in the supernatural gifts of the Holy Spirit. In the early church, it was an expected experience of all believers. However, it is not something that is mandatory in order to be saved but a gift of God and an empowerment of the person in the spiritual realm. It does not necessarily change the character of the person receiving the gift but, in counseling, it can be an extremely effective tool in helping clients grow in their Christian experience and strengthen them spiritually to overcome the flesh.

2. <u>We receive the baptism of the Holy Spirit by asking and acting in faith.</u> I suggest the following steps when asked to assist someone in receiving the baptism of the Holy Spirit.

    a. <u>Determine that they are clearly saved and born again.</u> (See how to be saved in the previous section.)

    b. <u>Determine what they currently believe about the baptism of the Holy Spirit and help them understand the principles presented above.</u>

    c. <u>Ask them if they believe that God wants to and will give them the baptism of the Holy Spirit with the evidence of speaking in tongues if they ask.</u> This is important because the baptism, like salvation, is received by faith. If they are not sure, suggest they study the subject further until they are convinced.

    d. <u>Explain that if they truly believe that God will give it to them, then they will act in faith, open their mouth, and begin speaking (but not in English) when you lay your hands on them and pray that they receive it.</u>

    e. <u>Lay your hands on them and pray in faith.</u> If you do not have the faith to believe that they will receive it or have not yet received the baptism of the Holy Spirit with the evidence of speaking in tongues yourself, have someone else pray with you who does have the faith that they will receive the baptism when you lay your hands on them and pray.

    f. <u>When they receive the baptism of the Holy Spirit, encourage them to continue praying in their new prayer language to edify themselves in the Spirit.</u>

3. <u>If, for some reason, they are not able to receive the baptism of the Holy Spirit, encourage them to continue seeking it.</u> God wants to give it to them, and it is only a matter of time until they will receive it as they continue to study the Word of God and become more convinced that what God's Word says is true.

The Principles of Prayer

Prayer is critical in order to effectively communicate with God, build a close relationship with Him and receive His promises. We, as Christians, must learn how to effectively pray in order to receive the answers to our prayers rather than attempt to rely primarily on our own efforts and hope that God may somehow mysteriously help us.

1. <u>We need prayer to obtain what we need.</u>

    Jas 4:2 Ye lust, and have not: ye kill, and desire to have, and cannot obtain: ye fight and war, yet ye have not, because ye ask not.

2. <u>Prayer is also our means of helping others.</u>

    1 Ti 2:1 I exhort therefore, that, first of all, supplications, prayers, intercessions, [and] giving of thanks, be made for all men;

3. <u>Through prayer, we can come boldly to receive mercy and grace in time of need.</u>

    Heb 4:16 Let us therefore come boldly unto the throne of grace, that we may obtain mercy, and find grace to help in time of need.

4. <u>Prayer is the key to our future.</u>

    Lu 21:36 Watch ye therefore, and pray always, that ye may be accounted worthy to escape all these things that shall come to pass, and to stand before the Son of man.

5. <u>Prayer changes us and promotes spiritual growth.</u>

    2 Co 3:18 But we all, with open face beholding as in a glass the glory of the Lord, are changed into the same image from glory to glory, [even] as by the Spirit of the Lord.

6. <u>We should pray in the name of Christ, relying on His merit, not ours.</u> We deserve nothing and are blessed only through the merits of Christ.

    Jo 14:13 And whatsoever ye shall ask in my name, that will I do, that the Father may be glorified in the Son.
    14 If ye shall ask any thing in my name, I will do [it].

7. <u>We should pray according to the will of God.</u>

    1 Jo 5:14 And this is the confidence that we have in him, that, if we ask any thing according to His will, he heareth us:

    15 And if we know that he hear us, whatsoever we ask, we know that we have the petitions that we desired of him.

8. <u>The Spirit of God will help us pray according to His will.</u>

    Ro 8:26 Likewise the Spirit also helpeth our infirmities: for we know not what we should pray for as we ought: but the Spirit itself maketh intercession for us with groanings which cannot be uttered.

    27 And he that searcheth the hearts knoweth what [is] the mind of the Spirit, because he maketh intercession for the saints according to [the will of] God.

9. <u>We must persevere in prayer in order to ensure that our prayers will be answered.</u> We need to pray until we are assured we have the answer in our spirit, and then thank God for the answer until it is fully manifested in our lives.

    Lu 11:5 And he said unto them, Which of you shall have a friend, and shall go unto him at midnight, and say unto him, Friend, lend me three loaves;

    6 For a friend of mine in his journey is come to me, and I have nothing to set before him?

    7 And he from within shall answer and say, Trouble me not: the door is now shut, and my children are with me in bed; I cannot rise and give thee.

    8 I say unto you, Though he will not rise and give him, because he is his friend, yet because of his importunity he will rise and give him as many as he needeth.

10. <u>All prayers are not immediately answered.</u> There is a battle in the spirit realm that must also be won for the answer to be manifested.

    Lu 18:7 And shall not God avenge his own elect, which cry day and night unto him, though he bear long with them?

    Da 10:12 Then said he unto me, Fear not, Daniel: for from the first day that thou didst set thine heart to understand, and to chasten thyself before thy God, thy words were heard, and I am come for thy words.

    13 But the prince of the kingdom of Persia withstood me one and twenty days: but, lo, Michael, one of the chief princes, came to help me; and I remained there with the kings of Persia.

11. <u>Sin can hinder prayer.</u> We must examine ourselves, and if sin is the problem, repent and ask for forgiveness.

    Isa 59:2 But your iniquities have separated between you and your God, and your sins have hid [his] face from you, that he will not hear.

12. <u>Sometimes prayers are not answered because they are selfish.</u> God loves us so much that He will only give us what is truly good for us.

Jas 4:3 Ye ask, and receive not, because ye ask amiss, that ye may consume [it] upon your lusts.

13. <u>Valuing other things over God can hinder our prayers.</u>

Eze 14:3 Son of man, these men have set up their idols in their heart, and put the stumblingblock of their iniquity before their face: should I be enquired of at all by them?

14. <u>Refusing to give what we have to help others can hinder prayer.</u>

Pr 21:13 Whoso stoppeth his ears at the cry of the poor, he also shall cry himself, but shall not be heard.

Lu 6:38 Give, and it shall be given unto you; good measure, pressed down, and shaken together, and running over, shall men give into your bosom. For with the same measure that ye mete withal it shall be measured to you again.

15. <u>Treating our mate poorly can hinder our prayers.</u>

1 Pe 3:7 Likewise, ye husbands, dwell with [them] according to knowledge, giving honour unto the wife, as unto the weaker vessel, and as being heirs together of the grace of life; that your prayers be not hindered.

16. <u>The effective fervent prayer is the one that will be heard.</u> Rev. Homer Hodge states, "No one can command success and become a real praying soul unless intense application is the price. I am even now convinced the difference between the saints like Wesley, Flecher, Edwards, Brainerd, Bramwell, and ourselves is energy, perseverance, and the invincible determination to succeed or die in the attempt." (Bounds, 1997, P. 413) He went on to say, "We announce the law of prayer as follows: A Christian's prayer is a joint agreement of the will, the mind, the emotions, the conscience, the intellect, working in harmony at white heat. The body cooperates under certain conditions to make the prayer long enough and at a high voltage to insure tremendous supernatural and unearthly results." (p. 459)

Jas 5:16 Confess [your] faults one to another, and pray one for another, that ye may be healed. The effectual fervent prayer of a righteous man availeth much.

Counseling Methods and Techniques

1. <u>We need to learn to pray effectively in faith to see answered prayer.</u> This may take some time, but we should not only encourage our clients to pray but also should model praying as part of our therapy. I almost always close my counseling sessions with prayer. One of my clients also asked that we open the session in prayer. In addition to teaching our clients the principles of prayer, we can refer them to the many other good books on this subject.

2. <u>Pray until we know we have it, then thank God for it until we see it.</u> Confusion seems to exist between the Christians who say if you pray for something more than once, that you are praying in unbelief; and those who emphasize persevering prayer or "praying through." In actuality, there is no conflict here. If we have the faith in our spirit that we have what we are asking for, then praying once is sufficient; and in that faith, we should thank God that He has given the answer to us until it is manifested in our lives. However, if we do not have that knowing assurance in our spirit that we have it, we need to continue to build our faith and pray until that assurance comes from God.

The Principles of Thanksgiving, Praise and Worship

The Bible is clear that in our relationship with God, thanksgiving, praise and worship are important ingredients. Thanksgiving has to do with acknowledgment and appreciation for what God has done for us. Praise is a commendation in word or song for Who God is. Worship is making obeisance, reverence, having a feeling of awe or devotion toward, or providing service to God.

1. <u>We are to thank God for everything He does for us, in all circumstances.</u>

   Eph 5:20 Giving thanks always for all things unto God and the Father in the name of our Lord Jesus Christ;

2. <u>Thanksgiving is the first step in approaching God.</u>

   Ps 100:4 Enter into his gates with thanksgiving, and into his courts with praise: be thankful unto him, and bless his name.

3. <u>Thanksgiving can also be a sacrifice that is pleasing to God.</u>

   Ps 116:17 I will offer to thee the sacrifice of thanksgiving, and will call upon the name of the LORD.

   Hab 3:17 Although the fig tree shall not blossom, neither shall fruit be in the vines; the labour of the olive shall fail, and the fields shall yield no meat; the flock shall be cut off from the fold, and there shall be no herd in the stalls:

   18 Yet I will rejoice in the LORD, I will joy in the God of my salvation.

4. <u>Being thankful for what we have leads to more blessings.</u>

   Jer 30:19 And out of them shall proceed thanksgiving and the voice of them that make merry: and I will multiply them, and they shall not be few; I will also glorify them, and they shall not be small.

   2 Co 4:15 For all things are for your sakes, that the abundant grace might through the thanksgiving of many redound to the glory of God.

5. <u>We are to sing praises to God. When we do, God inhabits or manifests Himself in our praise.</u>

   Ps 21:13 Be thou exalted, LORD, in thine own strength: so will we sing and praise thy power.

   22:3 But thou art holy, O thou that inhabitest the praises of Israel.

6. <u>Praise is a powerful spiritual weapon.</u>

   2 Chr 20:21 And when he had consulted with the people, he appointed singers unto the LORD, and that should praise the beauty of holiness, as they went out before the army, and to say, Praise the LORD; for his mercy endureth for ever.

   22 And when they began to sing and to praise, the LORD set ambushments against the children of Ammon, Moab, and mount Seir, which were come against Judah; and they were smitten.

7. <u>Praising God significantly improves our emotional state.</u>

    Ps 42:11 Why art thou cast down, O my soul? and why art thou disquieted within me? hope thou in God: for I shall yet praise him, who is the health of my countenance, and my God.

    Isa 61:3 To appoint unto them that mourn in Zion, to give unto them beauty for ashes, the oil of joy for mourning, the garment of praise for the spirit of heaviness; that they might be called trees of righteousness, the planting of the LORD, that he might be glorified.

8. <u>We should praise Him for all He has done for us.</u>

    Ps 139:14 I will praise thee; for I am fearfully and wonderfully made: marvellous are thy works; and that my soul knoweth right well.

    145:4 One generation shall praise thy works to another, and shall declare thy mighty acts.

9. <u>We should praise Him by singing a new song and with instruments.</u>

    Ps 149:1 Praise ye the LORD. Sing unto the LORD a new song, and his praise in the congregation of saints.

    150:3 Praise him with the sound of the trumpet: praise him with the psaltery and harp.

    4 Praise him with the timbrel and dance: praise him with stringed instruments and organs.

    5 Praise him upon the loud cymbals: praise him upon the high sounding cymbals.

10. <u>Everyone should praise the Lord.</u>

    Ps 150:6 Let every thing that hath breath praise the LORD. Praise ye the LORD.

    Re 19:5 And a voice came out of the throne, saying, Praise our God, all ye his servants, and ye that fear him, both small and great.

    Mt 21:16 And said unto him, Hearest thou what these say? And Jesus saith unto them, Yea; have ye never read, Out of the mouth of babes and sucklings thou hast perfected praise?

11. <u>We should not praise ourselves.</u>

    Pr 27:2 Let another man praise thee, and not thine own mouth; a stranger, and not thine own lips.

12. <u>We are not to value the praise of men more than what God says about us.</u>

    Jo 12:43 For they loved the praise of men more than the praise of God.

13. <u>God's praise is based on the motivations of our hearts and the strength of our faith.</u>

    1 Co 4:5 Therefore judge nothing before the time, until the Lord come, who both will bring to light the hidden things of darkness, and will make manifest the counsels of the hearts: and then shall every man have praise of God.

    1 Pe 1:7 That the trial of your faith, being much more precious than of gold that perisheth, though it be tried with fire, might be found unto praise and honour and glory at the appearing of Jesus Christ:

14. <u>We are commanded to worship God.</u>

1 Chr 16:29 Give unto the LORD the glory due unto his name: bring an offering, and come before him: worship the LORD in the beauty of holiness.

Ps 29:2 Give unto the LORD the glory due unto his name; worship the LORD in the beauty of holiness.

15. <u>We are to reserve our worship only for God.</u>

Ex 34:14 For thou shalt worship no other god: for the LORD, whose name is Jealous, is a jealous God:

De 8:19 And it shall be, if thou do at all forget the LORD thy God, and walk after other gods, and serve them, and worship them, I testify against you this day that ye shall surely perish.

11:16 Take heed to yourselves, that your heart be not deceived, and ye turn aside, and serve other gods, and worship them.

16. <u>Satan also desires our worship.</u>

Lu 4:7 If thou therefore wilt worship me, all shall be thine.

8 And Jesus answered and said unto him, Get thee behind me, Satan: for it is written, Thou shalt worship the Lord thy God, and him only shalt thou serve.

17. <u>We must worship in Spirit and truth.</u>

Jo 4:23 But the hour cometh, and now is, when the true worshippers shall worship the Father in spirit and in truth: for the Father seeketh such to worship him.

24 God is a Spirit: and they that worship him must worship him in spirit and in truth.

Counseling Methods and Techniques

1. <u>We can learn to approach God through the model of the tabernacle.</u> As we thank Him, we enter the gates, we praise Him in the courts and we worship Him in the Holy of Holies. Each part of the tabernacle and the furniture within, teaches us what we must do to approach God's manifested presence. (For more information see *Made According to Pattern* (1974) by C. W. Slemming.)

   1. Jesus is the gate and only those who come through Him in thanksgiving may enter.

   2. The courts prevent unlawful approach. None can enter in without praise.

   3. The Altar of Sacrifice shows that we must accept Jesus' sacrifice for our sins.

   4. We must identify with this sacrifice as we offer the sacrifice of praise.

   5. The Laver shows us that we must be convicted and washed by the Word of God in order to worship in Spirit and truth.

   6. Only priests (those who are saved) may enter the Holy Place, and then only after they have been cleansed. We are to be priests and kings of God. (Revelations 1:6)

   7. The lamps show that we are to praise God along with His church, which is the light of the world.

8. The Shew Bread indicates that we are to participate in fellowship with the Lord as we enter into praise.

9. The Altar of Incense represents our prayers reaching up to God.

10. The curtain of the Holy of Holies, which was ripped in two, indicates that we can now approach God directly. It also indicates that we must rend or die to our self-life to truly enter into His presence.

11. The Holy of Holies could only be entered once a year with the blood of the sacrifice. Therefore, we can enter into worship only by the blood of Jesus, our lamb of sacrifice.

12. At the mercy seat we find cleansing for all our sins. Without this cleansing, we cannot enter His presence or truly worship God.

13. The Shekinah Glory represents the very presence of God Himself. It is in His manifested presence that we come into true worship.

14. The Ark of the Covenant represents our heart. Inside of our heart, we are to place the manna (the Word of God), the law (written in our hearts through Christ), and Aaron's rod that budded (the authority of God in our lives). These are essential for true worship and fellowship with God.

2. <u>True worship brings us into the presence of God and brings healing.</u> Experiencing the very presence of God takes our eyes off ourselves and strengthens our faith as nothing else can do. Praise and worship services in most churches provide this opportunity.

The Principles of Fasting

Although fasting is clearly established in the Bible and has historically been an important spiritual discipline of the church, today, it is seldom practiced in the majority of our churches. Fasting is especially important in breaking the power of the flesh and in reinforcing prayer.

1. <u>God calls us to fast.</u>

    Joe 2:15 Blow the trumpet in Zion, sanctify a fast, call a solemn assembly:.

2. <u>It is not a question of if you fast, but when.</u>

    Mt 6:16 Moreover <u>when ye fast,</u> be not, as the hypocrites, of a sad countenance: for they disfigure their faces, that they may appear unto men to fast. Verily I say unto you, They have their reward.
    17 But thou, <u>when thou fastest,</u> anoint thine head, and wash thy face;

3. <u>Fasting intensifies prayer and spiritual power.</u>

    Mr 9:28 And when he was come into the house, his disciples asked him privately, Why could not we cast him out?
    29 And he said unto them, This kind can come forth by nothing, but by prayer and fasting.

4. <u>Fasting intensifies our relationship, communication, and ability to discern the will of God.</u>

    Ac 13:2 As they ministered to the Lord, and fasted, the Holy Ghost said, Separate me Barnabas and Saul for the work whereunto I have called them.

5. <u>Fasting aids in our sanctification.</u>

    Ps 69:10 When I wept, [and chastened] my soul with fasting, that was to my reproach.

6. <u>Fasting assists in receiving answers from God.</u>

    Ezr 8:23 So we fasted and besought our God for this: and he was entreated of us.

7. <u>Fasting shows repentance and turns away wrath.</u>

    Jon 3:5 So the people of Nineveh believed God, and proclaimed a fast, and put on sackcloth, from the greatest of them even to the least of them.

8. <u>Fasting sets free the captives of the flesh and of Satan.</u>

    Isa 58:6 [Is] not this the fast that I have chosen? to loose the bands of wickedness, to undo the heavy burdens, and to let the oppressed go free, and that ye break every yoke?

9. <u>Fasting brings spiritual breakthroughs and revelation.</u>

    Da 9:3 And I set my face unto the Lord God, to seek by prayer and supplications, with fasting, and sackcloth, and ashes:

10. <u>One type of fast is the normal fast where we abstain from all food, but drink water.</u>

    Mt 4:2 And when he had fasted forty days and forty nights, he was afterward an hungred.

11. <u>An absolute fast is one where neither food nor water is taken.</u> It must be limited in length to avoid dehydration.

    Es 4:16 Go, gather together all the Jews that are present in Shushan, and fast ye for me, and neither eat nor drink three days, night or day: I also and my maidens will fast likewise; and so will I go in unto the king, which [is] not according to the law: and if I perish, I perish.

12. <u>A partial fast is one where pleasant food is not eaten.</u> It can be used at any time, even when heavy work is required.

    Da 10:3 I ate no pleasant bread, neither came flesh nor wine in my mouth, neither did I anoint myself at all, till three whole weeks were fulfilled.

13. <u>When fasting, we are not to find pleasure or do unnecessary labor, but to focus on God.</u>

    Isa 58:3 Wherefore have we fasted, [say they], and thou seest not? [wherefore] have we afflicted our soul, and thou takest no knowledge? Behold, in the day of your fast ye find pleasure, and exact all your labours.

14. <u>We are not to use fasting to try to get our way and win over others.</u>

Isa 58:4 Behold, ye fast for strife and debate, and to smite with the fist of wickedness: ye shall not fast as [ye do this] day, to make your voice to be heard on high.

5 Is it such a fast that I have chosen? a day for a man to afflict his soul? [is it] to bow down his head as a bulrush, and to spread sackcloth and ashes [under him]? wilt thou call this a fast, and an acceptable day to the LORD?

15. <u>Fasting is for breaking wicked habits, overcoming anxiety and breaking free from oppression.</u>

Isa 58:6 [Is] not this the fast that I have chosen? to loose the bands of wickedness, to undo the heavy burdens, and to let the oppressed go free, and that ye break every yoke?

16. <u>We should use fasting to help others and to deal with our own issues.</u>

Isa 58:7 [Is it] not to deal thy bread to the hungry, and that thou bring the poor that are cast out to thy house? when thou seest the naked, that thou cover him; and that thou hide not thyself from thine own flesh?

17. <u>Fasting also helps to make us more healthy and vigorous, both physically and spiritually.</u> If it is used to help in weight loss, it must still be primarily focused on God.

Isa 58:8 Then shall thy light break forth as the morning, and thine health shall spring forth speedily: and thy righteousness shall go before thee; the glory of the LORD shall be thy rereward.

18. <u>God will respond to us if we seriously fast and are willing to change how we live and what we do.</u>

Isa 58:9 Then shalt thou call, and the LORD shall answer; thou shalt cry, and he shall say, Here I [am]. If thou take away from the midst of thee the yoke, the putting forth of the finger, and speaking vanity;

10 And [if] thou draw out thy soul to the hungry, and satisfy the afflicted soul; then shall thy light rise in obscurity, and thy darkness [be] as the noonday:

19. <u>Fasting can lead to continual guidance and blessing.</u>

Isa 58:11 And the LORD shall guide thee continually, and satisfy thy soul in drought, and make fat thy bones: and thou shalt be like a watered garden, and like a spring of water, whose waters fail not.

12 And [they that shall be] of thee shall build the old waste places: thou shalt raise up the foundations of many generations; and thou shalt be called, The repairer of the breach, The restorer of paths to dwell in.

20. <u>We must be careful to honor God in our fasting.</u>

Isa 58:13 If thou turn away thy foot from the sabbath, [from] doing thy pleasure on my holy day; and call the sabbath a delight, the holy of the LORD, honourable; and shalt honour him, not doing thine own ways, nor finding thine own pleasure, nor speaking [thine own] words:

14 Then shalt thou delight thyself in the LORD; and I will cause thee to ride upon the high places of the earth, and feed thee with the heritage of Jacob thy father: for the mouth of the LORD hath spoken [it].

Counseling Methods and Techniques

1. <u>Fasting is the most effective means for controlling the flesh.</u> This is true because the flesh desires to meet our needs in an excessive manner. Fasting is the denial of those needs. The flesh is selfish and fasting is self-less. The flesh resists fasting, but the Spirit thrives on it. Consequently, fasting helps us to be more spiritually sensitive.

2. <u>We need to learn how to effectively fast in order to see results.</u> We, as counselors, need to be able to teach our clients how to fast. Below are some of the points I try to explain when I teach a client how to fast.

    a. Spiritual aspects
        1. Enter fasting with positive faith.
        2. Base your fast on the Scriptures.
        3. Begin fasting when you are spiritually prepared.
        4. Do not set too long of a time as your goal when you fast for the first time.
        5. Give plenty of time to Bible reading.
        6. Set a specific spiritual objective.
        7. Avoid boastfulness.
        8. Keep a watchful check on your motives.

    b. Physical aspects of fasting
        1. Take proper care of your body—fasting cleans out toxins.
        2. If you have a medical limitation, use an appropriate type of fasting based on medical advice.
        3. Do not let physical discomfort deter you.
        4. Hunger will eventually disappear.
        5. Guard against constipation by eating fruit, etc. before and after.
        6. If you are drinking more than water, do not drink strong stimulants.
        7. Unless directed and supernaturally enabled by God, do not abstain from all fluids for more than 72 hours.
        8. Break your fast gradually.
        9. Any fast over two days will shrink your stomach—do not expand it again by overeating.

The Principles of Revelation

In the popular book and workbook *Experiencing God: Knowing and Doing the Will of God* (1990), Blackaby states that if a person is unable to hear from God, his Christian experience is in trouble at the most fundamental level. If a client has not yet learned to hear from God, it is impossible for them to be led by God or to walk according to the Spirit of God. If they cannot be led by God's Spirit, they will be at the mercy of their circumstances and will be little better off in making the critical decisions of life than an unbeliever.

1. <u>The first step in hearing from God is being willing to listen.</u> God seldom talks to those who do not want to listen to Him.

    Ge 3:8 And they heard the voice of the LORD God walking in the garden in the cool of the day: and Adam and his wife hid themselves from the presence of the LORD God amongst the trees of the garden.

Pr 3:5 Trust in the LORD with all thine heart; and lean not unto thine own understanding.

6 In all thy ways acknowledge him, and he shall direct thy paths.

2. <u>Sometimes God speaks and directs us through visions.</u>

Ac 11:5 I was in the city of Joppa praying: and in a trance I saw a vision, A certain vessel descend, as it had been a great sheet, let down from heaven by four corners; and it came even to me:

16:9 And a vision appeared to Paul in the night; There stood a man of Macedonia, and prayed him, saying, Come over into Macedonia, and help us.

3. <u>Sometimes He speaks to us through prophets.</u>

Jer 38:20 But Jeremiah said, They shall not deliver thee. Obey, I beseech thee, the voice of the LORD, which I speak unto thee: so it shall be well unto thee, and thy soul shall live.

4. <u>Sometimes through an audible voice.</u>

1 Sa 3:9 Therefore Eli said unto Samuel, Go, lie down: and it shall be, if he call thee, that thou shalt say, Speak, LORD; for thy servant heareth. So Samuel went and lay down in his place.

10 And the LORD came, and stood, and called as at other times, Samuel, Samuel. Then Samuel answered, Speak; for thy servant heareth.

5. <u>Sometimes He helps and directs us through the ministries of the church.</u>

Eph 4:11 And he gave some, apostles; and some, prophets; and some, evangelists; and some, pastors and teachers;

12 For the perfecting of the saints, for the work of the ministry, for the edifying of the body of Christ:

13 Till we all come in the unity of the faith, and of the knowledge of the Son of God, unto a perfect man, unto the measure of the stature of the fulness of Christ:

6. <u>Sometimes God speaks to us through circumstances.</u> Unfortunately, for many Christians this is their only method of hearing from God.

Ac 19:8 And he went into the synagogue, and spake boldly for the space of three months, disputing and persuading the things concerning the kingdom of God.

9 But when divers were hardened, and believed not, but spake evil of that way before the multitude, he departed from them, and separated the disciples, disputing daily in the school of one Tyrannus.

7. <u>God does not usually speak through cataclysmic events, visions or an audible voice, but through the small voice of our spirit's intuition.</u>

1 Ki 19:11 And he said, Go forth, and stand upon the mount before the LORD. And, behold, the LORD passed by, and a great and strong wind rent the mountains, and brake in pieces the rocks before the LORD; but the LORD was not in the wind: and after the wind an earthquake; but the LORD was not in the earthquake:

12 And after the earthquake a fire; but the LORD was not in the fire: and after the fire a still small voice.

Isa 30:21 And thine ears shall hear a word behind thee, saying, This is the way, walk ye in it, when ye turn to the right hand, and when ye turn to the left.

8. <u>God speaks most clearly through His infallible, inspired Word, the Bible.</u>

2 Ti 3:16 All scripture is given by inspiration of God, and is profitable for doctrine, for reproof, for correction, for instruction in righteousness:

17 That the man of God may be perfect, throughly furnished unto all good works.

2:15 Study to shew thyself approved unto God, a workman that needeth not to be ashamed, rightly dividing the word of truth.

9. <u>We must hear His voice to have a relationship with Him.</u>

Ps 95:7 For he is our God; and we are the people of his pasture, and the sheep of his hand. to day if ye will hear his voice,

8 Harden not your heart, as in the provocation, and as in the day of temptation in the wilderness:

10. <u>We learn to discern the difference between the voice of our soul and our spirit through studying the Word of God.</u>

Heb 4:12 For the word of God is quick, and powerful, and sharper than any twoedged sword, piercing even to the dividing asunder of soul and spirit, and of the joints and marrow, and is a discerner of the thoughts and intents of the heart.

11. <u>We perfect hearing His voice through our relationship with Him, just as a child or animal learns to know the voice of its mother or shepherd.</u>

Jo 10:3 To him the porter openeth; and the sheep hear his voice: and he calleth his own sheep by name, and leadeth them out.

4 And when he putteth forth his own sheep, he goeth before them, and the sheep follow him: for they know his voice.

16 And other sheep I have, which are not of this fold: them also I must bring, and they shall hear my voice; and there shall be one fold, and one shepherd.

27 My sheep hear my voice, and I know them, and they follow me:

12. <u>We can rely on God to re-direct us when we are contemplating going in the wrong direction.</u>

Ac 16:6 Now when they had gone throughout Phrygia and the region of Galatia, and were forbidden of the Holy Ghost to preach the word in Asia,

7 After they were come to Mysia, they assayed to go into Bithynia: but the Spirit suffered them not.

13. <u>It is the peace of God that helps us confirm God's direction in our decisions.</u>

Col 3:15 And let the peace of God rule in your hearts, to the which also ye are called in one body; and be ye thankful.

14. <u>Direct revelation comes through God's Spirit.</u> Revelation occurs when we believe that something is true in our spirit.

> 1 Co 2:9 But as it is written, Eye hath not seen, nor ear heard, neither have entered into the heart of man, the things which God hath prepared for them that love him.

> 10 But God hath revealed them unto us by his Spirit: for the Spirit searcheth all things, yea, the deep things of God.

> 11 For what man knoweth the things of a man, save the spirit of man which is in him? even so the things of God knoweth no man, but the Spirit of God.

> 12 Now we have received, not the spirit of the world, but the spirit which is of God; that we might know the things that are freely given to us of God.

15. <u>The natural man or unbeliever cannot receive the revelation of God.</u>

> 1 Co 2:14 But the natural man receiveth not the things of the Spirit of God: for they are foolishness unto him: neither can he know them, because they are spiritually discerned.

> Jo 3:3 Jesus answered and said unto him, Verily, verily, I say unto thee, Except a man be born again, he cannot see the kingdom of God.

Counseling Methods and Techniques

1. <u>We need to learn to hear and discern the voice of God.</u> Just as a wife learns the sound of her husband's voice by spending time with him, so we learn God's voice as we pray and listen for His response. Because God is a Spirit, most of the time this response will be an intuitive one in our spirit. Of course, God also speaks through an audible voice, visions, dreams, the gifts of the Spirit, and other people. We must learn through experience and the Word of God, the difference between our own mind, God's voice and the voice of Satan trying to deceive us. In order to teach the client that he will learn to know the voice of God by having an intimate relationship with Him, I sometimes use an example I learned from another minister. He had a woman come to the front of his church and face the altar with her back to the congregation. He asked her to identify her husband by his voice. He pointed to different men in the congregation and had each say "hello." When her husband said hello she knew immediately that it was he.

   In order to help a client know whether they are hearing from God, themselves, or Satan, I outline the characteristics of each. God is love. As such, He is loving, gentle and kind. He is never pushy or demanding. (See 1 Corinthians 13 and Galatians 5:22) He normally speaks through our spirit. Satan is pushy, demanding, and threatening. He attempts to plant thoughts into our mind. When we are speaking to ourselves, we hear what we are thinking in our mind; and it is the result of our own logic or emotions. I then suggest that they begin attempting to discern each of these voices in their own life. It is good to practice on small less important matters before attempting to know the will of God on major issues in our lives.

2. <u>We need to learn how to make God-directed choices.</u> I have taken some of the ideas presented by Bob Mumford in *Take Another Look at Guidance* (1971) and from the writings of George Muller (1984) to come up with a six-step method for receiving guidance from God. I teach it to my clients and use it myself. Whenever I have followed these principles, I have never missed what God was directing me to do.

   1. Get to the place where we are willing to do whatever God directs us to do.
   2. Is it in agreement with the Bible?

3. What is God saying in the Spirit?
4. Are the circumstances lining up?
5. If the first four steps are true, decide to follow the direction they suggest but ask God to make it very clear if we have reached the wrong conclusion.
6. Wait three days. If we continue to have the confirmation of the peace of God over those three days, do it.

3. <u>We can transform the truth in our mind to revelation in our spirit using the "If it is true…" method.</u> Because experience or action is the strongest type of evidence for our faith outside of the Word of God, I have the client state what the Word of God says and then act on it. As an example, "If it is true that God loves me and wants me to love others… how would I act?" Of course, I would try to act in loving ways toward others. "If it is true that God made me in His image and my worth does not depend on my performance or the approval of men and I am about to make a speech…how would I act?" Of course, I would make the speech as unto God and not allow myself to focus on how I was performing or what the audience was thinking about me. As we experience the Word of God in action, faith is built in our Spirit; and we have a revelation of God's truth. Another way is simply reading or listening to the Word of God over and over and meditating on it until it becomes revelation to us.

The Principles of the Conscience

Our conscience is that part of our Spirit that warns us when we are doing wrong. It may reflect the contents of our subconscious mind. When functioning normally, it can be a great asset but when it is either too strict or seared by repeated sin, it can become a detriment to our mental health.

1. <u>The healthy conscience reflects the law written in our subconscious mind.</u>

    Jer 31:33 But this shall be the covenant that I will make with the house of Israel; After those days, saith the LORD, I will put my law in their inward parts, and write it in their hearts; and will be their God, and they shall be my people.

    Ro 2:15 Which shew the work of the law written in their hearts, their conscience also bearing witness, and their thoughts the mean while accusing or else excusing one another;

2. <u>One of the functions of our conscience is to convict us of sin and teach us what is right and wrong.</u>

    Jo 8:9 And they which heard it, being convicted by their own conscience, went out one by one, beginning at the eldest, even unto the last: and Jesus was left alone, and the woman standing in the midst.

3. <u>We need to live in such a way as to maintain a conscience void of offense.</u>

    Ac 23:1 And Paul, earnestly beholding the council, said, Men and brethren, I have lived in all good conscience before God until this day.

    24:16 And herein do I exercise myself, to have always a conscience void of offence toward God, and toward men.

4. <u>A healthy conscience will bear witness in accordance with what God, through the Holy Ghost, affirms.</u>

    Ro 9:1 I say the truth in Christ, I lie not, my conscience also bearing me witness in the Holy Ghost,

5. <u>A conscience can become defiled through impure thoughts, incorrect thinking or legalism.</u>

1 Co 8:7 Howbeit there is not in every man that knowledge: for some with conscience of the idol unto this hour eat it as a thing offered unto an idol; and their conscience being weak is defiled.

10 For if any man see thee which hast knowledge sit at meat in the idol's temple, shall not the conscience of him which is weak be emboldened to eat those things which are offered to idols;

6. <u>If we believe something is acceptable to do and our conscience agrees, we should not make an issue of it with other people.</u> However, even if we believe it is okay, if doing it will offend another's conscience, we should not do it.

1 Co 10:25 Whatsoever is sold in the shambles, that eat, asking no question for conscience sake:

27 If any of them that believe not bid you to a feast, and ye be disposed to go; whatsoever is set before you, eat, asking no question for conscience sake.

28 But if any man say unto you, This is offered in sacrifice unto idols, eat not for his sake that shewed it, and for conscience sake: for the earth is the Lord's, and the fulness thereof:

29 Conscience, I say, not thine own, but of the other: for why is my liberty judged of another man's conscience?

7. <u>Lying and hypocrisy result in a seared conscience and lack of conviction.</u>

1 Ti 4:2 Speaking lies in hypocrisy; having their conscience seared with a hot iron;

8. <u>Our conscience is initially cleansed through baptism when we turn our backs on our old life of sin.</u>

1 Pe 3:21 The like figure whereunto even baptism doth also now save us (not the putting away of the filth of the flesh, but the answer of a good conscience toward God,) by the resurrection of Jesus Christ:

9. <u>The blood of Jesus can purge our conscience from past sins so that we can again serve God.</u>

Heb 9:14 How much more shall the blood of Christ, who through the eternal Spirit offered himself without spot to God, purge your conscience from dead works to serve the living God?

10:22 Let us draw near with a true heart in full assurance of faith, having our hearts sprinkled from an evil conscience, and our bodies washed with pure water.

10. <u>If our conscience and mind have been defiled by unbelief and lies, we need to renew our mind by purifying it through the truth of God.</u>

Tit 1:15 Unto the pure all things are pure: but unto them that are defiled and unbelieving is nothing pure; but even their mind and conscience is defiled.

11. <u>God's plan is living by faith, motivated by love, and having a good conscience in all we do.</u>

1 Ti 1:5 Now the end of the commandment is charity out of a pure heart, and of a good conscience, and of faith unfeigned:

3:9 Holding the mystery of the faith in a pure conscience.

12. <u>When we live right according to our conscience, we can rejoice in all we do.</u>

2 Co 1:12 For our rejoicing is this, the testimony of our conscience, that in simplicity and godly sincerity, not with fleshly wisdom, but by the grace of God, we have had our conversation in the world, and more abundantly to you-ward.

4:2 But have renounced the hidden things of dishonesty, not walking in craftiness, nor handling the word of God deceitfully; but by manifestation of the truth commending ourselves to every man's conscience in the sight of God.

13. <u>We should all endeavor to live our lives so that our conscience is clear even if others attempt to accuse us of wrongdoing.</u>

Heb 13:18 Pray for us: for we trust we have a good conscience, in all things willing to live honestly.

1 Pe 2:19 For this is thankworthy, if a man for conscience toward God endure grief, suffering wrongfully.

3:16 Having a good conscience; that, whereas they speak evil of you, as of evildoers, they may be ashamed that falsely accuse your good conversation in Christ.

Counseling Methods and Techniques

1. <u>To keep our conscience clear, we need to deal with our guilt.</u> To do so we must sort out real from false guilt. Real guilt is that which is a consequence of our sin. For this, we must repent, ask forgiveness from God and any others that we have offended and make restitution when possible. False guilt is that which others have placed on us about areas where we have done nothing wrong. It is not unusual for clients to feel guilty for not meeting the demands or suggestions of others for which they are not responsible. In these cases, the counselor should help identify the false guilt, encourage the client to drop it and set boundaries to prevent its reoccurrence. Of course, we must repent and ask forgiveness in areas where we are truly guilty.

2. <u>We must re-teach a defiled conscience.</u> Sometimes clients, especially for those brought up in legalistic churches, have overly active or defiled consciences. In this case, we need to help them get into God's Word and study the principles of grace until they receive a revelation of the love and unmerited favor of God toward them in spite of their shortcomings.

3. <u>We must renew our conscience if it is seared.</u> A seared conscience comes from repeated sin in our lives. As we continue to sin, eventually the level of conviction provided by our conscience becomes less and less. To renew our conscience, we must repent of the sin, deal with our denial and excuses and study God's Word until we again see sin as God sees it—rebellion against Him.

The Principles of Walking According to the Spirit

To walk according to the Spirit means to live a life directed by and in obedience to the Spirit of God. It requires that we yield our will completely to the will of God, effectively discern the leading of God's Spirit and carry out God's will. This is a learned process. It is essential for living a holy, sanctified Christian life.

1. <u>God's plan for our lives is to motivate us through the Spirit to do His will.</u>

Eze 36:27 And I will put my spirit within you, and cause you to walk in my statutes, and ye shall keep my judgments, and do [them].

2. <u>God has put aside our offenses and will not condemn us.</u> If we will walk after His Spirit, we will not feel condemned; and we will be able to have a loving relationship with Him.

    Ro 8:1 [There is] therefore now no condemnation to them which are in Christ Jesus, who walk not after the flesh, but after the Spirit.

3. <u>This inner walking according to the Spirit frees us to make right choices that lead to life and not to sin and death.</u> We are transformed from the inside out through our relationship with God.

    Ro 8:2 For the law of the Spirit of life in Christ Jesus hath made me free from the law of sin and death.

4. <u>Now, through what Jesus has done, we have the power to obey the law of God.</u>

    Ro 8:3 For what the law could not do, in that it was weak through the flesh, God sending his own Son in the likeness of sinful flesh, and for sin, condemned sin in the flesh:

    4 That the righteousness of the law might be fulfilled in us, who walk not after the flesh, but after the Spirit.

5. <u>We walk according to the Spirit by focusing our life on spiritual things.</u>

    Ro 8:5 For they that are after the flesh do mind the things of the flesh; but they that are after the Spirit the things of the Spirit.

6. <u>We must die to the flesh, which wars against the Spirit, in order to live effectively in the Spirit.</u>

    Ro 8:13 For if ye live after the flesh, ye shall die: but if ye through the Spirit do mortify the deeds of the body, ye shall live.

7. <u>This new spiritual life is based on a personal, intimate relationship with God.</u>

    Ro 8:14 For as many as are led by the Spirit of God, they are the sons of God.

    15 For ye have not received the spirit of bondage again to fear; but ye have received the Spirit of adoption, whereby we cry, Abba, Father.

    16 The Spirit itself beareth witness with our spirit, that we are the children of God:

8. <u>As we become identified with Him—although sometimes this means suffering with Him—the result is the glory of being part of His family and the rich reward that membership in the family of God brings.</u>

    Ro 8:17 And if children, then heirs; heirs of God, and joint-heirs with Christ; if so be that we suffer with [him], that we may be also glorified together.

9. <u>As we walk according to the Spirit, we are delivered from the bondage of the lusts of the flesh so that we can live a righteous life.</u>

    Ga 5:16 [This] I say then, Walk in the Spirit, and ye shall not fulfil the lust of the flesh.

17 For the flesh lusteth against the Spirit, and the Spirit against the flesh: and these are contrary the one to the other: so that ye cannot do the things that ye would.

10. <u>We are also delivered from legalism and trying to do things in our own strength to please God.</u>

Ga 5:18 But if ye be led of the Spirit, ye are not under the law.

11. <u>If we walk according to the Spirit, our character will reflect the Spirit of God.</u> We will be full of love and goodness and not envy, strife, or competition for prominence.

Ga 5:22 But the fruit of the Spirit is love, joy, peace, longsuffering, gentleness, goodness, faith,

23 Meekness, temperance: against such there is no law.

24 And they that are Christ's have crucified the flesh with the affections and lusts.

25 If we live in the Spirit, let us also walk in the Spirit.

26 Let us not be desirous of vain glory, provoking one another, envying one another.

Counseling Methods and Techniques

1. <u>We walk according to the Spirit by focusing on the things of the Spirit.</u> This is the meaning of Romans 8:5. We either give spiritual things or the flesh priority in our lives.

2. <u>To walk according to the Spirit, we must fully yield our lives to Him.</u> Walking according to the Spirit requires that we first decide that we really do want to fully follow God and let Him guide our lives. We can only walk according to the Spirit to the extent that we are willing to do what God asks us to do and to the degree that we are able to discern His direction for our lives. The principles of Lordship, discussed earlier, must be achieved before walking in the Spirit.

3. <u>We must learn how to walk according to the Spirit.</u> We learn by trying to hear the voice of God though our intuition and acting according to what we believe He has told us to do. As a new Christian, I used to dedicate a Saturday to practice walking in the Spirit. I would gather all of my Bibles, Christian books, songbooks and praise tapes. I would then fast to increase my spiritual sensitivity and ask God to show me what He wanted me to do moment by moment. I would read, sing, pray, dance, or just be quiet, as I believed He was directing me to do so. As a new Christian, my wife, Nancy, would ask God which route to take across Denver, Colorado, in order to avoid traffic jams. She did this to practice walking according to the Spirit.

Chapter 6

Principles of the Mind

Our mind is one of the most complex parts of the heart. The Bible uses this term to indicate the center of cognition or understanding which sometimes includes its predominate influence on our will and emotions. As a man thinks so is he. (Proverbs 23:7) The Bible suggests that our mind must be renewed. (Romans 12:2) Some of the functions of the mind include memory, logical thinking, sensory perception, thought, language, learning, problem solving, decision-making, intelligence and perception. In order to change our lives, we must change how we are thinking in our minds. We can choose what we think, what we entertain in our minds and what we let into our minds. By the way we look at or perceive things; we predispose how we organize data, what data we accept, what we believe, and how we will act. Clearly, the will and mind are closely intertwined.

It is an understatement to say that the mind has a profound influence on all the other aspects of our heart and behavior. It is clear that the Bible does not attempt to address how the mind physically functions or the many problems that might occur when it is not functioning as it should. The biblical principles of the mind address how, with a normally functioning mind, we should use this wonderful gift to achieve psychological and spiritual wholeness. The Bible primarily addresses four aspects of the mind: 1. The state or focus of our mind that influences the rest of the heart. 2. Establishing truth in the mind in order to provide accurate data for the process of thinking. 3. Our cognition or how we process data in our mind. 4. Using our thought process wisely to make right choices in our lives (wisdom).

The Principles of the State or Focus of the Mind

The Bible primarily discusses the state or focus of the mind as a characteristic of our mind.

1. <u>The state of our mind and heart determines the impact that the Word of God has on our lives.</u>

    Lu 8:11 Now the parable is this: The seed is the word of God.

    12 Those by the way side are they that hear; then cometh the devil, and taketh away the word out of their hearts, lest they should believe and be saved.

    13 They on the rock are they, which, when they hear, receive the word with joy; and these have no root, which for a while believe, and in time of temptation fall away.

    14 And that which fell among thorns are they, which, when they have heard, go forth, and are choked with cares and riches and pleasures of this life, and bring no fruit to perfection.

    15 But that on the good ground are they, which in an honest and good heart, having heard the word, keep it, and bring forth fruit with patience.

2. <u>We must have a willing mind.</u> A willing mind is one that wants to do something and influences our will to do it. It is in our mind that we determine what we want to do. Our minds are to be used to serve God. To do this, we must be willing to obey what God directs, control the imaginations of our thoughts, and direct our heart to seek and follow God.

   1 Chr 28:9 And thou, Solomon my son, know thou the God of thy father, and serve him with a perfect heart and with a willing mind: for the LORD searcheth all hearts, and understandeth all the imaginations of the thoughts: if thou seek him, he will be found of thee; but if thou forsake him, he will cast thee off for ever.

3. <u>A ready mind is one that wants to listen, learn or act.</u> It results in a teachable spirit.

   Ac 17:11 These were more noble than those in Thessalonica, in that they received the word with all readiness of mind, and searched the scriptures daily, whether those things were so.

4. <u>A right mind is one that is functioning properly and is free of outside negative spiritual influences.</u> It is focused on the things of God.

   Mr 5:15 And they come to Jesus, and see him that was possessed with the devil, and had the legion, sitting, and clothed, and in his right mind: and they were afraid.

5. <u>A sound mind is one that does not easily give in to fear or change what it believes.</u> It knows what is true and is not easily swayed.

   2 Ti 1:7 For God hath not given us the spirit of fear; but of power, and of love, and of a sound mind.

6. <u>A fervent mind is one which results in a strong desire or love for someone or something.</u>

   2 Co 7:7 And not by his coming only, but by the consolation wherewith he was comforted in you, when he told us your earnest desire, your mourning, your fervent mind toward me; so that I rejoiced the more.

7. <u>A humble mind or lowliness of mind comes from a mind which is not puffed up with its own greatness, importance or ability.</u>

   Ac 20:19 Serving the Lord with all humility of mind, and with many tears, and temptations, which befell me by the lying in wait of the Jews:

   Php 2:3 Let nothing be done through strife or vainglory; but in lowliness of mind let each esteem other better than themselves.

   Col 3:12 Put on therefore, as the elect of God, holy and beloved, bowels of mercies, kindness, humbleness of mind, meekness, longsuffering;

8. <u>A doubtful mind is one which has not yet reached a set conclusion concerning something.</u> A doubtful mind is easily changed.

   Lu 12:29 And seek not ye what ye shall eat, or what ye shall drink, neither be ye of doubtful mind.

9. <u>The Spirit of our mind determines the focus of our mind.</u> What we focus our mind on will then determine the direction of our entire heart. Our focus needs to be on God.

   Eph 4:23 And be renewed in the spirit of your mind;

10. <u>A vain mind is one which is focused on worthless or unimportant worldly things like our physical appearance or how much we possess in this life.</u>

    Eph 4:17 This I say therefore, and testify in the Lord, that ye henceforth walk not as other Gentiles walk, in the vanity of their mind,

11. <u>A fleshly mind is one which is focused on meeting the needs of the self through the flesh.</u> It results in walking according to the flesh.

    Col 2:18 Let no man beguile you of your reward in a voluntary humility and worshipping of angels, intruding into those things which he hath not seen, vainly puffed up by his fleshly mind,

12. <u>A wicked mind is one that is set on doing wickedness.</u>

    Pr 21:27 The sacrifice of the wicked is abomination: how much more, when he bringeth it with a wicked mind?

13. <u>A reprobate mind is one which refuses to think about God or acknowledge Him, but tries to function as its own god doing whatever it wants to do.</u>

    Ro 1:28 And even as they did not like to retain God in their knowledge, God gave them over to a reprobate mind, to do those things which are not convenient;

14. <u>To be shaken in mind is to reconsider our beliefs because of some significant event in our lives.</u>

    2 Th 2:2 That ye be not soon shaken in mind, or be troubled, neither by spirit, nor by word, nor by letter as from us, as that the day of Christ is at hand.

15. <u>We are not to focus on or worry about having our needs met or about the things of life.</u> Worry is an attempt to make ourselves feel in control when we are not. We are to pray and trust God instead.

    Mt 6:25 Therefore I say unto you, Take no thought for your life, what ye shall eat, or what ye shall drink; nor yet for your body, what ye shall put on. Is not the life more than meat, and the body than raiment?

    27 Which of you by taking thought can add one cubit unto his stature?

    34 Take therefore no thought for the morrow: for the morrow shall take thought for the things of itself. Sufficient unto the day is the evil thereof.

16. <u>We are to focus our thinking on all the good things of life; because if we think about positive and good things, our thinking will eventually lead to positive and good actions and emotions.</u>

    Php 4:8 Finally, brethren, whatsoever things are true, whatsoever things are honest, whatsoever things are just, whatsoever things are pure, whatsoever things are lovely, whatsoever things are of good report; if there be any virtue, and if there be any praise, think on these things.

17. <u>What we think about eventually determines what we do.</u> If we refuse to think lustful thoughts, we will never fall due to lust.

    Job 31:1 I made a covenant with mine eyes; why then should I think upon a maid?

18. <u>Our thoughts affect our emotions</u>

    Ps 94:19 In the multitude of my thoughts within me thy comforts delight my soul.

    Pr 21:5 The thoughts of the diligent tend only to plenteousness; but of every one that is hasty only to want.

19. <u>A mind focused on and trusting God leads to perfect peace in our emotions.</u>

    Isa 26:3 Thou wilt keep him in perfect peace, whose mind is stayed on thee: because he trusteth in thee.

20. <u>A renewed mind is one that is filled with the truth of God, focuses on His will and perceives the things of life from God's point of view.</u>

    Ro 12:2 And be not conformed to this world: but be ye transformed by the renewing of your mind, that ye may prove what is that good, and acceptable, and perfect, will of God.

Counseling Methods and Techniques

1. <u>We can and must control the direction of our mind.</u> Because we are so controlled by what comes out of our minds, we must be diligent to monitor the direction, focus or state of our minds. From the Bible verses presented above, it is clear that we must be careful to control what we are thinking about in our minds. We control the direction of our minds with our will. We can decide to change the direction of our minds if we choose to. We can simply refuse to think about certain things. However, it is much more effective to direct our minds in a particular direction rather than try to not think about something. For example, if we are thinking about a pink elephant it is easier to change the elephant's color than to just stop thinking about pink elephants.

2. <u>What we allow into our minds influences our focus and our thinking.</u> Consequently, we need to guard our minds and think on good things. (Philipians 4:8) Watching a particular movie or television show will usually start us thinking about the subject presented in that movie or show. If we primarily fill our mind with the things of God, our minds will become focused on the things of God.

The Principles of Truth

The Bible clearly tells us that all that God does is based on absolute truth—the way things <u>truly</u> are. God is not limited by perceptions or lack of knowledge but knows what is the absolute truth about everything: past, present and future. However, we, as people, "now see through a glass, darkly; but then face to face: now I know in part; but then shall I know even as also I am known." (1 Corinthians 13:12)

As human beings, we have many different types of input with different levels of reliability coming into our minds that must be processed in order to determine what is true. First, we have our physical senses of seeing, hearing, touch, smell and taste. These can be extended through instruments such as lenses, electron microscopes or microphones. These provide the basis of the scientific method, which attempts to determine truth through measurements and repeatability. Even the scientific method has major limitations and has difficulty when applied to complex human beings. Secular psychology is limited to research using the scientific method and to extrapolations concerning the nature of man. Others suggest that truth can also be obtained by such methods as "knowing yourself," ESP, witchcraft, "sacred writings," or fortune telling. We, as Christians, believe that we have additional sources of information concerning the truth: spiritual intuition, revelation, prophecy, the gifts of the Spirit, and the Word of God. Of all of these, we believe that the Word of God provides the most reliable source of the truth.

From these sources, what others tell us, what we read and see in movies and on television, as well as from our experiences, we form our perceptions of the truth. Our limitations, particularly because we do not know very much about the past and almost nothing about the future, are huge. Our attempts to know the truth provide both our greatest liability and the greatest possible opportunity for change. It is the lies that we believe about ourselves and our world that are the basis of our dysfunction, and it is replacing these lies that provides one of the greatest tools for change. Knowing the truth is a major part of what the Bible calls, "the renewing of your mind." This is the basis for the development of faith itself. Everything we are and will be depends upon what we know and believe.

Sometimes people become confused between what is the truth and what is a fact. The truth is what is absolutely true from the standpoint of God and facts are what we are currently experiencing through our physical senses. For example, we may be experiencing the symptoms of a cold with a runny nose. That is a fact. However, the Bible tells us "by His stripes we are healed." (Isaiah 53:5) That is the truth. The reason that facts and truth seem to contradict each other is simply because the truth has not yet been manifested as a fact. As another example, the Bible tells us that we are "…the righteousness of God in him [Christ]." (2 Corinthians 5:21) That is the truth, however, right now that righteousness may not yet be manifested as fact in our lives. It will finally manifest when we perceive ourselves as righteous and begin acting according to our faith.

1. <u>God is the source of all truth.</u>

   De 32:4 He is the Rock, his work is perfect: for all his ways are judgment: a God of truth and without iniquity, just and right is he.
   Ps 33:4 For the word of the LORD is right; and all his works are done in truth.

2. <u>God's truth is not relative but absolute and endures forever.</u>

   Ps 100:5 For the LORD is good; his mercy is everlasting; and his truth endureth to all generations.
   Isa 40:8 The grass withereth, the flower fadeth: but the word of our God shall stand for ever.

3. <u>God's laws are truth.</u>

   Ps 119:142 Thy righteousness is an everlasting righteousness, and thy law is the truth.

4. <u>God will teach us the truth if we will ask and wait on Him.</u>

   Ps 25:5 Lead me in thy truth, and teach me: for thou art the God of my salvation; on thee do I wait all the day.

5. <u>The Holy Spirit is the Spirit of truth that dwells in us and will tell us everything we need to know.</u>

   Jo 16:13 Howbeit when he, the Spirit of truth, is come, he will guide you into all truth: for he shall not speak of himself; but whatsoever he shall hear, that shall he speak: and he will shew you things to come.

6. <u>Since God cannot lie, the Word of God is truth.</u>

   1 Th 2:13 For this cause also thank we God without ceasing, because, when ye received the word of God which ye heard of us, ye received it not as the word of men, but as it is in truth, the word of God, which effectually worketh also in you that believe.

7. <u>Jesus is the full manifestation of the Word of God, is God, and was the living example of the Truth of God.</u>

   Jo 1: 14 And the Word was made flesh, and dwelt among us, (and we beheld his glory, the glory as of the only begotten of the Father,) full of grace and truth.

   14:6 Jesus saith unto him, I am the way, the truth, and the life: no man cometh unto the Father, but by me.

8. <u>We are born again by the truth of the Word of God.</u>

   1 Pe 1:23 Being born again, not of corruptible seed, but of incorruptible, by the word of God, which liveth and abideth for ever.

   Eph 1:13 In whom ye also trusted, after that ye heard the word of truth, the gospel of your salvation: in whom also after that ye believed, ye were sealed with that holy Spirit of promise,

9. <u>We will be judged by the truth.</u>

   Ps 96:13 Before the LORD: for he cometh, for he cometh to judge the earth: he shall judge the world with righteousness, and the people with his truth.

10. <u>The Word of God can be rightly and wrongly interpreted.</u> Consequently, it is imperative that Christians study it in depth and thoroughly understand God's Word.

    2 Ti 2:15 Study to shew thyself approved unto God, a workman that needeth not to be ashamed, rightly dividing the word of truth.

11. <u>Some people can learn but yet not understand the truth.</u>

    2 Ti 3:7 Ever learning, and never able to come to the knowledge of the truth.

12. <u>We are to live by and through God's Word.</u>

    Mt 4:4 But he answered and said, It is written, Man shall not live by bread alone, but by every word that proceedeth out of the mouth of God.

13. <u>We should pursue truth, wisdom, instruction and understanding.</u>

    Pr 23:23 Buy the truth, and sell it not; also wisdom, and instruction, and understanding.

14. <u>It is God's will that we be made whole and know the truth.</u>

    1 Ti 2:4 Who will have all men to be saved, and to come unto the knowledge of the truth.

15. Sanctification or wholeness comes through the truth of God's Word.

    Jo 17:17 Sanctify them through thy truth: thy word is truth.

    2 Th 2:13 But we are bound to give thanks alway to God for you, brethren beloved of the Lord, because God hath from the beginning chosen you to salvation through sanctification of the Spirit and belief of the truth:

16. Continuing in the Word leads to the truth, which makes us free from worldly bondage.

    Jo 8:31 Then said Jesus to those Jews which believed on him, If ye continue in my word, then are ye my disciples indeed;

    32 And ye shall know the truth, and the truth shall make you free.

17. When we receive what God says as our personal truth, we have written it on our hearts.

    Heb 8:10 For this is the covenant that I will make with the house of Israel after those days, saith the Lord; I will put my laws into their mind, and write them in their hearts: and I will be to them a God, and they shall be to me a people:

18. When we accept lies, both the mind and the conscience become defiled.

    Tit 1:15 Unto the pure all things are pure: but unto them that are defiled and unbelieving is nothing pure; but even their mind and conscience is defiled.

19. We must be careful not to entertain evil thoughts, or, like incubating snake eggs, they will hatch and bite us.

    Isa 59:4 None calleth for justice, nor any pleadeth for truth: they trust in vanity, and speak lies; they conceive mischief, and bring forth iniquity.

    5 They hatch cockatrice' eggs, and weave the spider's web: he that eateth of their eggs dieth, and that which is crushed breaketh out into a viper.

20. We are to possess the gates of our minds. Our minds are like gates, which determine what is let into them. We have authority over our thinking to determine what we allow into our minds as truth.

    Am 5:15 Hate the evil, and love the good, and establish judgment in the gate: it may be that the LORD God of hosts will be gracious unto the remnant of Joseph.

    Mt 7:13 Enter ye in at the strait gate: for wide is the gate, and broad is the way, that leadeth to destruction, and many there be which go in thereat:

Counseling Methods and Techniques

1. We must learn that God's Word is the absolute truth. We need to know that the Word of God is the only truly reliable source of the absolute truth. This can be difficult when what we experience with our senses (facts) contradicts God's Word. This can become a key issue in change when that change depends on our identity in Christ. However, Bible stories and actual life experiences can demonstrate that the reality of God is more reliable than that of this world. I use Josh McDowell's *Evidence That Demands A Verdict Vol I and II* (1972, 1975) to help clients establish their faith in God's Word.

2. <u>How we act can change what we think.</u> Because we are unified whole beings, our thinking affects our actions and our actions can affect our thinking. The term for this is dissonance. It is the irritation we feel when we act in one way while believing another. Acting according to what the Bible says is true, even if we are still struggling in our minds about the subject, will help us make the right decision. Eventually, our emotions will follow.

3. <u>We can change our thinking by exposing and dealing with subconscious assumptions.</u> One of the most difficult areas in counseling is trying to affect the unconscious assumptions that are held by the client. These assumptions are extremely important because this internalized "truth" about life is not usually challenged or even understood. The first step is to try to analyze and derive what these assumptions actually are. Analysis methods, especially "layer-caking," described later in this book under the principles of the heart section can help us understand these assumptions. Once they are identified, they can be examined in the light of the truth. Theophostic ministry can also be used to try to find the internalized assumptions or "lies" associated with past experiences.

The Principles of Cognition

The process of thinking about something is called cognition. It is how we process the data in our minds.

1. <u>Our thinking determines our choices.</u>

    Nu 36:6 This is the thing which the LORD doth command concerning the daughters of Zelophehad, saying, Let them marry to whom they think best; only to the family of the tribe of their father shall they marry.

2. <u>Our thinking process can lead to valid or invalid conclusions.</u>

    Lu 12:40 Be ye therefore ready also: for the Son of man cometh at an hour when ye think not.

    Jo 16:2 They shall put you out of the synagogues: yea, the time cometh, that whosoever killeth you will think that he doeth God service.

    5:39 Search the scriptures; for in them ye think ye have eternal life: and they are they which testify of me.

3. <u>The conclusions that we reach, based on how we process the data in our minds, greatly influences who we become.</u>

    Pr 23:7 For as he thinketh in his heart, so is he: Eat and drink, saith he to thee; but his heart is not with thee.

4. <u>We can know the truth and yet choose not to obey it.</u>

    Ga 5:7 Ye did run well; who did hinder you that ye should not obey the truth?

5. <u>We can purify our souls by choosing to obey the truth.</u> This produces a pure heart and love.

    1 Pe 1:22 Seeing ye have purified your souls in obeying the truth through the Spirit unto unfeigned love of the brethren, see that ye love one another with a pure heart fervently:

6. <u>How we think and imagine things in our mind can prepare our heart to either follow God or turn from Him and do evil.</u>

    1 Chr 29:18 O LORD God of Abraham, Isaac, and of Israel, our fathers, keep this for ever in the imagination of the thoughts of the heart of thy people, and prepare their heart unto thee:

    Mt 9:4 And Jesus knowing their thoughts said, Wherefore think ye evil in your hearts?

7. <u>We need to recognize the limitations of our logical thinking.</u> Spiritual revelation and intuition are many times superior to logic, especially when we are walking according to the Spirit or operating in one of the spiritual gifts.

    1 Co 8:2 And if any man think that he knoweth any thing, he knoweth nothing yet as he ought to know.

    2 Co 3:5 Not that we are sufficient of ourselves to think any thing as of ourselves; but our sufficiency is of God;

8. <u>God is able to do far more than we are able to ask for or comprehend in our minds.</u>

    Eph 3:20 Now unto him that is able to do exceeding abundantly above all that we ask or think, according to the power that worketh in us,

    Ec 8:17 Then I beheld all the work of God, that a man cannot find out the work that is done under the sun: because though a man labour to seek it out, yet he shall not find it; yea further; though a wise man think to know it, yet shall he not be able to find it.

9. <u>We must use the ability of our mind for our good when we remember and recall past events.</u> We must remember the good and important things of our lives, but forgive, process, and relegate as a part of our history the offenses of the past.

    Isa 46:8 Remember this, and shew yourselves men: bring it again to mind, O ye transgressors.

    Mr 14:72 And the second time the cock crew. And Peter called to mind the word that Jesus said unto him, Before the cock crow twice, thou shalt deny me thrice. And when he thought thereon, he wept.

10. <u>Another function of the mind is to think things through until we are absolutely convinced or persuaded that they are true.</u> This process can assist us in strongly establishing our faith.

    Ro 14:5 One man esteemeth one day above another: another esteemeth every day alike. Let every man be fully persuaded in his own mind.

11. <u>God knows all our thoughts.</u>

    Job 42:2 I know that thou canst do every thing, and that no thought can be withholden from thee.

12. <u>God takes our thoughts seriously.</u> Because the thoughts of the people during Noah's generation were continually evil, God brought destruction on the entire earth.

    Ge 6:5 And GOD saw that the wickedness of man was great in the earth, and that every imagination of the thoughts of his heart was only evil continually.

6 And it repented the LORD that he had made man on the earth, and it grieved him at his heart.

7 And the LORD said, I will destroy man whom I have created from the face of the earth; both man, and beast, and the creeping thing, and the fowls of the air; for it repenteth me that I have made them.

13. <u>God will judge our thoughts.</u>

1 Chr 28:9 And thou, Solomon my son, know thou the God of thy father, and serve him with a perfect heart and with a willing mind: for the LORD searcheth all hearts, and understandeth all the imaginations of the thoughts: if thou seek him, he will be found of thee; but if thou forsake him, he will cast thee off for ever.

14. <u>We can tell the righteous from the wicked by their thoughts.</u>

Pr 12:5 The thoughts of the righteous are right: but the counsels of the wicked are deceit.

Isa 59:7 Their feet run to evil, and they make haste to shed innocent blood: their thoughts are thoughts of iniquity; wasting and destruction are in their paths.

15. <u>We must realize that God knows our thoughts and holds us accountable for them.</u> If we need help to understand ourselves, God can reveal our thoughts to us through His Spirit and His Word.

Ps 119:59 I thought on my ways, and turned my feet unto thy testimonies.

139:23 Search me, O God, and know my heart: try me, and know my thoughts:

16. <u>If we are thinking wrong, we need to repent.</u>

Isa 55:7 Let the wicked forsake his way, and the unrighteous man his thoughts: and let him return unto the LORD, and he will have mercy upon him; and to our God, for he will abundantly pardon.

Ac 8:22 Repent therefore of this thy wickedness, and pray God, if perhaps the thought of thine heart may be forgiven thee.

17. <u>We are to control our thoughts and hold them captive so that they lead only to wanting to serve and obey God.</u>

2 Co 10:4 (For the weapons of our warfare are not carnal, but mighty through God to the pulling down of strong holds;)

5 Casting down imaginations, and every high thing that exalteth itself against the knowledge of God, and bringing into captivity every thought to the obedience of Christ;

18. <u>We are to use the armor (or truth of God) in our minds to filter the intruding thoughts that spirits use to gain entrance into our minds, in an attempt to control our will.</u>

Eph 6:14 Stand therefore, having your loins girt about with truth, and having on the breastplate of righteousness;

15 And your feet shod with the preparation of the gospel of peace;

16 Above all, taking the shield of faith, wherewith ye shall be able to quench all the fiery darts of the wicked.

17 And take the helmet of salvation, and the sword of the Spirit, which is the word of God:

18 Praying always with all prayer and supplication in the Spirit, and watching thereunto with all perseverance and supplication for all saints; by the armour of righteousness on the right hand and on the left,

Counseling Methods and Techniques

1. <u>Thought stopping can prohibit wrong thoughts from entering our minds.</u> This is defending the gate of our minds. When we recognize a thought, we can either entertain it; or we can refuse to think about it. To have a thought is not sin, but if we choose to dwell on an evil thought we become responsible for it and it becomes sin to us. There are a number of ways to stop thoughts: 1. We can simply say to ourselves, "Stop!" "Shut up Devil" or some other phrase to interrupt our thoughts. Then we can choose to think about something else. 2. A standard behavior modification technique is to place a rubber band on our wrist and snap it each time the thought attempts to enter our mind. 3. The client needs to be taught to bring every thought into the captivity of Jesus Christ in order to deal with imaginations and strongholds. We can state the truth or quote a Bible verse to debunk whatever thought has occurred. This is how Jesus stopped the temptations of the devil in the wilderness. (Matthew 4:4-11)

2. <u>The armor of God can protect our mind and our heart.</u> Satan has particular modes of attack, and God has provided defenses for us. Most Christians have recognized the importance of the armor of God as listed in Ephesians Chapter 6. These verses tell us that with this armor we will be able to stand up against Satan in difficult circumstances. Some have even gone to the lengths of acting out putting on the armor each morning. However, we should recognize that all of this armor is based on a strong faith in the truth of God. As long as we believe and stand on the truth, we are safe. From a counseling perspective we must help our clients to clearly understand, believe, and hold onto these principles, which form the very basis of the Christian life.

   Eph 6:14 Stand therefore, having your loins girt about with truth, and having on the breastplate of righteousness;

   15 And your feet shod with the preparation of the gospel of peace;

   16 Above all, taking the shield of faith, wherewith ye shall be able to quench all the fiery darts of the wicked.

   17 And take the helmet of salvation, and the sword of the Spirit, which is the word of God:

All of Satan's attacks can be stopped with the armor of God. Reviewing these well-known verses, we see that our armor consists of:

   a. <u>Loins girt about with truth.</u> Truth is the belt that holds all of the armor together. Until we know the truth of the Word of God, we will be at the mercy of the liar who will try to deceive us. To use this belt, we confront any lying attack by stating what we know to be true. We might state, "That's a lie devil," and then state the truth according to the Word of God.

   b. <u>The breastplate of righteousness.</u> The thought that we are inadequate or worthless, that we have sinned and cannot be forgiven, or that God is angry with us, are all strategies of the devil. These thoughts need to be refuted by the fact that we are now in Christ and Christ is in us, we have been forgiven for all our sins, we are clothed in Christ's robe of righteousness, Christ took our shame upon the cross, and we are now counted as righteous no matter how much we may have failed. This revelation of our righteousness through Christ needs to become part of our spirit (or subconscious mind), so that we can fend off all attacks on our perception of our righteousness.

c. <u>Feet shod with the preparation of the gospel of peace.</u> Our feet stand for our walk or how we act in life. The devil attacks with the thought that we will never be good enough or measure up to God's standards. The gospel or good news of peace is that we have been justified by what Christ has done and that we have the unmerited favor of God, which is not based on our works but the works of Christ.

d. <u>The shield of faith.</u> Our shield of faith is our first line of defense against the fiery darts or interjected thoughts of the devil. In Bible times, these darts were shot at enemy troops in order to catch their clothing on fire. Our clothing is our character and the devil wants us to forfeit our character by entertaining evil thoughts that he tries to plant in our minds. To use the shield, we simply state the truth that we believe to debunk any lie that the devil attempts to shoot into our minds.

e. <u>The helmet of salvation.</u> One of the devil's most common attacks is to try to convince the new or weak believer that he is not really saved. If he can convince us that we are not really saved and are going to hell, we will lose hope and quit trying to live the Christian life. He uses this lie and the lie that we have committed the unpardonable sin to destabilize those on the verge of mental collapse so that they will become mentally ill. We need to know Romans 10:9 and the other scriptures concerning salvation so that we cannot be fooled. (See the previous chapter concerning the principles of salvation.)

f. <u>The sword of the Spirit is the Word of God.</u> The Word of God is our main offensive weapon. We need to speak what it says and attack the lies of the devil wherever we find them. We also need to exercise the authority that God has given us over all the power of the enemy. We need to remember that Satan was defeated over 2000 years ago and that, at that time, he lost all of this authority and power. Today, he has power only to the extent that he can get us to believe his lies.

3. <u>We must filter what we choose to put into our minds.</u> The old computer saying, garbage in, garbage out, applies to our brains. We cannot hope to have our minds guide our lives if we have filled our data bases with lies and wrong interpretations concerning life, reality and God. The client must be challenged to guard vigilantly what he allows into his mind, since it will eventually affect his actions. Of course, in modern times, this includes what we read and what we see on television, at the movies, or on the Internet.

4. <u>We need to be careful what we say to ourselves in our minds.</u> Self-talk is an expression of how we perceive things in our lives. It is actually preaching to ourselves a positive or negative outlook on life. It eventually even affects our sub-conscious mind. Unfortunately, many clients, especially those who have been verbally abused as children, say negative things to themselves concerning their worth or capabilities. For example, if we have had a father who called us stupid, we might use these same words to ourselves when we make a mistake. This is extremely detrimental since we are actually verbally abusing ourselves and the Bible compares verbal abuse to murder. (Matthew 5:21-22) Thought stopping techniques or replacing negative thoughts with positive ones can be suggested when clients are destructively talking to themselves. Because negative self-talk usually becomes a habit or stronghold, it may be necessary to have the client set self-boundaries with consequences in order to stop it. If the client truly believes what they are saying to themselves is true, these lies will also have to be confronted.

The Principles of Wisdom

According to The New International Webster's Concise Dictionary of the English Language, edited by Sidney Landau (1997), wisdom is the following: "1. The ability to discern what is true and right and to make sound judgments based on such discernment. 2. Insight and intuition. 3. Common sense. 4. A high degree of knowledge; learning." The Bible strongly emphasizes the importance of wisdom and discusses two types: the wisdom of man and the wisdom of God. God considers man's wisdom to be foolishness when it rejects God's higher wisdom. God's wisdom is better than ours because it is based on absolute truth. He knows all things that will happen in the future and He cannot make a mistake. Even Solomon, who was possibly the wisest man on earth, failed when he decided to follow his own way and was led astray by his many wives.

1. <u>God is the true source of wisdom.</u>

    Da 2:20 Daniel answered and said, Blessed be the name of God for ever and ever: for wisdom and might are his:

    21 And he changeth the times and the seasons: he removeth kings, and setteth up kings: he giveth wisdom unto the wise, and knowledge to them that know understanding:

    Ps 51:6 Behold, thou desirest truth in the inward parts: and in the hidden part thou shalt make me to know wisdom.

2. <u>Wisdom begins through instruction and is perceived through understanding.</u>

    Pr 1:2 To know wisdom and instruction; to perceive the words of understanding;

    4:7 Wisdom is the principal thing; therefore get wisdom: and with all thy getting get understanding.

    5:1 My son, attend unto my wisdom, and bow thine ear to my understanding:

3. <u>We can gain it through discipline.</u>

    Pr 29:15 The rod and reproof give wisdom: but a child left to himself bringeth his mother to shame.

4. <u>We are to seek it out for ourselves.</u>

    Ec 1:17 And I gave my heart to know wisdom, and to know madness and folly: I perceived that this also is vexation of spirit.

    7:25 I applied mine heart to know, and to search, and to seek out wisdom, and the reason of things, and to know the wickedness of folly, even of foolishness and madness:

5. <u>It comes from studying the Word of God.</u>

    Col 3:16 Let the word of Christ dwell in you richly in all wisdom; teaching and admonishing one another in psalms and hymns and spiritual songs, singing with grace in your hearts to the Lord.

6. <u>God will give us wisdom if we ask Him for it.</u>

    Pr 2:6 For the LORD giveth wisdom: out of his mouth cometh knowledge and understanding.

Eph 1:17 That the God of our Lord Jesus Christ, the Father of glory, may give unto you the spirit of wisdom and revelation in the knowledge of him:

Jas 1:5 If any of you lack wisdom, let him ask of God, that giveth to all men liberally, and upbraideth not; and it shall be given him.

7. <u>God rewards those who seek wisdom and gives them success.</u>

2 Chr 1:11 And God said to Solomon, Because this was in thine heart, and thou hast not asked riches, wealth, or honour, nor the life of thine enemies, neither yet hast asked long life; but hast asked wisdom and knowledge for thyself, that thou mayest judge my people, over whom I have made thee king:

12 Wisdom and knowledge is granted unto thee; and I will give thee riches, and wealth, and honour, such as none of the kings have had that have been before thee, neither shall there any after thee have the like.

Pr 24:14 So shall the knowledge of wisdom be unto thy soul: when thou hast found it, then there shall be a reward, and thy expectation shall not be cut off.

8. <u>We are not to trust in our own wisdom. Doing so caused Satan's downfall.</u>

Isa 47:10 For thou hast trusted in thy wickedness: thou hast said, None seeth me. Thy wisdom and thy knowledge, it hath perverted thee; and thou hast said in thine heart, I am, and none else beside me.

Eze 28:17 Thine heart was lifted up because of thy beauty, thou hast corrupted thy wisdom by reason of thy brightness: I will cast thee to the ground, I will lay thee before kings, that they may behold thee.

9. <u>We are to seek after God's wisdom.</u>

Ro 11:33 O the depth of the riches both of the wisdom and knowledge of God! how unsearchable are his judgments, and his ways past finding out!

10. <u>Jesus is our wisdom.</u>

1 Co 1:30 But of him are ye in Christ Jesus, who of God is made unto us wisdom, and righteousness, and sanctification, and redemption:

11. <u>God resists the wisdom of man and counts it as foolishness because it rejects Him.</u>

1 Co 1:19 For it is written, I will destroy the wisdom of the wise, and will bring to nothing the understanding of the prudent.

20 Where is the wise? where is the scribe? where is the disputer of this world? hath not God made foolish the wisdom of this world?

21 For after that in the wisdom of God the world by wisdom knew not God, it pleased God by the foolishness of preaching to save them that believe.

3:19 For the wisdom of this world is foolishness with God. For it is written, He taketh the wise in their own craftiness.

12. <u>God is also able to give us a supernatural gift of the word of wisdom.</u>

   1 Co 12:8 For to one is given by the Spirit the word of wisdom; to another the word of knowledge by the same Spirit;

Counseling Methods and Techniques

1. <u>Our current problems are caused by our lack of wisdom.</u> We need to realize that it was our wisdom that got us into the problem, and it is our wisdom that has failed us repeatedly. One of our drug/alcohol counselors used to tell her clients; "Your best thinking got you here. Maybe you need to try something different this time."

2. <u>We need to value and obtain both natural and spiritual wisdom.</u> We need to teach our clients the value of wisdom and how to obtain it through both natural and supernatural means. As we study the Word of God and meditate on it, we can understand truth and learn true wisdom. If we ask God, He will give it to us; and as we get to know Jesus, we will become more like Him. This is true wisdom.

Chapter 7

Principles of Perception

To perceive is to become aware of something through the senses, to come to understand; to apprehend with the mind. (The New International Webster's Concise Dictionary of the English Language, 1997, edited by Sidney Landau) Perception is an interpretive function of the mind. Our experience in this world is determined by how we view or perceive things; and we will think, act and feel in accordance to these perceptions. Of course, these perception will be determined by what we believe is true, our experiences, and the conclusions we have reached concerning them. Our perceptions are critical, because we use them to evaluate everything around us. We will eventually act according to how we perceive things even if our perceptions are wrong. The overall way we perceive life as a whole is called our worldview. To the degree that our worldview and our perceptions match the absolute truth of how things really are, to that degree we will be healthy. To the degree that we believe lies about our world and perceive things inaccurately, to that degree we will not function as we should. There are three topics in the Bible concerning perception that are critical for healthy functioning: How we discern people and things, our identity in Christ, and our perception of the grace of God.

The Principles of Discernment

To discern means "To perceive, as with sight or mind; apprehend. 2. To discriminate mentally; recognize subtle differences. 3. To distinguish; discriminate." (The New International Webster's Concise Dictionary of the English Language, 1997, edited by Sidney Landau) Both discernment and judgment are used when discussing the evaluation of things or actions. Judgment is also used for the evaluation of a person or for the legal condemnation of a person. Because the Bible gives very different directions concerning the evaluation and judgment of people, I will limit our discussion of discernment to correctly perceive events, actions, experiences or things in a valid and true manner. (I will address judging people later in section on the principles of judgment and accountability.)

1. Correctly perceiving brings joy.

    Pr 21:15 It is joy to the just to do judgment: but destruction shall be to the workers of iniquity.

2. We are to discern what is good and bad.

    2 Sa 14:17 Then thine handmaid said, The word of my lord the king shall now be comfortable: for as an angel of God, so is my lord the king to discern good and bad: therefore the LORD thy God will be with thee.

3. God expects us to discern the meaning of the events of our lives and things to come.

    Lu 12:56 Ye hypocrites, ye can discern the face of the sky and of the earth; but how is it that ye do not discern this time?

4. <u>We are to discern the validity of the works or ministries of others, but not to legally judge them unless these ministries are under our authority.</u>

    Mt 7:16 Ye shall know them by their fruits. Do men gather grapes of thorns, or figs of thistles?

    17 Even so every good tree bringeth forth good fruit; but a corrupt tree bringeth forth evil fruit.

5. <u>We are expected to wisely judge personal controversies.</u>

    1 Co 6:2 Do ye not know that the saints shall judge the world? and if the world shall be judged by you, are ye unworthy to judge the smallest matters?

    5 I speak to your shame. Is it so, that there is not a wise man among you? no, not one that shall be able to judge between his brethren?

6. <u>God is pleased if we ask for discernment and will give many blessings if we desire and ask for it.</u>

    1 Ki 3:11 And God said unto him, Because thou hast asked this thing, and hast not asked for thyself long life; neither hast asked riches for thyself, nor hast asked the life of thine enemies; but hast asked for thyself understanding to discern judgment.

    12 Behold, I have done according to thy words: lo, I have given thee a wise and an understanding heart; so that there was none like thee before thee, neither after thee shall any arise like unto thee.

    13 And I have also given thee that which thou hast not asked, both riches, and honour: so that there shall not be any among the kings like unto thee all thy days..

7. <u>Discernment can be taught.</u>

    Eze 44:23 And they shall teach my people the difference between the holy and profane, and cause them to discern between the unclean and the clean.

8. <u>Discernment can be learned through experience and is a sign of maturity.</u>

    Heb 5:14 But strong meat belongeth to them that are of full age, even those who by reason of use have their senses exercised to discern both good and evil.

9. <u>Everything we do will eventually be tested to see if it is well-built on the foundation of Christ.</u>

    1 Co 3: 11 For other foundation can no man lay than that is laid, which is Jesus Christ.

    12 Now if any man build upon this foundation gold, silver, precious stones, wood, hay, stubble;

    13 Every man's work shall be made manifest: for the day shall declare it, because it shall be revealed by fire; and the fire shall try every man's work of what sort it is.

    14 If any man's work abide which he hath built thereupon, he shall receive a reward.

    15 If any man's work shall be burned, he shall suffer loss: but he himself shall be saved; yet so as by fire.

10. <u>Our desires are also a function of the mind and are a reflection of our perception of our needs.</u> They provide the basis for motivation.

Eph 2:3 Among whom also we all had our conversation in times past in the lusts of our flesh, fulfilling the desires of the flesh and of the mind; and were by nature the children of wrath, even as others.

Ps 37:4 Delight thyself also in the LORD; and he shall give thee the desires of thine heart.

Counseling Methods and Techniques

1. <u>Deal with the underlying fears to overcome obsessions.</u> It is the fear underlying the obsession that drives the client to focus so strongly on that specific problem. The more they focus on that problem, the bigger it gets until it consumes them. Many times the initial problem is based on an intuitive feeling that they have incorrectly discerned. Finding the underlying fear or feeling and dealing with it releases the person to again evaluate life in a more balanced way.

2. <u>Those with obsessions must again be taught discernment.</u> When a client is obsessed he sees everything through a single set of glasses. The saying is true that "for a kid with a hammer the whole world becomes a nail." The obsessed person gathers all sorts of evidence and tries to apply it to the area of his fear. His discernment usually becomes distorted. For example, the jealous person will see everything as signs of adultery. To teach discernment ask the client what other explanations there might be for the event. Next, have him evaluate which of his options is the most probable explanation.

The Principles of Our Identity in Christ

Possibly for Westerners, no area of the Bible is harder to grasp than that of our identity or position in Christ. We are so time-oriented that we find it hard to grasp that God operates outside of time; and, to Him, it is as if everything in the future has already taken place. If we truly believe what the Word of God says and act accordingly, these realities become manifested. By faith, God spoke the world into existence; and if we can learn to truly take God at His Word, through faith, we can experience the present and future that God has already provided for us. Because we act according to our perceptions, tremendous change can occur if we simply line up our perceptions about ourselves and our circumstances with what God has already spoken. We must remember that God cannot lie and what He says is truly reality. In *Sit, Walk, Stand,* Watchman Nee states, "Most Christians make the mistake of trying to walk in order to sit, but that is the reversal of the true order... If at the outset we try to do anything, we get nothing; if we seek to attain something, we miss everything. For Christianity begins not with a big DO, but with a big DONE...Whereas God worked six days and then enjoyed the Sabbath rest, Adam began his life with the Sabbath (having been created on the 6th day); for God works before He rests, while man must first enter into God's rest, and then alone can he work." (1957, pp. 11-13)

1. <u>God calls things that are not as if they are.</u> We need to realize that, to God, if we will simply believe Him and act on our belief, everything is already an accomplished fact. This is the conflict between truth and fact described earlier.

Ro 4:17 (As it is written, I have made thee a father of many nations,) before him whom he believed, [even] God, who quickeneth the dead, and calleth those things which be not as though they were.

2. We have been adopted as sons and daughters.

    Ro 8:15 For ye have not received the spirit of bondage again to fear; but ye have received the Spirit of adoption, whereby we cry, Abba, Father.

3. We are new spiritual creatures.

    2 Co 5:17 Therefore if any man [be] in Christ, [he is] a new creature: old things are passed away; behold, all things are become new.

4. He is in us.

    Jo 17:21 That they all may be one; as thou, Father, [art] in me, and I in thee, that they also may be one in us: that the world may believe that thou hast sent me.

5. We are in Him.

    1 Jo 4:13 Hereby know we that we dwell in him, and he in us, because he hath given us of his Spirit.

6. We are justified.

    Tit 3:7 That being justified by his grace, we should be made heirs according to the hope of eternal life.

7. We are sanctified.

    1 Co 1:30 But of him are ye in Christ Jesus, who of God is made unto us wisdom, and righteousness, and sanctification, and redemption:

8. We are glorified.

    Ro 8:30 Moreover whom he did predestinate, them he also called: and whom he called, them he also justified: and whom he justified, them he also glorified.

9. We are the righteousness of God in Him.

    2 Co 5:21 For he hath made him [to be] sin for us, who knew no sin; that we might be made the righteousness of God in him.

10. We are kings and priests.

    Re 5:10 And hast made us unto our God kings and priests: and we shall reign on the earth.

11. We are complete in Him through co-identification because we are in Him and He in us.

    Col 2:10 And ye are complete in him, which is the head of all principality and power:

11 In whom also ye are circumcised with the circumcision made without hands, in putting off the body of the sins of the flesh by the circumcision of Christ:

12 Buried with him in baptism, wherein also ye are risen with [him] through the faith of the operation of God, who hath raised him from the dead.

12. <u>We are more than conquerors in Him.</u>

Ro 8:37 Nay, in all these things we are more than conquerors through him that loved us.

13. <u>We are joint heirs with Jesus.</u>

Ro 8:17. And if children, then heirs; heirs of God, and joint-heirs with Christ; if so be that we suffer with [him], that we may be also glorified together.

14. <u>We are seated with Christ in Heavenly places with Him.</u>

Eph 2:5 Even when we were dead in sins, hath quickened us together with Christ, (by grace ye are saved;)

6 And hath raised [us] up together, and made [us] sit together in heavenly [places] in Christ Jesus:

15. <u>If we are one with Him, we have a common destiny.</u>

Ga 2:20 I am crucified with Christ: nevertheless I live; yet not I, but Christ liveth in me: and the life which I now live in the flesh I live by the faith of the Son of God, who loved me, and gave himself for me.

16. <u>God has provided for all our needs.</u>

Php 4:19 But my God shall supply all your need according to his riches in glory by Christ Jesus.

17. <u>We must know our position, reckon or rely on it, act according to it, and walk it out in our lives.</u>

Ro 6:6 Knowing this, that our old man is crucified with [him], that the body of sin might be destroyed, that henceforth we should not serve sin.

11 Likewise reckon ye also yourselves to be dead indeed unto sin, but alive unto God through Jesus Christ our Lord.

12 Let not sin therefore reign in your mortal body, that ye should obey it in the lusts thereof.

13 Neither yield ye your members [as] instruments of unrighteousness unto sin: but yield yourselves unto God, as those that are alive from the dead, and your members [as] instruments of righteousness unto God.

Counseling Methods and Techniques

1. <u>We must have a revelation that we are in Christ, and Christ is in us.</u> We can help the client understand these principles from the standpoint of God—outside of time—so that he can comprehend them with his mind. But, in order for them to significantly impact his life, these truths must become a revelation in his spirit.

2. <u>We must meditate on God's Word to know who we are in Christ.</u> We must study these principles, act according to them, and ask God for a spiritual revelation in order for them to change our outlook on life. The principle assumptions about life are stored in the subconscious mind, which is part of our human spirit. We must get the truth from our mind to our spirit.

3. <u>If we perceive ourselves differently, we will act differently.</u> Once we have a revelation of our position in Christ, a paradigm shift will occur. This is one of the most effective ways of changing from the inside out. A revelation or understanding in the spirit is something that is spiritually discerned, but may be assisted by gathering supporting data for our mind, emotions, and will that can influence our spirit. Faith in the spirit is the basis of revelation.

4. <u>Viewing our world as God does will change our lives.</u> Changing how we view our world can bring a significant change in our lives, especially if that new viewpoint is extremely optimistic. How we look at life determines the overall backdrop for how we experience it. If it is a dangerous and scary place, we are prone to be negative and expect the worst to happen. God's worldview is that Satan has been defeated; and, although we will have challenges in life, we can do everything required through Christ. Ultimately, we can overcome anything through Christ and we will win. Our worldview influences many aspects of our lives, especially our feelings of worth, how we value others, and our desire to compete with others in order to become successful in life. Most Christians have just accepted the lies of the world. Consequently, they find life a stressful place instead of entering into "the rest of God." (Hebrews 4:9-10) (For much more on this subject see my book *Faith Therapy*.)

The Principles of the Grace of God

As a general term, grace means that which is "pleasant or favored." In the Bible, it is used to mean the unmerited favor of God and, sometimes, the influence and power that God displays on our behalf due to that favor, mercy and kindness. The critical issue is how we perceive God. If we see him as a vindictive, punishing father, we will fear his judgment; but if we see him as an unconditionally loving friend, we will seek His presence in our lives.

1. <u>One of God's primary characteristics is grace or unmerited favor toward everyone.</u>

   Ne 9:31 Nevertheless for thy great mercies' sake thou didst not utterly consume them, nor forsake them; for thou art a gracious and merciful God.

   Ps 103:8 The LORD is merciful and gracious, slow to anger, and plenteous in mercy.

2. <u>Jesus was characterized by grace, and God's grace came to us through Him.</u>

   Jo 1:14 And the Word was made flesh, and dwelt among us, (and we beheld his glory, the glory as of the only begotten of the Father,) full of grace and truth.

   17 For the law was given by Moses, but grace and truth came by Jesus Christ.

3. <u>We are justified by grace.</u>

   Ro 3:24 Being justified freely by his grace through the redemption that is in Christ Jesus:

4. <u>Grace is a free gift that sets us free from the law and sin.</u>

   Ro 5:15 But not as the offence, so also is the free gift. For if through the offence of one many be dead, much more the grace of God, and the gift by grace, which is by one man, Jesus Christ, hath abounded unto many.

6:14 For sin shall not have dominion over you: for ye are not under the law, but under grace.

5. Grace is obtained through faith.

    Ro 5:2 By whom also we have access by faith into this grace wherein we stand, and rejoice in hope of the glory of God.

6. Grace sets us free from the law so that we can do anything, but we must be careful not to use God's grace as an occasion for the flesh. If we do, we may again find ourselves in bondage to sin.

    1 Co 6:12 All things are lawful unto me, but all things are not expedient: all things are lawful for me, but I will not be brought under the power of any.

7. Grace is not a license to sin.

    Ro 6:15 What then? shall we sin, because we are not under the law, but under grace? God forbid.

8. Grace cannot be obtained by works.

    Ro 11:6 And if by grace, then is it no more of works: otherwise grace is no more grace. But if it be of works, then is it no more grace: otherwise work is no more work.

9. Grace is supposed to result in works.

    1 Co 15:10 But by the grace of God I am what I am: and his grace which was bestowed upon me was not in vain; but I laboured more abundantly than they all: yet not I, but the grace of God which was with me.

10. Trying to accomplish things (the law) in our own strength works against the grace of God and is called "falling from grace."

    Ga 2:21 I do not frustrate the grace of God: for if righteousness come by the law, then Christ is dead in vain.
    5:4 Christ is become of no effect unto you, whosoever of you are justified by the law; ye are fallen from grace.

11. Grace functions best when we admit our inability and trust God to accomplish what is needed.

    2 Co 12:9 And he said unto me, My grace is sufficient for thee: for my strength is made perfect in weakness. Most gladly therefore will I rather glory in my infirmities, that the power of Christ may rest upon me.
    Jas 4:6 But he giveth more grace. Wherefore he saith, God resisteth the proud, but giveth grace unto the humble

12. We must have a revelation of grace in order to experience all that it provides for us.

    Col 1:6 Which is come unto you, as it is in all the world; and bringeth forth fruit, as it doth also in you, since the day ye heard of it , and knew the grace of God in truth:

13. <u>We are saved by grace.</u>

   Eph 2:5 Even when we were dead in sins, hath quickened us together with Christ, (by grace ye are saved;)

   2 Ti 1:9 Who hath saved us, and called us with an holy calling, not according to our works, but according to his own purpose and grace , which was given us in Christ Jesus before the world began,

14. <u>God's grace results in sufficiency in everything.</u>

   2 Co 9:8 And God is able to make all grace abound toward you; that ye, always having all sufficiency in all things, may abound to every good work:

15. <u>Ministry comes by grace.</u>

   Eph 3:7 Whereof I was made a minister, according to the gift of the grace of God given unto me by the effectual working of his power.

16. <u>Grace can give us strength.</u>

   2 Ti 2:1 Thou therefore, my son, be strong in the grace that is in Christ Jesus.

   Tit 3:7 That being justified by his grace, we should be made heirs according to the hope of eternal life.

17. <u>Because of grace we can approach God with assurance in time of need.</u>

   Heb 4:16 Let us therefore come boldly unto the throne of grace, that we may obtain mercy, and find grace to help in time of need.

18. <u>We also must have grace in ourselves in order to serve God acceptably.</u> It provides the basis for loving others.

   Heb 12:28 Wherefore we receiving a kingdom which cannot be moved, let us have grace, whereby we may serve God acceptably with reverence and godly fear:

19. <u>Grace can be multiplied and grown as we know God and Jesus more.</u>

   2 Pe 1:2 Grace and peace be multiplied unto you through the knowledge of God, and of Jesus our Lord,

   3:18 But grow in grace, and in the knowledge of our Lord and Saviour Jesus Christ. To him be glory both now and for ever. Amen.

Counseling Methods and Techniques

1. <u>We must realize that the law is a trap to be avoided.</u> The law separates us from God, since failing to obey it is sin, and sin causes shame. When we are told to do something according to the law, we either rebel or try to do it in our own strength and fail. Either way, we are wrongly motivated and this leads to sin. The Pharisees attempted to obey the law fully; and, as a result, they became more evil

than even the common people. When we attempt to make ourselves better in our own strength, we are focusing on meeting our own needs and, therefore, become more self-centered or selfish. When we try to perform, we end up with performance self-worth; and when we try to please others, we end up with approval self-worth, both of which put us on an emotional roller coaster. The Apostle Paul addressed this in Romans 7:19, "For the good that I would I do not: but the evil which I would not, that I do." Finally, he concludes in verse 24, "O wretched man that I am! Who shall deliver me from the body of this death?" (For more on the law see my book *Revelations That Will Set You Free*.)

2. <u>We must understand that we are no longer under the law.</u> Since Christ fulfilled the law and we are in Christ and Christ is in us, all things are now lawful for us, but as the Apostle Paul so aptly put it, "…not all things are expedient for me." (1 Corinthians 6:12)

3. <u>We must understand how God's grace sets us free.</u> I explain it this way. We have God's unmerited favor toward us because He loves us. Our faith in God is based on His love for us because when we realize He loves us and has our best interest in mind, we realize we can trust and rely on Him. We are justified (just as if we had never sinned), because Jesus paid the penalty for our past, present, and future sins on the cross. Therefore, we are reconciled to God and are guaranteed of His favor in everything, without regard to our works or actions. Consequently, we can always know that since we have God's favor, He will meet all our needs, do what is best for us and answer our prayers. Because all of our needs have been and will always be met through God's grace, we are freed from our selfish attempt to meet our own needs through the flesh and are delivered from our selfishness, which is the basis of sin.

Because of His unmerited favor, we are free to do anything without affecting our relationship with God. No matter what we do, because we are in Christ and Christ is in us, God will always love us and favor us. This freedom delivers us from being motivated to live for God out of fear, obligation or guilt; It allows us to act out of gratitude and love for Him. We are deterred from sinning because we will still get the consequences of our sin, and, because God loves us so much, He will still discipline us when necessary. We now do what He asks because we realize He has our best interests in mind and that what He desires for us is truly in our best interest. However, we now do it by relying on His grace and strength, out of love for Him and His kingdom. Therefore, we are saved, or made completely whole, by grace. Sometimes I also use the chart entitled "Freedom Through Grace" from my book *Revelations That Will Set You Free* to help my clients clearly understand this critical concept.

Chapter 8

Principles for Meeting Needs

Each of us has basic physical and psychological needs. Our psychological needs include a need to feel worthwhile, a need to feel significant, a need to feel secure and a need for acceptance or love. Attempts to meet these needs are the basis of much of what motivates us in life and are the basis of our selfishness, which underlies our sin nature. These are the needs of the self. When we attempt to meet these needs by our own efforts, we are meeting our needs through the flesh. The Greek word *sarx*, translated as the flesh, can also refer to our physical body, our human nature with its cravings, or the sensuous animal nature of man that is prone to sin. The Bible warns us that in our flesh dwells no good thing. (Romans 7:18) Although it is impossible to reform the desires of the flesh, it is possible to control them by meeting these needs through faith and dying to the self and the flesh through the Spirit. It is God's purpose to deliver us from this self-centeredness through faith that He can be trusted to meet all of our needs.

The Principles of Walking in the Flesh

1. <u>A person is walking according to the flesh when he focuses on meeting his own needs and relies on his own efforts to get his needs met.</u>

   Ro 8:5 For they that are after the flesh do mind the things of the flesh; but they that are after the Spirit the things of the Spirit.

   Ps 81:12 So I gave them up unto their own hearts' lust: and they walked in their own counsels.

2. <u>Lust is not of God, but of the world, which passes away.</u> We are not to lust for or strongly desire evil things which attempt to meet these needs.

   1 Jo 2:16 For all that is in the world, the lust of the flesh, and the lust of the eyes, and the pride of life, is not of the Father, but is of the world.

   17 And the world passeth away, and the lust thereof: but he that doeth the will of God abideth for ever.

3. <u>Walking in the flesh results in fulfilling the desires of the flesh.</u>

   Eph 2:3 Among whom also we all had our conversation in times past in the lusts of our flesh, fulfilling the desires of the flesh and of the mind; and were by nature the children of wrath, even as others.

4. <u>Lust leads to sin.</u>

   Jas 1:14 But every man is tempted, when he is drawn away of his own lust, and enticed.

15 Then when lust hath conceived, it bringeth forth sin: and sin, when it is finished, bringeth forth death.

5.   The flesh battles with the Spirit for the control of the soul.

Ga 5:17 For the flesh lusteth against the Spirit, and the Spirit against the flesh: and these are contrary the one to the other: so that ye cannot do the things that ye would.

6.   Resisting temptation or trying to do right through the flesh will eventually fail.

Mt 26:41 Watch and pray, that ye enter not into temptation: the spirit indeed is willing, but the flesh is weak.

Ro 7:18 For I know that in me (that is, in my flesh,) dwelleth no good thing: for to will is present with me; but how to perform that which is good I find not.

7.   We are not to make any provisions to fulfill the lust of the flesh.

Ro 13:14 But put ye on the Lord Jesus Christ, and make not provision for the flesh, to fulfil the lusts thereof.

Ga 5:13 For, brethren, ye have been called unto liberty; only use not liberty for an occasion to the flesh, but by love serve one another.

8.   Those who walk according to the flesh cannot please God.

Ro 8:8 So then they that are in the flesh cannot please God.

9.   Walking according to the flesh will produce many destructive practices, which can eventually end in the loss of our salvation.

Ga 5:19 Now the works of the flesh are manifest, which are these; Adultery, fornication, uncleanness, lasciviousness,

20 Idolatry, witchcraft, hatred, variance, emulations, wrath, strife, seditions, heresies,

21 Envyings, murders, drunkenness, revellings, and such like: of the which I tell you before, as I have also told you in time past, that they which do such things shall not inherit the kingdom of God.

10. Sowing or feeding the flesh will end in corruption.

Ga 6:7 Be not deceived; God is not mocked: for whatsoever a man soweth, that shall he also reap.

8 For he that soweth to his flesh shall of the flesh reap corruption; but he that soweth to the Spirit shall of the Spirit reap life everlasting.

11. God's covenants require that we cut away or die to the control of the flesh in our lives. In the Old Testament circumcision symbolized this.

Ge 17:14 And the uncircumcised man child whose flesh of his foreskin is not circumcised, that soul shall be cut off from his people; he hath broken my covenant.

Jer 4:4 Circumcise yourselves to the LORD, and take away the foreskins of your heart, ye men of Judah and inhabitants of Jerusalem: lest my fury come forth like fire, and burn that none can quench it, because of the evil of your doings.

Ro 2:29 But he is a Jew, which is one inwardly; and circumcision is that of the heart, in the spirit, and not in the letter; whose praise is not of men, but of God.

12. <u>We escape lust through believing that God will meet our needs according to His promises.</u>

2 Pe 1:4 Whereby are given unto us exceeding great and precious promises: that by these ye might be partakers of the divine nature, having escaped the corruption that is in the world through lust.

13. <u>Fasting is the first step in breaking the power of the flesh.</u>

Isa 58:6 Is not this the fast that I have chosen? to loose the bands of wickedness, to undo the heavy burdens, and to let the oppressed go free, and that ye break every yoke?

14. <u>The ultimate answer for overcoming the lust of the flesh and doing right is to walk according to the Spirit.</u>

Ga 5:16 This I say then, Walk in the Spirit, and ye shall not fulfill the lust of the flesh.

Ro 8:4 That the righteousness of the law might be fulfilled in us, who walk not after the flesh, but after the Spirit.

15. <u>We are obligated to walk according to the Spirit and mortify the deeds of the flesh, or we will eventually die spiritually.</u>

Ro 8:12 Therefore, brethren, we are debtors, not to the flesh, to live after the flesh.

8:13 For if ye live after the flesh, ye shall die: but if ye through the Spirit do mortify the deeds of the body, ye shall live.

16. <u>When we walk according to the Spirit, we do not feel the condemnation that accompanies walking according to the flesh.</u>

Ro 8:1 There is therefore now no condemnation to them which are in Christ Jesus, who walk not after the flesh, but after the Spirit.

Counseling Methods and Techniques

1. <u>Deliverance from the flesh can be difficult.</u> It quickly becomes clear that when a person is walking in the flesh, he is in spiritual bondage. This is because the flesh provides an opening for the spirits of lust to take more and more control of the person. Because the person is trying to meet his needs through the flesh, he usually does not want to be delivered. Eventually, due to the heavy consequences that result from walking according to the flesh, he will be willing to repent. At this opportune moment, he needs to repent, renounce his desire to meet his needs through the things of the flesh, begin fasting, and fully immerse himself in the things of God until the power of the flesh is fully broken. (For a more detailed plan, see the biblical model in *Revelations That Will Set You Free* for overcoming the flesh based on the story of Esther.)

2. <u>A "dog fight" illustrates the battle between flesh and spirit.</u> Although there are now many different variations of this story, this is how I heard it as a young Christian. An evangelist was preaching on an unnamed Native American reservation. As he was walking down the street, he met one of his recent converts who had had a reputation as the reservation drunk, tough guy, and womanizer. When he inquired how the new Christian was doing, the Indian replied, "I don't know. It's like there is a big dog fight going on in my head. My old, bad dog that wants me to go back to the bars, is fighting with this new good dog that wants me to go to church, love my wife, and tell others about Christ." The evangelist smiled and asked, "Which one is winning." The Indian replied, "I guess the one I feed the most!" In each of us there is a battle going on between the flesh (the bad dog) and the Spirit (the good dog). I usually use this story to explain to a new convert what he needs to do after he has been saved. To win that battle he must starve the bad dog, feed the good dog and not quit!

With those who have been heavily addicted or might have a strong possibility of falling back into besetting sins, I add to this story. I ask, "What would it mean in the fight between the two dogs if the Indian goes back to the bar and gets drunk again?" The answer I am looking for is that "the bad dog is winning." I then ask, "What should the Indian do then? Should he just say I must not have been saved or this does not work so I'll just go out to the bar and feed the bad dog a t-bone steak?" Of course not. He should get a scoop shovel and get a 50 pound bag of dog food and stuff it down the good dog until he is strong enough to defeat the bad dog. In this way, I try to insure that any relapse will not end in backsliding. I actually had a relationship addicted client find different church services every night for a month in order to permanently break off an abusive dating relationship.

The Principles of Self-worth

Self-worth is the measure of how we value ourselves. It is possibly the most basic of our psychological needs. It has many dimensions, but is addressed mostly in the Bible in terms of pride, humility and meekness. Pride is a defense mechanism against low self-worth or the feeling we get when we are taking credit for who we are or what we have accomplished. Since none of us made ourselves, provided our own talents, or are truly self-sufficient, we should not take credit for who we are. Therefore, pride is a rejection of God's rightful place in our lives. Consequently, God resists all prideful efforts.

Most often if we feel inadequate in our life we are driven to meet this need by making ourselves feel adequate through accomplishments or approval and oscillate between feeling worthless and prideful depending on the circumstances of our lives. This results in a competitive spirit, comparing ourselves with others, and a critical or judgmental spirit trying to bring others down to our level. Humility is not having a low evaluation of ourselves but an accurate one from God's point of view. God wants us to value ourselves as He values us. He was willing to send His own Son to die for us while we were yet sinners. We are the objects of His love without regard to our works or performance. God has chosen to resist the proud and assist the humble. God also chooses to greatly reward the meek—those humble persons who have totally yielded themselves to God and accepted His will for their lives.

1. <u>Pride is not from God, but is of the world.</u> It is our attempt in our own flesh to feel valuable when, in truth, we are only one of six billion people in a world so small it is hardly noticeable in the universe.

   1 Jo 2:16 For all that is in the world, the lust of the flesh, and the lust of the eyes, and the pride of life, is not of the Father, but is of the world.

2. <u>Pride is actually the sin of rebellion against God which was first committed by the devil long ago.</u> It says that we see ourselves as equal to God, that we want to exalt ourselves above Him, that we owe Him nothing, and that we want to become self-sufficient without Him. It is interesting how we as

created creatures somehow think we do not need the one who created us. The "theory" of evolution is just that—an attempt to come up with some explanation for our creation that will allow us to deny our Creator and any obligation to Him.

Isa 14:12 How art thou fallen from heaven, O Lucifer, son of the morning! how art thou cut down to the ground, which didst weaken the nations!

13 For thou hast said in thine heart, I will ascend into heaven, I will exalt my throne above the stars of God: I will sit also upon the mount of the congregation, in the sides of the north:

Ps 10:4 The wicked, through the pride of his countenance, will not seek after God: God is not in all his thoughts.

3. <u>God opposes the proud.</u> He does this for our good. If our worth is based on what we have done or what others think of us, we will become slaves to our circumstances or the opinions of others. This results in performance self-worth, the competition of the rat race, and an emotional roller coaster that can only make our lives miserable. God loves us too much to allow this to happen.

Pr 16:5 Every one that is proud in heart is an abomination to the LORD: though hand join in hand, he shall not be unpunished.

Le 26:19 And I will break the pride of your power; and I will make your heaven as iron, and your earth as brass:

Job 33:17 That he may withdraw man from his purpose, and hide pride from man.

4. <u>Pride gives an opening to Satan, removes us from God's protection, and results in destruction and shame.</u> If we proudly want to run our own lives, God will let us; but we should not expect His help or protection if we do. He must allow the consequences of life to prove to us that we are not self-sufficient and that we cannot be our own God.

Pr 16:18 Pride goeth before destruction, and an haughty spirit before a fall.

11:2 When pride cometh, then cometh shame: but with the lowly is wisdom.

5. <u>Pride leads to taking advantage of others, causes conflict and defiles the heart.</u> If we are competing with others in order to make ourselves worthwhile, we will be tempted to do whatever it takes to win and will live in contention with others. People attempt to rely on themselves, because they do not trust God to meet their needs. Since they must take care of themselves, they are prone to all sorts of evil.

Ps 10:2 The wicked in his pride doth persecute the poor: let them be taken in the devices that they have imagined.

Pr 13:10 Only by pride cometh contention: but with the well advised is wisdom.

Mr 7: 21 For from within, out of the heart of men, proceed evil thoughts, adulteries, fornications, murders,

22 Thefts, covetousness, wickedness, deceit, lasciviousness, an evil eye, blasphemy, pride, foolishness:

23 All these evil things come from within, and defile the man.

6. <u>God requires us to be humble.</u> Humility is just an honest evaluation of our worth from the viewpoint of God. We are His creation. We have nothing that He has not given us. We are no better than others.

Nothing we can do is of true significance without His help. We do not have enough information to direct our own lives. We are all selfish sinners with a tendency to do evil in order to get our needs met at the expense of others. If God had not saved us, we would be doomed to a selfish, wasted, bitter life, ending in the destruction of hell. We are of true worth only because He loves us.

Mic 6:8 He hath shewed thee, O man, what is good; and what doth the LORD require of thee, but to do justly, and to love mercy, and to walk humbly with thy God?

7. Humility is also seeing ourselves and others through the loving eyes of God—of infinite worth and more valuable than the rest of His creation. Because He loves us, He made us in His image and said that we are very good. Through His grace and unmerited favor, we are worth as much to Him as His very own Son, Jesus. This truth is more clearly expressed below in the New Living Translation of John 17:23.

    Ps 8: 3 When I consider thy heavens, the work of thy fingers, the moon and the stars, which thou hast ordained;

    4 What is man, that thou art mindful of him? and the son of man, that thou visitest him?

    5 For thou hast made him a little lower than the angels, and hast crowned him with glory and honour.

    6 Thou madest him to have dominion over the works of thy hands; thou hast put all things under his feet:

    Jo 17:23 I in them and you in me, all being perfected into one. Then the world will know that you sent me and will understand that you love them as much as you love me. (NLT)

8. We can escape judgment by humbling ourselves before God. God does not want to punish us, but He must at least correct us. If we humble ourselves and repent, we are no longer in need of correction.

    2 Chr 7:14 If my people, which are called by my name, shall humble themselves, and pray, and seek my face, and turn from their wicked ways; then will I hear from heaven, and will forgive their sin, and will heal their land.

    12:7 And when the LORD saw that they humbled themselves, the word of the LORD came to Shemaiah, saying, They have humbled themselves; therefore I will not destroy them, but I will grant them some deliverance; and my wrath shall not be poured out upon Jerusalem by the hand of Shishak.

    32:26 Notwithstanding Hezekiah humbled himself for the pride of his heart, both he and the inhabitants of Jerusalem, so that the wrath of the LORD came not upon them in the days of Hezekiah.

9. Humble persons are exalted and are greatest in the Kingdom of God. This is because they are open to God's direction and are therefore more useful and effective in His kingdom. No matter how talented we are, if we refuse to be obedient we are of little use to Him.

    Mt 18:4 Whosoever therefore shall humble himself as this little child, the same is greatest in the kingdom of heaven.

    Lu 18:14 I tell you, this man went down to his house justified rather than the other: for every one that exalteth himself shall be abased; and he that humbleth himself shall be exalted.

10. <u>God chooses those who are seen as the weak and foolish in this world to do His work so that He will get the glory.</u> Of course, they are also more open to His direction and know clearly how much they need His help.

1 Co 1:26 For ye see your calling, brethren, how that not many wise men after the flesh, not many mighty, not many noble, are called:

27 But God hath chosen the foolish things of the world to confound the wise; and God hath chosen the weak things of the world to confound the things which are mighty;

28 And base things of the world, and things which are despised, hath God chosen, yea, and things which are not, to bring to nought things that are:

29 That no flesh should glory in his presence.

11. <u>Because we are all equal, God wants us to value each other as much as He loves and values us, esteeming others as better than ourselves.</u> Humility is a prerequisite for the development of unconditional love.

1 Th 5:13 And to esteem them very highly in love for their work's sake. And be at peace among yourselves.

Php 2:3 Let nothing be done through strife or vainglory; but in lowliness of mind let each esteem other better than themselves.

12. <u>We are to judge ourselves by the amount of faith and trust we have in God and by how Christ-like we are.</u> We are only useful in the Kingdom of God to the degree that we trust and obey the King.

Ro 12:3 For I say, through the grace given unto me, to every man that is among you, not to think of himself more highly than he ought to think; but to think soberly, according as God hath dealt to every man the measure of faith.

Eph 4:13 Till we all come in the unity of the faith, and of the knowledge of the Son of God, unto a perfect man, unto the measure of the stature of the fulness of Christ:

13. <u>Meekness is totally yielding ourselves to the will of God, relying on Him, and not demanding our rights.</u> It has been clearly demonstrated in the lives of Moses and Jesus.

Nu 12:3 (Now the man Moses was very meek, above all the men which were upon the face of the earth.)

Mt 11:29 Take my yoke upon you, and learn of me; for I am meek and lowly in heart: and ye shall find rest unto your souls.

21:5 Tell ye the daughter of Sion, Behold, thy King cometh unto thee, meek, and sitting upon an ass, and a colt the foal of an ass.

14. <u>Because the meek are totally yielded to and trust in God's plan for them, they have abundant peace.</u> Nothing seems to bother them.

Ps 37:11 But the meek shall inherit the earth; and shall delight themselves in the abundance of peace.

15. <u>We are called to develop a meek and quiet spirit.</u>

Zep 2:3 Seek ye the LORD, all ye meek of the earth, which have wrought his judgment; seek righteousness, seek meekness: it may be ye shall be hid in the day of the LORD'S anger.

1 Pe 3:4 But let it be the hidden man of the heart, in that which is not corruptible, even the ornament of a meek and quiet spirit, which is in the sight of God of great price.

16. <u>Because the meek totally trust in Him and do not demand their own rights, they are greatly rewarded by God.</u> A father wants to bless the child that demands nothing, but trusts him to meet all of his needs. Because the child believes the father loves him and has his best interest in mind, he wants to do whatever the father desires for him to do. This type of child will truly inherit everything that his father can possibly give him.

Ps 22:26 The meek shall eat and be satisfied: they shall praise the LORD that seek him: your heart shall live for ever.

147:6 The LORD lifteth up the meek: he casteth the wicked down to the ground.

149:4 For the LORD taketh pleasure in his people: he will beautify the meek with salvation.

Isa 29:19 The meek also shall increase their joy in the LORD, and the poor among men shall rejoice in the Holy One of Israel.

Mt 5:5 Blessed are the meek: for they shall inherit the earth.

Counseling Methods and Techniques

1. <u>Pride can be overcome by facing our insecurity and glorifying God.</u> When we understand that pride is either a self-defense mechanism used when we feel unworthy or insecure, or an attempt to take credit for something we have done ourselves, we can deal with the underlying causes. When we feel pride rising up, we need to identify what has happened. Either, we are feeling insecure or things are going so well we are tempted to think that our prosperity is our own doing, instead of a blessing from God. We must immediately stop the thought of pride by dealing with our insecurity or declaring that everything that we have is from God. If we allow pride into our lives thinking that we can run our own lives, God will resist us. We should give the glory to God for whatever we have been tempted to be prideful about. Overcoming pride can be a constant battle, but it must be won. At one point in my life, God revealed to me that every major failure that I had experienced was due to allowing pride in my life. Today, I avoid it like the plague that it actually is!

2. <u>We can humble ourselves by seeing things from God's perspective.</u> We need to recognize that we have nothing that God did not give us, that without His help we can do nothing of lasting value, and that we are truly nothing compared to God and His creation. Humility is simply taking an honest evaluation of ourselves from God's perspective. According to the Bible, this evaluation should be based on how much faith or trust we have in God, not in our own efforts or success.

3. <u>We become meek by giving up all our rights to God.</u> We are to present ourselves a living sacrifice for use in the Kingdom of God. (Romans 12:1) Truly meek persons are so interested in doing good for the Kingdom of God, that they cannot be offended by how they are treated or by what others do to them, if what happens turns out to be a benefit to God.

4. <u>We should not confuse self-worth or value with significance.</u> Self-worth has to do with our inherent value and is based solely on the love of God and the price God was willing to pay to redeem us through the sacrifice of His Son on the cross. No amount of money, performance, approval, accomplishments

or morals can make us any more worthwhile. God loves all of His kids equally! Significance has to do with our function or performance and will be addressed in the next section.

5. <u>Align our perceptions with the biblical truth.</u> I usually begin by asking clients to tell me what, in their mind, makes a person more or less worthwhile. I then show them that what they said fits the world formula of self-worth = performance + approval + morals. I then debunk the world's system using the arguments discussed and models for dealing with self-worth in my books *Faith Therapy* and *Transformation!*

6. <u>Do not interpret offenses as affecting our worth as a person.</u> The greatest damage from an offense occurs when we accept that what has been done to us says something important about our worth as a person. In fact, very few of the offenses in our lives were done intentionally to send us a specific message concerning our worth. Most offences are the results of miscommunication, other's selfish attempts to defend themselves, escalation during conflicts, and problems in the other person's life. Our most usual response to someone hurting us should be, "They have a problem, I'll pray for them."

   When, as young children we cannot gain the approval of our fathers, we seldom can see that it is our father who is at fault. Instead, we take what is done personally and perceive that it must mean that we are in some way inadequate. This leads to a low self-evaluation of ourselves which eventually results in low self-worth. However, when we are grown, we understand that most problems are not our fault and have nothing to do with our value as a person. A secular method, sometimes used to change the person's thinking, is to suggest that the grown up person (who understands that it was not their fault) have a conversation with the "inner child" who was hurt, to help them understand what has really happened.

7. Change how we perceive our hurts. Because emotions are basically thermometers of our perceptions, the most effective way to deal with emotions is to identify why we are feeling the way we are and deal with the misperceptions. We must first realize that offenses will happen to everyone. Even though Jesus was perfect, others still did offensive things to Him. Consequently, the fact that others offend us does not necessarily mean that there is something wrong with us. Jesus suggested that we should be of good cheer in the middle of our tribulation, because we know that we will overcome in the end and that God will work everything for our good.

   Mt 18:7 Woe unto the world because of offences! for it must needs be that offences come; but woe to that man by whom the offence cometh!

   Lu 17:1 Then said he unto the disciples, It is impossible but that offences will come: but woe unto him, through whom they come!

   Jo 16:33 These things I have spoken unto you, that in me ye might have peace. In the world ye shall have tribulation: but be of good cheer; I have overcome the world.

8. <u>Change how we handle offenses.</u> If we mishandle the emotions created by the events of our lives, they are transformed from hurts into wounds. What we do with them determines their effect on us. If we choose not to forgive, hold onto our hurts, obsess about them, and retain our right to get vengeance on those who hurt us, we will become bitter and our hurts will become long-term wounds that will result in further damage to our emotions. Jesus made it clear that the one who will not forgive is "turned over to the tormentors" (Matthew 18:34) and we must forgive others if we want to be forgiven (Luke 6:37). We must give up control of our lives and trust God for justice, especially in situations over which we have no control. (See the principles of justice and forgiveness later in this book.)

9. <u>Correctly deal with shame and failures.</u> Another factor in developing low self-worth is that we incorrectly deal with the shame of our failures. When we chose to hide and deny our failures, they are

changed from "I did a bad thing" to "I am a bad person." This affects how we feel about ourselves. Of course, we understand that neither of these factors are valid indicators of our worth since our worth does not depend on our performance, how others view us, or even how well we have obeyed the commands of God. Our worth must be based solely on the fact that God, who cannot lie, made us in His image, said we are very good, and loves, likes, favors and values us just the way we are.

10. <u>Build our faith that God loves and values us without works.</u> It is not good enough to read what the Bible has to say, but we must make it a part of us through study and meditation. We must study the biblical principles presented in this chapter and meditate on them until they become part of our spirit. When they do, we will be able to accept ourselves as we are simply because we "know" that God loves and values us without any performance or works on our part.

The Principles of Significance

Significance has to do with how important we are, how well we perform, and what we accomplish in life. In our society, if we do well we are said to be successful. While our worth should not be based on our performance, our significance is a measure of our performance and our position in life. Again, the problem is that man and God view things very differently. Man sees the world as a zero-sum game—What one gets, the other does not get. The result is a selfish competition for the scarce resources of life. The one who has the most things, popularity or power is the winner. Instead, God rejects all selfishly motivated accomplishments as "filthy rags," and rewards those who do His will motivated by love. Since all of us have a different mission and He has given us different talents in accordance with our mission, we should not compare ourselves with each other but press forward to accomplish that which He has called us to do motivated by love for Him. (See *Faith Therapy* for an in-depth discussion of this subject.)

1. <u>Each of us has a particular mission on earth.</u>

   Jer 1:5 Before I formed thee in the belly I knew thee; and before thou camest forth out of the womb I sanctified thee, and I ordained thee a prophet unto the nations.

   Ga 1:15 But when it pleased God, who separated me from my mother's womb, and called me by his grace,

   16 To reveal his Son in me, that I might preach him among the heathen; immediately I conferred not with flesh and blood:

2. <u>Because each of us has a different mission, we should not compare ourselves with anyone else or compete with each other.</u>

   2 Co 10:12 For we dare not make ourselves of the number, or compare ourselves with some that commend themselves: but they measuring themselves by themselves, and comparing themselves among themselves, are not wise.

3. <u>God has also given us different talents that are appropriate to our mission.</u> Some of us are five, two or one talent people. We make a mistake if we try to be something that God did not design us to be. One pastor said this, "I was never any good to God until I realized that He had not called me to be somebody great."

   Mt 25:15 And unto one he gave five talents, to another two, and to another one; to every man according to his several ability; and straightway took his journey.

4. <u>God judges us by what we have done with what He has entrusted to us.</u> The more we have been given, the more He expects of us.

   Mt 25:20 And so he that had received five talents came and brought other five talents, saying, Lord, thou deliveredst unto me five talents: behold, I have gained beside them five talents more.

   21 His lord said unto him, Well done, thou good and faithful servant: thou hast been faithful over a few things, I will make thee ruler over many things: enter thou into the joy of thy lord.

   22 He also that had received two talents came and said, Lord, thou deliveredst unto me two talents: behold, I have gained two other talents beside them.

   23 His lord said unto him, Well done, good and faithful servant; thou hast been faithful over a few things, I will make thee ruler over many things: enter thou into the joy of thy lord.

5. <u>Only those who do not use their talents will be rejected.</u> God only asks that we do our best with what He has given us. Of course, a good attitude will help. It is fear and not relying on God that keeps us from being successful in the sight of God. Faith opposes and overcomes fear.

   Mt 25:24 Then he which had received the one talent came and said, Lord, I knew thee that thou art an hard man, reaping where thou hast not sown, and gathering where thou hast not strawed:

   25 And I was afraid, and went and hid thy talent in the earth: lo, there thou hast that is thine.

   26 His lord answered and said unto him, Thou wicked and slothful servant, thou knewest that I reap where I sowed not, and gather where I have not strawed:

   27 Thou oughtest therefore to have put my money to the exchangers, and then at my coming I should have received mine own with usury.

6. <u>The more we use our talents, the more we will be given.</u> We are to compete against ourselves to be the best servant possible.

   Mt 25:28 Take therefore the talent from him, and give it unto him which hath ten talents.

   29 For unto every one that hath shall be given, and he shall have abundance: but from him that hath not shall be taken away even that which he hath.

   30 And cast ye the unprofitable servant into outer darkness: there shall be weeping and gnashing of teeth.

7. <u>God has a specific mission for everyone in the church.</u>

   1 Co 12:14 For the body is not one member, but many.

   15 If the foot shall say, Because I am not the hand, I am not of the body; is it therefore not of the body?

   16 And if the ear shall say, Because I am not the eye, I am not of the body; is it therefore not of the body?

   17 If the whole body were an eye, where were the hearing? If the whole were hearing, where were the smelling?

   18 But now hath God set the members every one of them in the body, as it hath pleased him.

8. <u>God judges our significance in the Kingdom of God by what we have done for Jesus out of love for Him.</u> All worldly accomplishments and those motivated by selfishness will be rejected.

1 Co 3:13 Every man's work shall be made manifest: for the day shall declare it, because it shall be revealed by fire; and the fire shall try every man's work of what sort it is.

14 If any man's work abide which he hath built thereupon, he shall receive a reward.

9. <u>All of our attempts to be righteous in our own strength are filthy rags.</u> This is because all we do without trusting in God is motivated by selfishness. Everything that is not based on faith is sin. (Romans 14:23)

   Isa 64:6 But we are all as an unclean thing, and all our righteousnesses are as filthy rags; and we all do fade as a leaf; and our iniquities, like the wind, have taken us away.

10. <u>We can take no credit for what we do because He made us, gave us our talents and our call, delivered us from our selfishness, and motivated us with His love.</u> Without what God has done for us, we can do nothing of lasting value or virtue.

    1 Co 4: 7 For who maketh thee to differ from another? and what hast thou that thou didst not receive? now if thou didst receive it, why dost thou glory, as if thou hadst not received it?

Counseling Methods and Techniques

1. <u>The first step to significance is becoming saved.</u> Without it, everything we do will be motivated by trying to meet the needs of the self; and everything motivated by selfishness to God is filthy rags. (Isaiah 64:6)

2. <u>We must confront our client's worldly concepts about life and the world, and replace them with God's truth.</u> We must help our clients see that the world's system does not make sense and that through it, everyone, including themselves, will eventually lose. When they realize this, they will be more open to learning and applying God's ways in their lives. I usually use an example to show them that the world's system always ends in failure. I ask them if they were good at a particular sport, as an example, high jumping. If they were the best in their school, they would then compete in the State championships, and then the regionals, and finally the Olympics. Even if they won the gold metal in the Olympics, they would still have to win it again in four years. Eventually, they would lose in the Olympics or have to retire. The point is that in the world's system of success, the more talented you are the higher you will rise and the harder the competition; and the higher you rise before you fail, the greater the consequences of your failure. In God's system, everyone wins; because He only expects us to do our best based on the talents He gave us (The Parable of the Talents). Each of us has our own specific race to run, so that we are only in competition with ourselves. In addition, God values us all equally and that value is not dependent on our performance, but on His unconditional love. I then explain that they choose God's system by believing in Him and yielding to His call on their lives.

3. <u>We must exit the world's rat race and compete only with ourselves.</u> In order to do this, We must accept God's view of our life. It is not true that we are all competing against each other. Instead, we all have a different mission and different talents. God, alone, will be the judge of our performance and He will judge us according to how well we carried out the specific mission He has given us, motivated by our love for Him.

4. <u>We must realize that only those things done for God are worthwhile.</u> It is so easy for us to be caught up again in the rat race of the world. Many times, I challenge the client that he does not have the ability, without God, to do anything of significance in life. God is not impressed with our worldly accomplishments. Mark 8:36 asks, "For what shall it profit a man, if he shall gain the whole world, and lose his own soul?"

5. <u>Teach the client God's concept of success.</u> We are only successful to the extent we find God's will for our lives and carry it out with His assistance, yielded to His will. Here, I use the example of John the Baptist. I compare John's success from the world's point of view and his success from God's point of view (as expressed by Jesus). (Luke 7:28)

6. <u>Change how we process our failures and success.</u> Feeling like we are on an emotional roller coaster ride is a sign that we are still elated by our success and shamed by our failures; at least in our own eyes and the eyes of others. Instead, we must realize that we can do nothing of significance without God and, therefore, He must get the credit for everything that we do. Otherwise, we have fallen into the trap of pride and may find that God Himself will resist our efforts. (James 4:6) If we take our successes or failures personally, we are again seeing them as ours, not God's. We are to be obedient to follow His commands, trust Him to provide all we need, and do our best. That is all He asks. The rest is up to Him. His point of view is what counts, not ours. If we cannot make it happen in our own strength, then the outcome is up to Him. If we see what we have done as a success, we are to be thankful; and if we see it as a failure, we are to trust Him to turn it for our good. (Romans 8:28)

The Principles of Security

Eventually all of us will face situations in our lives where we feel insecure. This is especially true when dealing with the problem of protection from harm or catastrophe. The attack on the World Trade Center showed us just how powerless we were to stop terrorist attacks. Our natural response to feelings of insecurity or powerlessness is to try to control things. Unfortunately, many persons have not learned that the more you try to control people, the more they rebel against the control; and the more a person tries to control all of his circumstances the more out of control things seem to get. Our only hope for absolute control and protection is to turn the control of our lives over to God, who alone is capable of controlling everything. (See my book *Faith Therapy* for a more in-depth discussion of this subject.)

1. <u>We cannot, in our own efforts, become completely secure in this life.</u>

   Ec 8:8 There is no man that hath power over the spirit to retain the spirit; neither hath he power in the day of death: and there is no discharge in that war; neither shall wickedness deliver those that are given to it.

2. <u>We either trust God, or we trust in ourselves.</u> We will never be secure by trusting in ourselves. In fact, the opposite is true. When we trust in ourselves, we are telling God that we will provide our own security in life. God will allow us to try until we learn by our consequences that we cannot do it.

   Mt 6:24 No man can serve two masters: for either he will hate the one, and love the other; or else he will hold to the one, and despise the other. Ye cannot serve God and mammon.

3. <u>God has promised to take care of us just like He cares for all of His creation.</u>

   Mt 6:25 Therefore I say unto you, Take no thought for your life, what ye shall eat, or what ye shall drink; nor yet for your body, what ye shall put on. Is not the life more than meat, and the body than raiment?

   26 Behold the fowls of the air: for they sow not, neither do they reap, nor gather into barns; yet your heavenly Father feedeth them. Are ye not much better than they?

4. <u>We must have faith that God will meet all our needs in the same wonderful way that He takes care of all of the rest of His creation.</u>

   Mt 6:28 And why take ye thought for raiment? Consider the lilies of the field, how they grow; they toil not, neither do they spin:

   29 And yet I say unto you, That even Solomon in all his glory was not arrayed like one of these.

   30 Wherefore, if God so clothe the grass of the field, which to day is, and to morrow is cast into the oven, shall he not much more clothe you, O ye of little faith?

5. <u>We are to trust God so much that we do not worry about things as insignificant as food or clothing.</u>

   Mt 6:31 Therefore take no thought, saying, What shall we eat? or, What shall we drink? or, Wherewithal shall we be clothed?

   32 (For after all these things do the Gentiles seek:) for your heavenly Father knoweth that ye have need of all these things.

6. <u>We are to make God's kingdom and doing His will our top priority.</u> If we do this, He promises to meet all our needs.

   Mt 6:33 But seek ye first the kingdom of God, and his righteousness; and all these things shall be added unto you.

7. <u>When we have put our trust in God, we should not even be concerned about what could happen tomorrow.</u>

   Mt 6:34 Take therefore no thought for the morrow: for the morrow shall take thought for the things of itself. Sufficient unto the day is the evil thereof.

8. <u>God will provide the protection and security we need if we will abide and trust in His protection by following His direction and doing His will.</u>

   Ps 91:1 He that dwelleth in the secret place of the most High shall abide under the shadow of the Almighty.

   2 I will say of the LORD, He is my refuge and my fortress: my God; in him will I trust.

   3 Surely he shall deliver thee from the snare of the fowler, and from the noisome pestilence.

   4 He shall cover thee with his feathers, and under his wings shalt thou trust: his truth shall be thy shield and buckler.

   5 Thou shalt not be afraid for the terror by night; nor for the arrow that flieth by day;

   6 Nor for the pestilence that walketh in darkness; nor for the destruction that wasteth at noonday.

   7 A thousand shall fall at thy side, and ten thousand at thy right hand; but it shall not come nigh thee.

   10 There shall no evil befall thee, neither shall any plague come nigh thy dwelling.

   11 For he shall give his angels charge over thee, to keep thee in all thy ways.

   12 They shall bear thee up in their hands, lest thou dash thy foot against a stone.

13 Thou shalt tread upon the lion and adder: the young lion and the dragon shalt thou trample under feet.

14 Because he hath set his love upon me, therefore will I deliver him: I will set him on high, because he hath known my name.

15 He shall call upon me, and I will answer him: I will be with him in trouble; I will deliver him, and honour him.

16 With long life will I satisfy him, and shew him my salvation.

9. <u>Even in the most difficult circumstances, we can count on God's protection if we remain in a caring relationship with Him and allow Him to shepherd our lives.</u>

Ps 23:1 The LORD is my shepherd; I shall not want.

2 He maketh me to lie down in green pastures: he leadeth me beside the still waters.

3 He restoreth my soul: he leadeth me in the paths of righteousness for his name's sake.

4 Yea, though I walk through the valley of the shadow of death, I will fear no evil: for thou art with me; thy rod and thy staff they comfort me.

5 Thou preparest a table before me in the presence of mine enemies: thou anointest my head with oil; my cup runneth over.

6 Surely goodness and mercy shall follow me all the days of my life: and I will dwell in the house of the LORD for ever.

Counseling Methods and Techniques

1. <u>We must realize that true security comes only from God.</u> It is important to build faith in the client that they can trust God for absolute protection if they are willing to meet God's requirements. From Psalm 91, we see that God provides absolute protection to those who trust and rely in Him. We can take ourselves out of that protection through willful disobedience, tempting God and pride. We tempt God when we take unreasonable chances or refuse to do our part by being responsible in life. God resists pride and it provides an opportunity for Satan to attack. We know that God will work everything for our good if we love Him and fit into His plans (Romans 8:28) but we must meet these requirements. Of course, we must realize that sometimes from God's eternal viewpoint and total understanding of the future, what He views as in our best interest may initially be perceived by us as evil, while in fact it is for our good. Consider the story of Joseph being sold as a slave, which eventually resulted in his elevation to second ruler of Egypt and the salvation of his entire family. (Genesis 37-46) (See my book *Faith Therapy* for a complete description and chart of the principles of protection from catastrophe.)

2. <u>We trust God for our security when we realize how powerless we are.</u> Sometimes I say that I pity very talented and favored people because they will not realize how powerless they really are until they have reached greater heights of success and have experienced greater failures. The Apostle Paul said in 2 Corinthians 12:10, "Therefore I take pleasure in infirmities, in reproaches, in necessities, in persecutions, in distresses for Christ's sake: for when I am weak, then am I strong." It is only when we realize how weak we really are that we truly rely on Christ and acquire true power. Recognizing our powerlessness is also the first step in Alcoholics Anonymous' 12-step program.

3. <u>Attempts to be in control of our lives lead to a greater loss of control.</u> People who attempt to feel secure through controlling others must be confronted with the fact that control never works in the long run and will result in the destruction of their relationships as well as frustration in life. The only things we can really control are our own actions, thoughts, attitudes and feelings. As soon as we try

to control others and take away their free will, they will rebel; and we will have to escalate control until it reaches a violent level and the relationship is destroyed. I sometimes use the examples of the Soviet Union and Iraq. In the Soviet Union, millions of people were killed in an attempt to control them and yet the system failed. In Iraq, Saddam Hussein even used torture to frighten his subjects into submission. He eventually was removed from power. If we try to control our circumstances, we will become very frustrated with life since "doing the impossible takes a little longer." In fact, we will put ourselves at the mercy of our circumstances and feel like we are on an emotional roller coaster. Attempting to control others and the circumstances around us is a clear sign of insecurity. The only true way to be in control is to turn all control of our lives over to the only One who is in absolute control—God.

The Principles of Love

Love is the ultimate level of Christian attainment and is the very essence of God Himself. Unfortunately, in our society, this concept has become so confused and perverted that many people have lost sight of its sacrificial quality and its importance in healthy relationships. God's type of love is best understood as "having another person's best interests in mind." Without this type of love, relationships will not last and marriages ultimately fail. Love is the opposite of selfishness because it gives and selfishness only takes. God even calls us to love our enemies unconditionally. (See my book *Faith Therapy* for a more in-depth discussion of this subject.) In the verses that follow, I will use the Weymouth New Testament (wey) in order to express these concepts more clearly. All other verses will continue to be from the Authorized Version of the King James Bible (av).

1. <u>Love, as a way of life, transcends everything else.</u>

    1 Co 12:31... And now I will point out to you a way of life which transcends all others. (wey)

2. <u>Whatever I do that is not motivated by true love counts for nothing.</u>

    1 Co 13:1 If I can speak with the tongues of men and of angels, but am destitute of Love, I have but become a loud-sounding trumpet or a clanging cymbal.

    2 If I possess the gift of prophecy and am versed in all mysteries and all knowledge, and have such absolute faith that I can remove mountains, but am destitute of Love, I am nothing.

    3 And if I distribute all my possessions to the poor, and give up my body to be burned, but am destitute of Love, it profits me nothing. (wey)

3. <u>All the other things that we think are important pass away and are imperfect.</u>

    1 Co 13:8 But if there are prophecies, they will be done away with; if there are languages, they will cease; if there is knowledge, it will be brought to an end.

    9 For our knowledge is imperfect, and so is our prophesying; (wey)

4. <u>The perfect state of the future is based on love.</u> Therefore, we should put away the childish ways of this world and focus on becoming a loving, mature Christian.

    1 Co 13:10 but when the perfect state of things is come, all that is imperfect will be brought to an end.

    11 When I was a child, I talked like a child, felt like a child, reasoned like a child: when I became a man, I put from me childish ways. (wey)

5. <u>Current things will be replaced by true intimacy with God and others.</u>

    1 Co 13:12 For the present we see things as if in a mirror, and are puzzled; but then we shall see them face to face. For the present the knowledge I gain is imperfect; but then I shall know fully, even as I am fully known. (WEY)

6. <u>Love is the most important of eternal things.</u>

    1 Co 13:13 And so there remain Faith, Hope, Love—these three; and of these the greatest is Love. (WEY)

7. <u>Agape or God's type of love is benevolence toward everyone.</u>

    1 Co 13:4 Love is patient and kind. Love knows neither envy nor jealousy. Love is not forward and self-assertive, nor boastful and conceited.

    5 She does not behave unbecomingly, nor seek to aggrandize herself, nor blaze out in passionate anger, nor brood over wrongs.

    6 She finds no pleasure in injustice done to others, but joyfully sides with the truth.

    7 She knows how to be silent. She is full of trust, full of hope, full of patient endurance.

    8 Love never fails. (WEY)

8. <u>Human love is based on someone else meeting our needs.</u> Most human relationships are based on conditional or selfish love. We love others because we believe they have our best interests in mind and will meet out needs. If we perceive that they are against us or that they are no longer useful to meet out needs, conflict arises and we usually break off the relationship.

    Lu 7:41 There was a certain creditor which had two debtors: the one owed five hundred pence, and the other fifty.

    42 And when they had nothing to pay, he frankly forgave them both. Tell me therefore, which of them will love him most?

    43 Simon answered and said, I suppose that [he], to whom he forgave most. And he said unto him, Thou hast rightly judged.

9. <u>Lust is not true love because it is only selfish.</u> Because it does not truly satisfy, it results in a continuing demand for more.

    2 Sa 13:4 And he said unto him, Why [art] thou, [being] the king's son, lean from day to day? wilt thou not tell me? And Amnon said unto him, I love Tamar, my brother Absalom's sister.

    15 Then Amnon hated her exceedingly; so that the hatred wherewith he hated her [was] greater than the love wherewith he had loved her. And Amnon said unto her, Arise, be gone.

10. <u>The very essence of God is love.</u>

    1 Jo 4:7 Beloved, let us love one another: for love is of God; and every one that loveth is born of God, and knoweth God.

    8 He that loveth not knoweth not God; for God is love.

11. <u>God's love is not based on the desirability or the performance of the object.</u>

    Ro 5:8 But God commendeth his love toward us, in that, while we were yet sinners, Christ died for us.

12. <u>Love leads to a desire to please and obey.</u> If we love someone, we want to please them and if we feel loved and believe that the other person has our best interests in mind, we will want to obey them.

    Jo 14:23 Jesus answered and said unto him, If a man love me, he will keep my words: and my Father will love him, and we will come unto him, and make our abode with him.

    24 He that loveth me not keepeth not my sayings: and the word which ye hear is not mine, but the Father's which sent me.

    1 Jo 2:5 But whoso keepeth his word, in him verily is the love of God perfected: hereby know we that we are in him.

13. <u>The measure of love is what we are willing to sacrifice for it.</u> The more we love, the more we want the very best for those we love. Our measure of love is determined by what we are willing to sacrifice for it. There is no greater expression of love than to sacrifice our very lives for someone else.

    Jo 3:16 For God so loved the world, that he gave his only begotten Son, that whosoever believeth in him should not perish, but have everlasting life.

    15:13 Greater love hath no man than this, that a man lay down his life for his friends.

14. <u>We, as Christians, are to be known for our love one for another.</u>

    Jo 13:34 A new commandment I give unto you, That ye love one another; as I have loved you, that ye also love one another.

    35 By this shall all [men] know that ye are my disciples, if ye have love one to another.

15. <u>We are to love everyone unconditionally just as God does.</u>

    Mt 5:44 But I say unto you, Love your enemies, bless them that curse you, do good to them that hate you, and pray for them which despitefully use you, and persecute you;

    46 For if ye love them which love you, what reward have ye? do not even the publicans the same?

    47 And if ye salute your brethren only, what do ye more [than others]? do not even the publicans so?

    48 Be ye therefore perfect, even as your Father which is in heaven is perfect.

16. <u>Love provides the motivation to work for God's kingdom.</u> Love is manifested in action.

    2 Co 5:14 For the love of Christ constraineth us; because we thus judge, that if one died for all, then were all dead:

    12:15 And I will very gladly spend and be spent for you; though the more abundantly I love you, the less I be loved.

    1 Jo 3:16 Hereby perceive we the love [of God], because he laid down his life for us: and we ought to lay down [our] lives for the brethren.

17 But whoso hath this world's good, and seeth his brother have need, and shutteth up his bowels [of compassion] from him, how dwelleth the love of God in him?

18 My little children, let us not love in word, neither in tongue; but in deed and in truth.

17. We shall never be separated from the love of God.

Ro 8:35 Who shall separate us from the love of Christ? [shall] tribulation, or distress, or persecution, or famine, or nakedness, or peril, or sword?

37 Nay, in all these things we are more than conquerors through him that loved us.

38 For I am persuaded, that neither death, nor life, nor angels, nor principalities, nor powers, nor things present, nor things to come,

39 Nor height, nor depth, nor any other creature, shall be able to separate us from the love of God, which is in Christ Jesus our Lord.

Counseling Methods and Techniques

1. Those who seek love do not find it, but those who give it freely, get it abundantly. Clients seeking to find the fulfillment of love in the world can be challenged with this "paradox of love." The paradox of love states that "those who directly seek or demand love never find it, but those who liberally give it away receive it in abundance." The point is that trying to meet the need for love by direct means fails. A large majority of clients that are struggling to be loved are desperately trying to obtain love and, therefore, cannot find it. What works is to seek God's kingdom, receive love from Him and give love to others without any strings attached. (Matthew 6:33)

2. The analogy of the emotional train helps us "get our love back." When clients understand that their emotions are the caboose of the train which follows their will, mind, and actions, it becomes clear that they can only control their emotions through deciding to love, changing their perceptions of the person or situation, and acting in a loving way. Eventually the caboose (their emotions) will follow the rest of the train.

4. Praying for our enemies can lead to loving them. This is because prayer is an action that has the other person's best interest in mind. It is actually acting in a loving way. Our loving action (praying) affects our thoughts. In order to act in this way, we must have already changed our will in relationship to them. Consequently, following the model of the emotional train mentioned above, if we decide to love, convince our mind, and act accordingly, eventually our emotions (the caboose) will follow.

5. Teach attachment theory. Attachment theory provides a new frame of reference for understanding personal conflict. Until people understand that each of us have different attachment styles and that these are at the core of how we relate to others, they tend to see everything as personal attacks or abandonment. This makes the other person an enemy and it is very difficult to reconcile enemies. Ongoing fighting or entrenched problems with love are many times "love fights" or attachment problems. Both persons desperately want to feel loved by the other one. By teaching attachment theory, identifying the attachment style of each, and re-interpreting their fighting as attempts to make the other person safe for them again, the entire picture can be transformed. (For a fuller explanation of attachment theory, see *Faith Therapy* or *Attachments* (2002) by Clinton and Sibcy.)

6. Help them use their faith in God to develop a secure attachment style in this life. Secure attachment styles only come through the experience of being secure in our attachments. Although it is possible to feel secure in this world, true security only comes from a trusting relationship with God, the ultimate attachment figure. Secure attachments increase our feelings of security and lead to feelings of being

loved. They also provide the basis from which we can love others unconditionally. (See the chart in my book *Faith Therapy* that outlines how secure attachment provides the basis for developing agape love.)

The Principles of Lust

Perhaps one of the areas of life most prone to difficulty in our society today is the struggle to overcome lust in our lives. Lust is a selfish, consuming, counterfeit for love. It has been reported that at a Promise Keepers meeting two-thirds of the men admitted to having periodic struggles with sexual lust. When this is added to the problems in our society over a quest for money, eating and buying things, the magnitude of this problem becomes readily apparent.

But what does this word lust mean? In the Greek three words can be translated lust. *Orexis* is translated lust in conjunction with homosexuality and means "a desire, longing, craving for, an eager desire, lust or appetite." *Pathos* can also be translated as inordinate affection or lust. It means "whatever befalls one, whether it be sad or joyous." It can also mean a passionate deed, either good or bad. *Epithumia* is translated as lust, concupiscence, desire, or to lust after. It means a "desire, a craving, a longing, a desire for what is forbidden, a lust, and it denotes a strong desire of any kind, both good and bad." It is many times preceded by a descriptive term indicating the type of desire.

1. <u>When our basic needs of the self for worth, significance, security, and acceptance are not fulfilled in life, this can lead to strong desires or lusts.</u> A desire becomes a lust when we attempt to meet it through the flesh. Since meeting our needs through the flesh can never fully satisfy us, we enter a never-ending cycle of wanting more and more.

   Ge 3:6 And when the woman saw that the tree [was] good for food (physical needs), and that it [was] pleasant to the eyes (wanting things that make us feel secure) , and a tree to be desired to make [one] wise (worth and significance) , she took of the fruit thereof, and did eat, and gave also unto her husband with her; and he did eat. (love or acceptance)

2. <u>Our basic lusts are for sensuous desires (love), things (that make us feel secure), and worth and significance.</u>

   1 Jo 2:15 Love not the world, neither the things that are in the world. If any man love the world, the love of the Father is not in him.

   16 For all that is in the world, the lust of the flesh, (sensuous desires) and the lust of the eyes, (desire for nice things) and the pride of life (striving for worth and significance), is not of the Father, but is of the world.

3. <u>Lust resides in the heart of a man who wants to run his own life and meet his own needs.</u>

   Ps 81:11 But my people would not hearken to my voice; and Israel would none of me.

   12 So I gave them up unto <u>their own hearts'</u> lust: and they walked in their own counsels.

   13 Oh that my people had hearkened unto me, and Israel had walked in my ways!

4. <u>Lust can bring terrible consequences.</u>

   Ro 1:27 And likewise also the men, leaving the natural use of the woman, burned in their lust one toward another; men with men working that which is unseemly, and receiving in themselves that recompence of their error which was meet.

5. <u>Lust becomes stronger when we are told not to do something.</u>

    Ro 7:7 What shall we say then? Is the law sin? God forbid. Nay, I had not known sin, but by the law: for I had not known lust, except the law had said, Thou shalt not covet.

    8 But sin, taking occasion by the commandment, wrought in me all manner of concupiscence. For without the law sin was dead.

6. <u>God commands us not to lust after evil things.</u>

    1 Co 10:6 Now these things were our examples, to the intent we should not lust after evil things, as they also lusted.

7. <u>Those who do not know God try to meet their needs through lust, which results in abuse and taking advantage of others.</u>

    1 Th 4:4 That every one of you should know how to possess his vessel in sanctification and honour;

    5 Not in the lust of concupiscence, even as the Gentiles which know not God:

    6 That no man go beyond and defraud his brother in any matter: because that the Lord is the avenger of all such, as we also have forewarned you and testified.

8. <u>Lusts dissipate our lives and make us unfruitful for God.</u>

    Mr 4:19 And the cares of this world, and the deceitfulness of riches, and the lusts of other things entering in, choke the word, and it becometh unfruitful.

9. <u>Lusts make us vulnerable to temptation and threatens to destroy the quality of this life and the life to come.</u>

    1 Ti 6:9 But they that will be rich fall into temptation and a snare, and into many foolish and hurtful lusts, which drown men in destruction and perdition.

    2 Ti 3:6 For of this sort are they which creep into houses, and lead captive silly women laden with sins, led away with divers lusts,

10. <u>Lust results in a loss of spiritual discernment.</u>

    2 Ti 4:3 For the time will come when they will not endure sound doctrine; but after their own lusts shall they heap to themselves teachers, having itching ears;

11. <u>The devil, who is filled with lust, can take advantage of our vulnerability to such an extent that it can even lead to lying and murder.</u>

    Jo 8:44 Ye are of your father the devil, and the lusts of your father ye will do. He was a murderer from the beginning, and abode not in the truth, because there is no truth in him. When he speaketh a lie, he speaketh of his own: for he is a liar, and the father of it.

    Tit 3:3 For we ourselves also were sometimes foolish, disobedient, deceived, serving divers lusts and pleasures, living in malice and envy, hateful, and hating one another.

12. <u>Lust wars against our very soul: mind, will, emotions and spirit.</u>

   1 Pe 2:11 Dearly beloved, I beseech you as strangers and pilgrims, abstain from fleshly lusts, which war against the soul;

13. <u>Those who continue in lust become increasingly corrupt as time passes.</u>

   2 Pe 2:10 But chiefly them that walk after the flesh in the lust of uncleanness, and despise government. Presumptuous are they, selfwilled, they are not afraid to speak evil of dignities.

   18 For when they speak great swelling words of vanity, they allure through the lusts of the flesh, through much wantonness, those that were clean escaped from them who live in error.

   Jude 1:16 These are murmurers, complainers, walking after their own lusts; and their mouth speaketh great swelling words, having men's persons in admiration because of advantage.

14. <u>Lust can result in God giving us up to our own uncleanness so that we will learn from our consequences.</u>

   Ro 1:24 Wherefore God also gave them up to uncleanness through the lusts of their own hearts, to dishonour their own bodies between themselves:

15. <u>Lust eventually leads to sin and death.</u>

   Jas 1:14 But every man is tempted, when he is drawn away of his own lust, and enticed.

   15 Then when lust hath conceived, it bringeth forth sin: and sin, when it is finished, bringeth forth death.

16. <u>Our vulnerability to lust is based on the ignorant belief that fulfilling our lust can really meet our needs.</u>

   1 Pe 1:14 As obedient children, not fashioning yourselves according to the former lusts in your ignorance:

17. <u>The antidote for lust is believing and acting on the promise of God that He will meet all our needs.</u> Since God's love and provision truly meets our needs, we are fully satisfied and are no longer motivated to seek to meet our needs through the flesh.

   2 Pe 1:4 Whereby are given unto us exceeding great and precious promises: that by these ye might be partakers of the divine nature, having escaped the corruption that is in the world through lust.

   Jas 4:2 Ye lust, and have not: ye kill, and desire to have, and cannot obtain: ye fight and war, yet ye have not, because ye ask not.

18. <u>We must put off all lust from our lives.</u>

   Eph 4:22 That ye put off concerning the former conversation the old man, which is corrupt according to the deceitful lusts;

   Col 3:5 Mortify therefore your members which are upon the earth; fornication, uncleanness, inordinate affection, evil concupiscence, and covetousness, which is idolatry:

Tit 2:12 Teaching us that, denying ungodliness and worldly lusts, we should live soberly, righteously, and godly, in this present world;

19. <u>In addition to putting off lust and any provision to fulfill our lust, we must seek God, purify our heart, and replace our lust with an intimate relationship with Jesus.</u>

    2 Ti 2:22 Flee also youthful lusts: but follow righteousness, faith, charity, peace, with them that call on the Lord out of a pure heart.

    Ro 13:14 But put ye on the Lord Jesus Christ, and make not provision for the flesh, to fulfil the lusts thereof.

20. <u>Either, we will live in lust or in the will of God; we cannot have both!</u>

    1 Pe 4:2 That he no longer should live the rest of his time in the flesh to the lusts of men, but to the will of God.

    3 For the time past of our life may suffice us to have wrought the will of the Gentiles, when we walked in lasciviousness, lusts, excess of wine, revellings, banquetings, and abominable idolatries:

21. <u>We are to do whatever it takes to eradicate lust from our lives.</u>

    Mt 5:28 But I say unto you, That whosoever looketh on a woman to lust after her hath committed adultery with her already in his heart.

    29 And if thy right eye offend thee, pluck it out, and cast it from thee: for it is profitable for thee that one of thy members should perish, and not that thy whole body should be cast into hell.

    30 And if thy right hand offend thee, cut it off, and cast it from thee: for it is profitable for thee that one of thy members should perish, and not that thy whole body should be cast into hell.

22. <u>The ultimate answer to overcoming lust is to walk according to the Spirit.</u>

    Ga 5:16 This I say then, Walk in the Spirit, and ye shall not fulfil the lust of the flesh.

Counseling Methods and Techniques

1. <u>We must view lust as poison.</u> The client will not usually be victorious over lust until he realizes that he must confront lust before it has taken hold in the mind, will, or emotions. Consequently, I suggest the analogy to clients that lust is poison. We cannot take even one drop of it or we will eventually die. Just as one drink leads to another, so one taste of lust brings us into a bondage that will destroy our spiritual discernment, our desire for God, and our motivation to accomplish His will in our lives. Lust really brings death to all that is good in life.

2. <u>Life has only two modes or experiences: freedom or bondage.</u> I explain to the client that he will either experience complete freedom or he will be in bondage. It is not true that he can have a small taste of lust and return immediately to a life of freedom from lust. Even one taste will so affect him that it will take a significant recovery effort to escape again from the bondage that he has brought upon himself. This is because lust affects our will and our desire to do what is right and undermines our ability to do it.

    Sometimes I use a skit our drama team performed at an outreach concert as an illustration. In the first scene, a man walked onto the stage with a small monkey on his shoulder. A second actor tried to warn him about "monkeys" but he liked this one and it could not hurt anything since it was so small. In the second scene, the monkey had grown significantly but the man explained that he had it completely under control and it did whatever he wanted it to do. Again, he was warned, but he refused to listen. Finally, in the third scene a huge ape lumbered onto the stage holding the man upside down by the ankles. He said, "Now I see what you were warning me about." Unfortunately, many of us will not listen until we experience the bondage that results from entertaining a little lust in our lives.

The Principles of Dying to the Self and the Flesh

Self-centeredness or selfishness is the underlying basis of the sin problem. The psychological needs of the self, which are a need to feel worthwhile, to be significant, to be secure, and to be loved and accepted, drive us to attempt to meet these needs through the flesh. In secular counseling, the goal is to help the client to better meet the needs of the self and to learn to meet these needs in a more socially acceptable way. Without faith, it is impossible to truly deal with the problem of the selfishness within. Through faith, God calls us to give up immediate gratification for the far greater rewards of the Kingdom of God. These principles of dying to the self-life lead us to learn to serve God and His interests as we, by faith, know that He will take care of our needs because He loves us. It is a life exchange of our natural life (psuche) for the life of God (Zoe). Jim Elliott, who was martyred as a missionary in South America, put it this way: "He is no fool who gives up what he cannot keep to have that which he cannot lose." (*Through Gates of Splendor*, Elisabeth Elliott, 1986)

1. <u>Man looks at his self or natural life as something to be nurtured and preserved.</u>

   Eph 5:29 For no man ever yet hated his own flesh; but nourisheth and cherisheth it…
   Php 2:21 For all seek their own, not the things which are Jesus Christ's.

2. <u>This striving to meet the needs of the self results in the evil symptoms of self-focus or selfishness. This focus is the basis of evil in the world.</u>

   2 Ti 3:2 For men shall be lovers of their own selves, covetous, boasters, proud, blasphemers, disobedient to parents, unthankful, unholy,

   3 Without natural affection, trucebreakers, false accusers, incontinent, fierce, despisers of those that are good,

   4 Traitors, heady, highminded, lovers of pleasures more than lovers of God;

3. <u>Trying to meet these needs through the flesh leads to a life dominated by the flesh with its accompanying consequences.</u>

   Ga 5:19 Now the works of the flesh are manifest, which are [these]; Adultery, fornication, uncleanness, lasciviousness,

   20 Idolatry, witchcraft, hatred, variance, emulations, wrath, strife, seditions, heresies,

   21 Envyings, murders, drunkenness, revellings, and such like: of the which I tell you before, as I have also told [you] in time past, that they which do such things shall not inherit the kingdom of God.

4. <u>Carnal Christians are Christians in which the pursuit of self and the flesh still predominate.</u>

   1 Co 3:3 For ye are yet carnal: for whereas [there is] among you envying, and strife, and divisions, are ye not carnal, and walk as men?

4 For while one saith, I am of Paul; and another, I [am] of Apollos; are ye not carnal?

5.   If Christ died for us, we should be willing to give up our self-life to live for Him.

2 Co 5:15 And [that] he died for all, that they which live should not henceforth live unto themselves, but unto him which died for them, and rose again.

6.   We must die to soulical affection.

Mt 10:37 He that loveth father or mother more than me is not worthy of me: and he that loveth son or daughter more than me is not worthy of me.

38 And he that taketh not his cross, and followeth after me, is not worthy of me.

39 He that findeth his life shall lose it: and he that loseth his life for my sake shall find it.

7.   We must die to self-will.

Mt 16:24 Then said Jesus unto his disciples, If any [man] will come after me, let him deny himself, and take up his cross, and follow me.

25 For whosoever will save his life shall lose it: and whosoever will lose his life for my sake shall find it.

26 For what is a man profited, if he shall gain the whole world, and lose his own soul? or what shall a man give in exchange for his soul?

8.   Dying to the self is our reasonable service and is necessary for fulfilling God's purpose in our lives.

Ro 12:1 I beseech you therefore, brethren, by the mercies of God, that ye present your bodies a living sacrifice, holy, acceptable unto God, [which is] your reasonable service.

2 And be not conformed to this world: but be ye transformed by the renewing of your mind, that ye may prove what [is] that good, and acceptable, and perfect, will of God.

9.   This dying to self must be done on a daily basis.

1 Co 15:31 I protest by your rejoicing which I have in Christ Jesus our Lord, I die daily.

10. We must learn to esteem riches and possessions lightly.

Mt 19:23 Then said Jesus unto his disciples, Verily I say unto you, That a rich man shall hardly enter into the kingdom of heaven.

24 And again I say unto you, It is easier for a camel to go through the eye of a needle, than for a rich man to enter into the kingdom of God.

11. We must die to our soul-life in order to produce the fruit of eternal life.

Jo 12:24 Verily, verily, I say unto you, Except a corn of wheat fall into the ground and die, it abideth alone: but if it die, it bringeth forth much fruit.

25 He that loveth his life shall lose it; and he that hateth his life in this world shall keep it unto life eternal.

12. <u>We must be more concerned about honoring God than caring what men think about us.</u>

    Mr 8:38 Whosoever therefore shall be ashamed of me and of my words in this adulterous and sinful generation; of him also shall the Son of man be ashamed, when he cometh in the glory of his Father with the holy angels.

13. <u>We must walk according to the Spirit in order not to fulfill the desires of the flesh.</u> Because the Spirit directly opposes the flesh, it is the most important factor in motivating and helping us to die to our soul-life and flesh.

    Ga 5:16 This I say then, Walk in the Spirit, and ye shall not fulfil the lust of the flesh.

Counseling Methods and Techniques

1. <u>We must give up worldly desires if we want God's abundant life.</u> It is an exchange process like emptying a glass of water, so it can be filled with air. If we are not willing to dump out the water of this life, we will never be filled with the Spirit of God. We only experience the abundant life of God to the degree we are willing to give up the desires of this life.

2. <u>If we will not crucify the flesh, we will receive its manifestations.</u> These manifestations of the flesh are listed in Galatians 5:19. These deeds are sin and they will eventually destroy the very life we are trying to preserve. Usually, this can be aptly demonstrated by examining the client's efforts in the flesh and the resulting consequences that have led the client to come to counseling in the first place. King Saul was removed as King because he refused to completely destroy the Amalekites which are a type of the flesh (1 Samuel 28:18). If we will not fully crucify the flesh in our lives, God may not be able to fully accomplish through us what He has called us to do in our lives.

3. <u>If we try to rely on both the flesh and the Spirit, we will eventually lose everything.</u> We must help the client understand that without the death of his flesh, he cannot produce the fruit of eternal life. We will either have one or the other. Those who try to ride the fence and have both, lose both.

4. <u>If we focus on the things of God, worldly things become less important.</u> What we spend our time on increases in value and in importance in our lives. The old chorus says it best: "Turn your eyes upon Jesus, look full in His wonderful face, and the things of earth will grow strangely dim in the light of His glory and grace." (Helen Lemmel, 1922)

5. <u>We are to seek servanthood instead of prominence.</u> Even large secular companies have reached the conclusion that they can increase production by taking the position that they are there to help the employee do his job better and to help him meet his needs. Servant leadership is dying to self. This is the position that God took in sending us His Son.

6. <u>We need to rely on God's power, not our own.</u> We should help the client to want to do things God's way, relying on God's strength and power; not his own. If the client tries to do what he wants, tries to do it in his own strength, or tries to do God's work His way, he will fail and feel overwhelmed with the demands of life. God says that His assignment is easy and if we do it His way, it will bring rest to our souls. (Matthew 11:30)

Chapter 9

The Principles of Motivation

The Principles of Motivation

When our perceived needs are not met, we are automatically motivated to act in a way to meet those needs. Emotions, such as fear or anger that are based on our perceptions of our circumstances, motivate us to action. The possibility of positive or negative consequences, which might result from our actions, may also influence us to act or refrain from those actions. An excessive desire or motivation for the wrong things in life or a lack of motivation to change what is wrong in our lives can become difficult obstacles in the counseling process. Sometimes a lack of motivation is a sign that the client is smoking marijuana, is having an affair in a troubled marriage, is depressed, is "burnt out," has lost his vision for his life, or has lost hope in the future. At other times, it simply indicates that the de-motivators outnumber the motivators. God has His own methods for providing motivation in our lives.

1. <u>When goals are thwarted for a significant period of time, we can lose heart.</u>

   Pr 13:12 Hope deferred maketh the heart sick: but when the desire cometh, it is a tree of life.

2. <u>The world has no real basis for hope in the future.</u> The people of the world are simply playing the lottery of life and can expect only a mixture of good and bad results. Without salvation, they cannot look forward to the blessings of heaven and, therefore, have no real hope.

   Eph 2:12 That at that time ye were without Christ, being aliens from the commonwealth of Israel, and strangers from the covenants of promise, having no hope, and without God in the world:

3. <u>Hope is faith in the future.</u>

   Ro 8:24 For we are saved by hope: but hope that is seen is not hope: for what a man seeth, why doth he yet hope for?
   4:18 Who against hope believed in hope, that he might become the father of many nations, according to that which was spoken, So shall thy seed be.

4. <u>One reason for a lack of motivation is that our faith is shaken and we no longer have hope in God.</u> Many of the Psalms beautifully illustrate this situation and our ability to lift ourselves above it by focusing our thoughts on God.

   Ps 42:5 Why art thou cast down, O my soul? and why art thou disquieted in me? hope thou in God: for I shall yet praise him for the help of his countenance.

78:7 That they might set their hope in God, and not forget the works of God, but keep his commandments:

5. <u>When hope in God is lost, we tend to turn to the evil imaginations of the flesh.</u>

    Jer 18:12 And they said, There is no hope: but we will walk after our own devices, and we will every one do the imagination of his evil heart.

6. <u>Our promised hope of salvation comes through the grace or the unmerited favor of God, which never fails.</u> Therefore, because it does not depend on our performance or even our morals, we can always be assured that God will provide for us, no matter what happens.

    2 Th 2:16 Now our Lord Jesus Christ himself, and God, even our Father, which hath loved us, and hath given us everlasting consolation and good hope through grace,

    Tit 1:2 In hope of eternal life, which God, that cannot lie, promised before the world began;

7. <u>God's first method of motivation is to send us His Word and reward those who follow it with a prosperous life.</u>

    Jos 1:8 This book of the law shall not depart out of thy mouth; but thou shalt meditate therein day and night, that thou mayest observe to do according to all that is written therein: for then thou shalt make thy way prosperous, and then thou shalt have good success.

    De 10:13 To keep the commandments of the LORD, and his statutes, which I command thee this day for thy good?

8. <u>God's second method is to turn those who refuse to know and follow His Word over to their own devices to learn from their own consequences.</u>

    Jer 18:12 And they said, There is no hope: but we will walk after our own devices, and we will every one do the imagination of his evil heart.

    Ps 81:12 So I gave them up unto their own hearts' lust: and they walked in their own counsels.

9. <u>God's third method is to eventually bring judgment, or heavy consequences, on those who ignore God's Word and His correction.</u>

    Ro 2:5 But after thy hardness and impenitent heart treasurest up unto thyself wrath against the day of wrath and revelation of the righteous judgment of God;

    Pr 29:1 He, that being often reproved hardeneth his neck, shall suddenly be destroyed, and that without remedy.

Counseling Methods and Techniques

1. <u>God's three methods of motivation help a client to change.</u> We should make it clear to clients that learning, understanding, and obeying the Word of God provides a shelter from consequences and judgment. If we continue doing the same thing and do not learn from our consequences, eventually we will receive even larger consequences or judgment. God knows everything that we do and will do whatever is needed to help us repent, turn from sin and become whole.

2. <u>A parachute analogy demonstrates the truth that most of us really trust God only when everything else fails.</u> I use this illustration to help the client understand that he will probably try, in his own efforts, to make life work for him until everything he tries to do fails. Only then will he fully and completely put his trust in God. I ask my clients if they actually believe that parachutes work? Most people believe that they do. I then ask them if they were standing on the top of a very high cliff if they would jump off and try the parachute. Most people say they would not. That is how we are as people. We would rather rely on something we think we can really trust—ourselves and solid ground—than to take a chance on someone or something else; even God. I then ask what they would do if the ledge they are standing on suddenly collapsed and they began to fall. If they are truly honest, they would probably try to jump for the solid ground or grab onto anything they could including rocks or trees. They would use the parachute only after they had tried everything they could do to save themselves and all other hope vanished. Until we realize that, without God, there is no hope of a full and abundant life, most of us will not fully rely on God. I many times suggest that the fact that they are currently in such a desperate situation can be a blessing if they will use it to give up their own efforts and try the parachute (God).

3. <u>We can overcome inaction by evaluating motivators and de-motivators.</u> When clients will not act, although they say they are convinced that they should act, it is a sign that they are perceiving that the de-motivators exceed the motivators in this situation. We can help the client analyze what is causing the resistance by listing what he sees as the motivation to act and the motivation not to act. Reducing the de-motivators and increasing the motivators through reframing the situation can usually remove the impasse.

4. <u>Failure to do homework results in doing it in the counseling session.</u> If a client consistently fails to do homework assignments, the counselor can make it clear that assignments that are incomplete will be finished in the next counseling session. I explain that it is their choice whether to do assignments at home at no charge, or to pay me to help them complete them in the next session. Doing homework in session will increase the number of sessions required, slow their progress in treatment, and increase the cost of their counseling. By doing so, I demonstrate a clear example of boundaries and natural consequences.

The Principles of Consequences

As we have seen, God uses consequences as motivation. Another name for the principles of consequences might be the principle of sowing and reaping. The choices we make in life will inevitably result in consequences now and many times later in our lives. It is by these consequences that we learn to repeat those things that brought us desired results, and we learn not to do those things that produce negative results. In psychology, this is called behavior modification. In a way, God uses behavior modification to motivate us to do what is right and to obey Him. These principles have been preached primarily in the church as they apply to giving and receiving of tithes and offerings, but they actually apply to all aspects of our lives.

Throughout the entire Bible, it is clear that what we do determines, in the long run, what we get back; and this determines how our lives ultimately turn out. These basic principles apply to everyone without exception. These methods are called operant conditioning in secular psychology and have even been used successfully in mental institutions as token economies. However, for the Christian, we have promises and blessings that even exceed this natural law of sowing and reaping.

1. <u>The law of sowing and reaping will never end as long as the world stands.</u>

   Ge 8:22 While the earth remaineth, seedtime and harvest, and cold and heat, and summer and winter, and day and night shall not cease.

2. <u>We choose our consequences by what we do.</u> In addition to the verses below, when the children of Israel entered the promised land, God directed them to declare from Mount Gerizim, all of His blessings for those who keep His covenant and from Mount Ebal, all the curses for those who do not keep it. (Deuteronomy 27:12-28:68)

   De 30:19 I call heaven and earth to record this day against you, [that] I have set before you life and death, blessing and cursing: therefore choose life, that both thou and thy seed may live:

   11:27 A blessing, if ye obey the commandments of the LORD your God, which I command you this day:

   28 And a curse, if ye will not obey the commandments of the LORD your God, but turn aside out of the way which I command you this day, to go after other gods, which ye have not known.

3. <u>These blessings and cursings extend to future generations.</u>

   Ex 34:7 Keeping mercy for thousands, forgiving iniquity and transgression and sin, and that will by no means clear [the guilty]; visiting the iniquity of the fathers upon the children, and upon the children's children, unto the third and to the fourth [generation].

4. <u>They apply to the salvation of souls.</u>

   Jo 4:36 And he that reapeth receiveth wages, and gathereth fruit unto life eternal: that both he that soweth and he that reapeth may rejoice together.

   37 And herein is that saying true, One soweth, and another reapeth.

5. <u>These principles apply to the struggle between the flesh and Spirit.</u>

   Ga 6:7 Be not deceived; God is not mocked: for whatsoever a man soweth, that shall he also reap.

   8 For he that soweth to his flesh shall of the flesh reap corruption; but he that soweth to the Spirit shall of the Spirit reap life everlasting.

6. <u>They apply to our finances and giving.</u>

   2 Co 9:6 But this [I say], He which soweth sparingly shall reap also sparingly; and he which soweth bountifully shall reap also bountifully.

   8 And God is able to make all grace abound toward you; that ye, always having all sufficiency in all things, may abound to every good work:

7. <u>Even if we have sown evil and deserve to reap judgment, we can repent and obtain mercy from the Lord.</u>

   Isa 55:7 Let the wicked forsake his way, and the unrighteous man his thoughts: and let him return unto the LORD, and he will have mercy upon him; and to our God, for he will abundantly pardon.

8. <u>God gives much more back than we give to Him.</u>

Mal 3:10 Bring ye all the tithes into the storehouse, that there may be meat in mine house, and prove me now herewith, saith the LORD of hosts, if I will not open you the windows of heaven, and pour you out a blessing, that [there shall] not [be room] enough [to receive it].

11 And I will rebuke the devourer for your sakes, and he shall not destroy the fruits of your ground; neither shall your vine cast her fruit before the time in the field, saith the LORD of hosts.

9. We can claim the promise of a hundredfold blessing.

    Mr 10:30 But he shall receive an hundredfold now in this time, houses, and brethren, and sisters, and mothers, and children, and lands, with persecutions; and in the world to come eternal life.

10. Our future in Him is wonderful and glorious. We, as Christians, are not limited to the law of sowing and reaping. Through the Spirit, anything is possible.

    Am 9:13 Behold, the days come, saith the LORD, that the plowman shall overtake the reaper, and the treader of grapes him that soweth seed; and the mountains shall drop sweet wine, and all the hills shall melt.

Counseling Methods and Techniques

1. The client will eventually learn from his mistakes. Even mentally ill clients can learn from their consequences. It is not our job, as counselors, to "make our clients change," but God's method of sowing and reaping consequences will eventually lead them to want change no matter how determined they are to resist it. Many times, I will help them to understand where their actions are leading them and ask if that is where they really want to go? As an example, if they are sowing selfish love they should not be surprised if that is what they are receiving back from others. If they want unconditional love, that is what they will have to sow.

2. Sowing and reaping can change our actions. Each of us, after we are saved, has an ongoing conflict between the flesh and the Spirit in our minds for the control of our will. The answer to victory is simple: sow to the Spirit and you will reap life everlasting. (Galatians 6:8) I remember one woman who read the Bible for three days straight to win the battle over her will. If we sow to the Spirit, we will eventually act according to the Spirit.

3. God's promises motivate us to do His will. All the covenants and promises of God can provide motivation for us to act according to His will. The more we realize He loves us (and has our best interests in mind) and the more we experience His blessings, the more we will want to do His will. Finally, our growing faith in God and the resulting blessings may eventually motivate us to have the faith to believe for a hundredfold return.

4. We can pray for a crop failure. If we believe in the principles of sowing and reaping, and we realize we have planted bad seed in our lives, we can repent and ask the Lord for mercy. God promises Christians much more than we should expect according to the law of sowing and reaping, and He is also willing to grant us a crop failure if we repent and ask Him for it.

The Principles of Fear

Fear is motivation to flee from danger. Ignoring this gift can lead to disaster. Unfortunately, many times this gift, which was given to us for our good, can overwhelm us and bring negative consequences. The New Testament Greek word *Phobeo* makes this clear since its primary meaning is "to put to flight by terrifying." When used as "the fear of God" it can also mean, "to reverence, venerate, to treat with deference or reverential obedience." Fearing or trusting God drives worldly fear from our lives. Praising God in all of our circumstances, as an expression of our faith that He will turn everything for our good (Romans 8:28), can help us overcome our fears.

1. <u>Worldly fear opposes faith and is the result of not fully trusting God.</u>

   Mt 8:26 And he saith unto them, Why are ye fearful, O ye of little faith? Then he arose, and rebuked the winds and the sea; and there was a great calm.

   Mr 4:40 And he said unto them, Why are ye so fearful? how is it that ye have no faith?

2. <u>We should not be fearful of worldly things because we know and believe that God has our best interests in mind and that He will always meet all our needs.</u>

   Lu 12:32 Fear not, little flock; for it is your Father's good pleasure to give you the kingdom.

3. <u>God has not sent us a spirit of bondage to fear, but a spirit of childlike trust.</u> Bondage is the result of trusting ourselves instead of God. We should not rely on psychological defenses because although they keep others out, they many times prevent us from receiving the blessing that God has for us. Trusting God sets us free from fear without the use of psychological defense mechanisms.

   Ro 8:15 For ye have not received the spirit of bondage again to fear; but ye have received the Spirit of adoption, whereby we cry, Abba, Father.

   Heb 13:6 So that we may boldly say, The Lord is my helper, and I will not fear what man shall do unto me.

4. <u>We should confront fear with the power of God, the love He has for us, and correct biblical thinking.</u> How we perceive a situation in our minds determines the emotions that we will experience. Emotions, including fear, are just "thermometers" of our perceptions about a specific situation. If we are afraid, it means we do not truly possess and trust God's perfect love and concern for us. If we concentrate on God, we will perceive Him as more powerful and our fears will have to retreat.

   2 Ti 1:7 For God hath not given us the spirit of fear; but of power, and of love, and of a sound mind.

   1 Jo 4:18 There is no fear in love; but perfect love casteth out fear: because fear hath torment. He that feareth is not made perfect in love.

5. <u>Sometimes fear must be overcome step-by-step.</u> An example of this strategy was used to conquer Jericho, the city of fear. This method has been called systematic desensitization.

   Jos 6:3 And ye shall compass the city, all ye men of war, and go round about the city once. Thus shalt thou do six days.

   4 And seven priests shall bear before the ark seven trumpets of rams' horns: and the seventh day ye shall compass the city seven times, and the priests shall blow with the trumpets.

6. <u>We get the victory over fear by declaring our faith that our God can be trusted and is greater than our circumstances.</u>

Jos 6:5 And it shall come to pass, that when they make a long blast with the ram's horn, and when ye hear the sound of the trumpet, all the people shall shout with a great shout; and the wall of the city shall fall down flat, and the people shall ascend up every man straight before him.

7. <u>As we trust God, prayer and thanksgiving provide freedom from anxiety.</u> Praising and worshiping God for His power helps us build our confidence in God and can help us overcome our fear in the day of trouble. We must believe that, even in these circumstances, God will work everything for our good.

   Php 4:6 Be careful for nothing; but in every thing by prayer and supplication with thanksgiving let your requests be made known unto God.

   7 And the peace of God, which passeth all understanding, shall keep your hearts and minds through Christ Jesus.

   Ps 59:16 But I will sing of thy power; yea, I will sing aloud of thy mercy in the morning: for thou hast been my defence and refuge in the day of my trouble.

Counseling Methods and Techniques

1. <u>Confronting fear is always the best policy.</u> When we run from our fears, they seem to get stronger. This is because we have just added the agreement of our will and actions to the thoughts that created the emotions of fear. If instead, we confront our fears, we take a stand in our will, mind and actions that we will not allow them to rule over us.

2. <u>We can overcome difficult fears one step at a time.</u> In secular counseling, this process is called systematic desensitization. In the Bible, we are taught this method in the conquering of the city of Jericho. (Joshua 6) The children of Israel silently marched around the city of Jericho for six days in order to strengthen their faith that they could conquer the city. They then declared their faith with a victory shout, and the walls of fear came tumbling down. This method suggests slowly confronting our fears one step at a time as we grow in confidence that the next step can be overcome. As we progress step-by-step, we can eventually face our greatest fear. Sometimes, this is done as a mental process before it is acted out in the physical world. A common example of this method in most of our lives was learning to dive off the high diving board. First, we overcome our fear of water by learning to swim. Then we learned to jump off the side of the pool. Later, we dove off a low diving board until we had enough confidence to jump off the high board.

3. <u>Fear can be overcome by focusing on God instead of our problems.</u> This method is taught in the story of the exodus from Egypt, when God instructed Moses to make a bronze snake on a pole. If an Israelite, who had been bitten by a deadly snake, looked at the snake on the pole; they were healed. (Numbers 21:8) The snake on the pole represented Jesus taking our sin upon Himself. When we focus on God, our problems seem to get smaller. When we focus on our problems, they and our fears increase.

4. <u>Experiencing the love of God casts out all fear.</u> One answer for dealing with fear is to develop a close personal relationship with God. When, in our intimate relationship with God, we realize that He really loves and cares for us and that He will protect us, we are not so afraid of what will happen to us.

5. <u>We can overcome anxiety by praising God in all situations.</u> When we do this, we are acting on our faith that even in the current negative circumstances, God will work everything for our good. (Romans 8:28) Our praise is an outward expression of our faith, and it helps us focus on the greatness of God. Praising God, as an expression of faith, breaks the power of fear and anxiety and will help us face our circumstances positively. It is declaring the truth of Romans 8:18, "For I reckon that the

sufferings of this present time are not worthy to be compared with the glory which shall be revealed in us."

6. <u>Anxiety disorders are generalized fears.</u> The source of these fears must be discovered in order to deal with them effectively. The core issue is a perception that life is threatening in some aspect. If a person has been anxious all of his life, the precipitating problem may come from childhood experiences or learned perceptions about life. If the anxiety began at a particular point in the client's life, a particular event can usually be identified that significantly influenced how the client now views his life. In order to alleviate the anxiety, the way the client views his situation must be changed from fear to faith in God to protect him. The client must trust God in order to face his fear. (See the plan for overcoming an anxiety disorder later in this book.)

7. <u>Panic attacks result from a cycle of fear.</u> Panic attacks are short-lived periods of panic where the client feels he is having a heart attack or some other medical problem, which could result in death. Because the client focuses on his bodily responses, he becomes increasingly fearful and actually precipitates the panic. As an example, some incident from the past or present triggers a fearful response in the client. He notices that his heart is pounding more rapidly than usual (a physical response to fear). Because he is afraid that something must be wrong, he becomes more fearful so his heart pounds even more rapidly. This makes him even more afraid, so he starts hyperventilating. This makes him dizzy and he fears he may pass out. This confirms to him that something is very seriously wrong; and, maybe, he will die. This cycle continues until the client is certain that he is dying. At this point, an ambulance is usually called. However, in most cases the panic subsides in about ten minutes. Unfortunately, many times this experience is so traumatic that the client now fears having another attack and may begin avoiding driving or going out in public. If the client does not face his fear, it can lead to agoraphobia. Treatment includes educating the client about panic attacks, using relaxation and controlled breathing to alleviate the symptoms, developing plans to minimize the impact on the client's life, and identifying and dealing with the underlying fear issue. From a faith standpoint, the client must trust that God will protect him in all circumstances, work everything for his good, and that even death itself is not a serious enough event to justify out-of-control panic. Faith that everything is in God's hands can help to calm the client in any circumstance.

8. <u>Phobias are excessive irrational fears.</u> Phobias are irrational fears that make a person extremely afraid of certain objects or situations. Over one hundred different phobias have been identified. Systematic desensitization has been shown to be about ninety percent effective in overcoming all phobias. It is simply a behavior modification plan for facing the fear a little at a time. One cannot be relaxed and afraid at the same time. Using a hierarchy ranked from events that would make the client mildly fearful to the most fearful event imaginable, the client attempts to stay relaxed as he faces one fear after another. When he is able to remain relaxed when facing one fearful event, he moves on to face a more threatening event, first in his mind and later in real life. Eventually, he will be able to face the most fearful stimulus. Adding faith in God and possibly even picturing Jesus walking with the client through the situation can be an effective addition to this method. The Bible states that we are to cast all of our cares upon God. (1 Peter 5:7)

9. <u>A series of fearful reactions caused by past experiences of extreme trauma is called Post Traumatic Stress Disorder.</u> The person may have flash backs, fearful reactions, and continue to be traumatized by the events even years after they have occurred. The experience dramatically affects how the person thinks and feels about life. Faith must be applied to these past experiences so that they may be healed and so that they will no longer affect the current life of the client. Theophostic Ministry (Smith, 1996) is usually the most effective intervention because the emotions that accompany the experiences themselves must be modified.

10. <u>Obsessions are an attempt to feel in control.</u> A milder form of obsession is worry. These are an attempt to feel in control of a situation by focusing our thoughts on the situation. Unfortunately,

when we think about our problems they usually become more significant in our minds. When we perceive them as larger, we have even more to worry or obsess about. Consequently, our problems grow. The answer is to focus more on the solution to our problems and on our faith in God.

11. <u>Compulsions are an attempt to compensate for obsessions that feel out of control.</u> Compulsions are an attempt to make ourselves feel that we are in control when we are actually feeling out of control and insecure, by trying to over-control some other aspect of our lives. As an example, we might feel compelled to check that the front door is locked numerous times before we can feel secure in the house. In this case, we may be trying to compensate for an obsessive fear that we might be fired at work. Howard Hughes attempted to compensate for fears of failure by washing his hands and trying to protect himself from germs. (Barlett and Steele, 1997) Identifying and developing faith for our true fears and insecurity can greatly help us to overcome these types of compulsions.

The Principles of Anger

Anger is similar to fear in its effect on our body. It is energy to resolve problems or injustices. It has been given as a gift to us so that we will have the motivation and energy to overcome our problems. Unfortunately, it too can be used incorrectly with major consequences. When we bury it, anger can lead to bitterness and sickness. There are a number of Greek words for anger and wrath so it is necessary to carefully interpret verses on this subject. *Orge* means "a strong controlled passion or impulse." *Thumos* is usually translated wrath and means "an agitated condition or outburst which quickly blazes and subsides." *Paraorgismos* is stronger but more short lived than *Orge*. *Cholao* means "to be enraged."

1. <u>Anger is energy to resolve problems and to bring justice.</u> We need anger in order to resolve our problems. Since we are made in the image of God,we need to learn to use anger correctly as God does.

   Nah 1:3 The LORD is slow to anger, and great in power, and will not at all acquit the wicked: the LORD hath his way in the whirlwind and in the storm, and the clouds are the dust of his feet.

   Ps 30:5 For his anger endureth but a moment; in his favour is life: weeping may endure for a night, but joy cometh in the morning.

2. <u>The wrong use of anger can be a destructive curse to us.</u>

   Ge 49:7 Cursed be their anger, for it was fierce; and their wrath, for it was cruel: I will divide them in Jacob, and scatter them in Israel.

3. <u>We can control the amount of anger that we have by how we perceive our problems and by what we say.</u> If we take things personally or perceive that the other person did things intentionally, we will be angrier. If we tell ourselves that they have a problem and that what they have done says nothing about us, we will be less agitated. We can actually talk to ourselves in such a way that our anger level decreases.

   Pr 15:1 A soft answer turneth away wrath: but grievous words stir up anger.

4. <u>We must not react to a situation, but take time to think it through and respond to it.</u> Sometimes this requires taking an anger break to calm ourselves down. Taking time to evaluate the situation instead of reacting to it is called being slow to anger.

   Pr 16:32 He that is slow to anger is better than the mighty; and he that ruleth his spirit than he that taketh a city.

Jas 1:19 Wherefore, my beloved brethren, let every man be swift to hear, slow to speak, slow to wrath:

5. <u>We are to use our anger to resolve our problems and to bring justice speedily.</u> Sometimes taking dramatic action is the only option when we have done everything else that can be done. Jesus cleared the moneychangers from the temple Himself when he realized that the Pharisees and leaders themselves were involved in the corruption.

Jo 2:13 And the Jews' passover was at hand, and Jesus went up to Jerusalem,

14 And found in the temple those that sold oxen and sheep and doves, and the changers of money sitting:

15 And when he had made a scourge of small cords, he drove them all out of the temple, and the sheep, and the oxen; and poured out the changers' money, and overthrew the tables;

6. <u>If we cannot resolve the problem, we are to give it and our anger to God.</u>

Ro 12:19 Dearly beloved, avenge not yourselves, but rather give place unto wrath: for it is written, Vengeance is mine; I will repay, saith the Lord.

7. <u>Sometimes the best thing to do is just drop our anger.</u> However, if we do this we must be sure we are not stuffing it. If we stuff it, it will erupt at a different and inappropriate time and place.

Pr 19:11 The discretion of a man deferreth his anger; and it is his glory to pass over a transgression.

8. <u>We are to resolve our anger issues before we go to bed.</u> This is critical because we will start the next day with whatever anger remains from the previous day. Since we have only one anger level, if we are still very angry from events from the previous day, we will only have a small margin of anger control remaining until we blow up on the following day.

Eph 4:26 Be ye angry, and sin not: let not the sun go down upon your wrath:

9. <u>We are not to provoke others to anger.</u> If we do, we may only be increasing contention and strife. We will usually receive the unpleasant consequences of that anger!

Pr 20:2 The fear of a king is as the roaring of a lion: whoso provoketh him to anger sinneth against his own soul.

Eph 6:4 And, ye fathers, provoke not your children to wrath: but bring them up in the nurture and admonition of the Lord.

10. <u>Problems with anger and wrath in our lives can become a stronghold.</u> The adrenaline that accompanies anger can become an addictive agent.

Pr 19:19 A man of great wrath shall suffer punishment: for if thou deliver him, yet thou must do it again.

Counseling Methods and Techniques

1. <u>We can control the amount of anger by how we perceive the situation.</u> Anger is energy to resolve a problem. It is also a secondary emotion. Since anger is an emotion, it is controlled by how we choose to look at a situation. The amount of anger we create is significantly different when we look at a circumstance or problem as unintentional or an accident, or when we believe it was intentionally done. We can either say "they have a problem and I will pray for them," or we can blame ourselves. We can either perceive it as a small problem or a catastrophe.

2. <u>The first step in anger management is to realize that we are angry.</u> We need to identify feelings, physical symptoms, self-talk, and actions that signal that we are angry. It is impossible to deal with something we do not realize is happening. Since anger is a secondary emotion, it is created only when we are also experiencing more primary emotions like hurt, betrayal, powerlessness, or worthlessness. Numerous physical signs like increased heartbeat, tension, sweating, flushed face, and agitation are clear signs of anger (and sometimes fear). We tend to talk faster, pace and obsess in our minds when we are afraid or angry. In any case, the counselor may need to assist the client to learn how he can most effectively identify his anger as soon as possible.

3. <u>We need to take an "anger break" in order to have time to control our anger.</u> Unless we do, we will probably react negatively instead of respond in a correct, reasonable way. I tend to avoid the term "time out" because it can be interpreted as punishment for a child. However, I suggest a specific plan for use by my clients. It has three steps.

   a. <u>When clients feel that they or anyone else is becoming angry, they are to state that they need to take an "anger break."</u> They and any other persons involved are to suspend the discussion for thirty minutes so that all involved have time to de-anger, think about the problem, and let the tension between them subside. If they are at home, they should go to separate rooms and return after the break. It is important to specify the amount of time and return to resolve the problem so that the other person does not perceive the break as abandonment.

   b. <u>If the other person refuses to take the break, the person calling for the strife break has the right to retire to the nearest bathroom and lock the door so that he or she can take the required break.</u> The thirty minutes does not start until the pursuing person quits talking. I even suggest, if necessary, that they stash earplugs and a good magazine in the bathroom for such occasions. A variant of this anger or strife break, suggested by an associate pastor I know, is to spend the time praying for the other person.

   c. <u>In extreme cases, if the other person refuses to take the break and might be so violent as to try to break through the bathroom door, that person has the right to leave the home and go to a public place from which they can call after the thirty minutes.</u> If an anger problem still exists, they can hang up and continue to call back at thirty-minute intervals until they are able to resolve the problem and return home. If not, the problem should be taken to counseling.

4. <u>We need to de-anger or talk ourselves down from high levels of anger.</u> We need the appropriate level of anger for effectively solving the problem. In our domestic violence therapy group, I give the illustration of a greased playground slide with ten steps. Each step relates to an increasing level of anger. After climbing the tenth step and getting on the greased slide, there is little chance of stopping a rapid descent and an angry crash. The steps for anger management include: 1. Identify the fact that you are angry. 2. Take a "time out" or "anger break" so that you have time to respond instead of react. 3. During the break, de-anger or talk yourself down to a reasonable level by rationally evaluating the situation and deciding what will be the most effective action to bring the desired result. Then everyone involved should pray about the planned solution and other individuals involved in the situation. For Christians who have the baptism of the Holy Spirit this is an excellent time to pray in the Spirit. This method of anger management is extremely effective in most situations.

5. <u>We need to use our anger to resolve the situation, give it to God or drop it.</u> These are the three acceptable uses of anger. Since anger is energy to resolve problems or injustices, we should use it first for its primary purpose—to resolve the problem. In cases where we have done everything we can do, but are unable to resolve the problem, we should give our anger to God. In cases where the problem is insignificant and not worth the effort, we should drop it.

6. <u>We should avoid the wrong uses of anger.</u> In counseling, I use the illustration that anger is like a stick of dynamite. The size of the stick depends on how large we perceive the problem. Aggression is using our anger to attack or violate another's rights, because they have violated ours. This is like having someone hand us a stick of lit dynamite and throwing it back at them. Displacement is when we take out our anger on someone who is not involved in the problem. This is like having someone hand us a lit stick of dynamite and throwing it at somebody else. Depression is caused by turning anger inward. This is like someone handing us a lit stick of dynamite, and we stick it in our mouth and wait for it to explode. Passive-aggression is when we covertly get back at someone. It is like sneaking the lit stick of dynamite into the back pocket of the person who gave it to you. Finally, stuffing anger is internalizing it and not using it to resolve the problem for which it was intended. This is like thinking that we are putting out the fuse and sticking it into our pocket. In actuality, it is apt to go off at any time. If it does not, soon we will have our pockets full of dynamite and when someone comes by with a match, we will experience a tremendous explosion.

7. <u>We should not take offenses personally.</u> We need to resolve the problem, not the person. Unfortunately, many times we can get confused between what is the real problem to be resolved and the personal issues involved in the problem. A classic example is given in the movie "Godfather I." In this film, the gangs of Chicago have a disagreement concerning whether they should be involved in selling illegal drugs. Instead of using their energy to resolve the problem and reach some agreement, they start shooting members of the other gangs. At a meeting after the other gang had shot the Godfather's dad seven times, a member of the other gang states, "But don't take it personally." The Godfather responds by killing two of the other gang members. By the end of the movie, almost all of the gang leaders had been murdered yet they were no closer to resolving the question than before. They did not use their anger to resolve the problem, but personalized it, and ended up destroying each other. (The Godfather, directed by Francio Coppla, 1972) Unfortunately, many times we do the same. The Bible is clear in its condemnation of such a use of anger. We are not to compare ourselves with others, blame others, judge others, envy others, compete with others or expect them to be the primary source to meet our needs. We are to love our enemies, pray for them and do good to them as we trust God to vindicate us and provide for all our needs. Jesus even forgave the Roman soldiers who taunted Him, whipped Him, mocked Him, and crucified Him. The problem was not the Roman soldiers; it was sin in the Roman soldiers.

8. <u>We can use an anger diagram to teach anger management.</u> I use the chart on the following page. It summarizes all the steps that we have just discussed.

Anger Management

Event

↓

Perception of the event determines the
amount of anger

↓

Identify that you are angry

↓

Time out, anger, or strife break

↓

De-anger or talking yourself down
Avoid the greased slide

↓

Choice of how to use anger

Wrong uses   Right uses

Aggression   Fix the problem
Displacement   Give it to God
Depression   Drop it
Passive-aggression
Stuffing it   Solve problem by sundown
Personalizing it

Start the new day without built-up anger

Chapter 10

The Principles of Action

Principles of Action

Our actions are the result of what we think, perceive, believe, focus on, feel and decide to do. They say more than words can say about who we are. They are the sum of what our heart has decided to do. If we do not act in a certain way, it is because at least some part of our heart is not in agreement. Our actions in turn determine what we experience, think and feel, and affect what we will do the next time. Consequently, it is clear that actions are a potentially significant agent for change in our lives.

1. <u>We are to do everything with thanksgiving in God's name as if we were working directly for Him.</u> This helps us do our very best even for incompetent bosses or in bad circumstances. Otherwise, our minds can be overwhelmed by the responsibilities and conflicts of life.

   Col 3:17 And whatsoever ye do in word or deed, do all in the name of the Lord Jesus, giving thanks to God and the Father by him.

2. <u>We should realize that God will reward us according to what we do.</u> He knows our every thought and motivation, therefore, we cannot fool Him.

   Pr 24:12 If thou sayest, Behold, we knew it not; doth not he that pondereth the heart consider it? and he that keepeth thy soul, doth not he know it? and shall not he render to every man according to his works?

   Ec 12:14 For God shall bring every work into judgment, with every secret thing, whether it be good, or whether it be evil.

3. <u>What we try to accomplish in our own strength ends in frustration and in the long run counts for nothing.</u>

   Ec 1:14 I have seen all the works that are done under the sun; and, behold, all is vanity and vexation of spirit.

   2:11 Then I looked on all the works that my hands had wrought, and on the labour that I had laboured to do: and, behold, all was vanity and vexation of spirit, and there was no profit under the sun.

4. <u>We should do our best in everything we do, since we have only a short time on earth and a limited number of things we can accomplish.</u>

Ec 9:10 Whatsoever thy hand findeth to do, do it with thy might; for there is no work, nor device, nor knowledge, nor wisdom, in the grave, whither thou goest.

5. <u>We should live a life of good works so that God gets the credit for what we do.</u> He will reward us for what we have done for Him. Of course, we should be motivated by love and not primarily for the reward we will receive.

    Mt 5:16 Let your light so shine before men, that they may see your good works, and glorify your Father which is in heaven.

    16:27 For the Son of man shall come in the glory of his Father with his angels; and then he shall reward every man according to his works.

6. <u>Because God does not immediately judge every work, some people think they are getting away with evil and continue to do evil things.</u>

    Ec 8:11 Because sentence against an evil work is not executed speedily, therefore the heart of the sons of men is fully set in them to do evil.

7. <u>God is more interested in what we actually do than our good intentions.</u>

    Mt 21:28 But what think ye? A certain man had two sons; and he came to the first, and said, Son, go work to day in my vineyard.

    29 He answered and said, I will not: but afterward he repented, and went.

    30 And he came to the second, and said likewise. And he answered and said, I go, sir: and went not.

    31 Whether of them twain did the will of his father? They say unto him, The first. Jesus saith unto them, Verily I say unto you, That the publicans and the harlots go into the kingdom of God before you.

8. <u>God will work with us to accomplish His will.</u>

    Mr 16:20 And they went forth, and preached every where, the Lord working with them, and confirming the word with signs following. Amen.

9. <u>When we work with God, He leads and helps us in all we do because we follow His directions. Consequently, great things are accomplished.</u>

    Jo 5:17 But Jesus answered them, My Father worketh hitherto, and I work.

    20 For the Father loveth the Son, and sheweth him all things that himself doeth: and he will shew him greater works than these, that ye may marvel.

10. <u>The very basis of working for God is believing and having a personal relationship with Him.</u>

    Jo 14:12 Verily, verily, I say unto you, He that believeth on me, the works that I do shall he do also; and greater works than these shall he do; because I go unto my Father.

    15:4 Abide in me, and I in you. As the branch cannot bear fruit of itself, except it abide in the vine; no more can ye, except ye abide in me.

5 I am the vine, ye are the branches: He that abideth in me, and I in him, the same bringeth forth much fruit: for without me ye can do nothing.

11. <u>We show that we have truly been saved by how our lives are changed and the works that we do.</u>

Ac 26:20 But shewed first unto them of Damascus, and at Jerusalem, and throughout all the coasts of Judaea, and then to the Gentiles, that they should repent and turn to God, and do works meet for repentance.

Ro 2:15 Which shew the work of the law written in their hearts, their conscience also bearing witness, and their thoughts the mean while accusing or else excusing one another;)

12. <u>If we love God and are willing to fit into his plans, He works behind the scenes in order to turn everything, even our failures, for our good.</u> He has and will always have our best interest in mind.

Ro 8:28 And we know that all things work together for good to them that love God, to them who are the called according to his purpose.

13. <u>Everything that we do will be recorded and evaluated by God.</u> What we have done for and through Him will be rewarded.

1 Co 3:13 Every man's work shall be made manifest: for the day shall declare it, because it shall be revealed by fire; and the fire shall try every man's work of what sort it is.

14 If any man's work abide which he hath built thereupon, he shall receive a reward.

15 If any man's work shall be burned, he shall suffer loss: but he himself shall be saved; yet so as by fire.

Heb 6:10 For God is not unrighteous to forget your work and labour of love, which ye have shewed toward his name, in that ye have ministered to the saints, and do minister.

14. <u>The struggles that we go through in this life change our character and result in great rewards.</u>

2 Co 4:17 For our light affliction, which is but for a moment, worketh for us a far more exceeding and eternal weight of glory;

15. <u>God will provide all we need to enable us to do what He has called us to do.</u>

2 Co 9:8 And God is able to make all grace abound toward you; that ye, always having all sufficiency in all things, may abound to every good work:

16. <u>God is the author of all that we do and all we accomplish.</u>

Eph 2:10 For we are his workmanship, created in Christ Jesus unto good works, which God hath before ordained that we should walk in them.

3:7 Whereof I was made a minister, according to the gift of the grace of God given unto me by the effectual working of his power.

20 Now unto him that is able to do exceeding abundantly above all that we ask or think, according to the power that worketh in us,

17. <u>We are to do everything through faith.</u>

    Ro 12:6 Having then gifts differing according to the grace that is given to us, whether prophecy, let us prophesy according to the proportion of faith;

    Mt 21:21 Jesus answered and said unto them, Verily I say unto you, If ye have faith, and doubt not, ye shall not only do this which is done to the fig tree, but also if ye shall say unto this mountain, Be thou removed, and be thou cast into the sea; it shall be done.

18. <u>Actions and work need to be balanced with rest.</u> If we are driven to perform in order to feel worthwhile, the resulting imbalance can significantly affect our relationships and health.

    Ge 2:2 And on the seventh day God ended his work which he had made; and he rested on the seventh day from all his work which he had made.

    Ex 23:12 Six days thou shalt do thy work, and on the seventh day thou shalt rest: that thine ox and thine ass may rest, and the son of thy handmaid, and the stranger, may be refreshed.

19. <u>If we will do what God has called us to do, and not add additional challenges of our own, our burden in this life will be light; and we will not be stressed out or overwhelmed by life.</u>

    Mt 11:28 Come unto me, all ye that labour and are heavy laden, and I will give you rest.

    29 Take my yoke upon you, and learn of me; for I am meek and lowly in heart: and ye shall find rest unto your souls.

    30 For my yoke is easy, and my burden is light.

20. <u>God wants us ultimately to do everything for and through Him, while we rest in His strength.</u>

    Heb 4:10 For he that is entered into his rest, he also hath ceased from his own works, as God did from his.

Counseling Methods and Techniques

1. <u>We are to do everything as unto God.</u> Since many times our actions are hindered by relationship problems with people, we need to learn to do absolutely everything as though we were doing it all for God. In fact, this is exactly what we should be doing. If we do this, we will be delivered from trying to please people instead of doing what God tells us to do. Since we are to do everything ultimately for Christ, we can work at our job for Him even if we do not like our boss. Instead of serving him, we are serving Christ.

2. <u>We must break the dance of anger and conflict.</u> Conflicts, many times, become patterns that have been described as dances. Each person does something, the other reacts, and then the first reacts to the reaction. To break a dance, only one person needs to do something differently.

Principles of Confession

Confession, or what we say, is another specific way in which we can choose to act. Confession is actually preaching directly to ourselves. How many times have we heard the lie, "Sticks and stones can break my bones but words can never hurt me?" What we say does have a very significant effect on our lives even in the natural realm. In the realm of the Spirit, its effect is even more important.

1. <u>Words control our lives and are difficult to bring under control.</u>

   Jas 3:6 And the tongue [is] a fire, a world of iniquity: so is the tongue among our members, that it defileth the whole body, and setteth on fire the course of nature; and it is set on fire of hell.

   8 But the tongue can no man tame; [it is] an unruly evil, full of deadly poison.

2. <u>Words hurt or help other people.</u>

   Pr 15:1 A soft answer turneth away wrath: but grievous words stir up anger.

   16:24 Pleasant words [are as] an honeycomb, sweet to the soul, and health to the bones.

   26:22 The words of a talebearer [are] as wounds, and they go down into the innermost parts of the belly.

3. <u>We will be judged by our words.</u>

   Mt 12:36 But I say unto you, That every idle word that men shall speak, they shall give account thereof in the day of judgment.

   37 For by thy words thou shalt be justified, and by thy words thou shalt be condemned.

4. <u>Our words can bring salvation.</u>

   Ac 11:14 Who shall tell thee words, whereby thou and all thy house shall be saved.

5. <u>Spiritual power can accompany our words.</u>

   Mr 16:20 And they went forth, and preached every where, the Lord working with [them], and confirming the word with signs following. Amen.

   1 Co 2:4 And my speech and my preaching [was] not with enticing words of man's wisdom, but in demonstration of the Spirit and of power:

6. <u>Confession of sin is necessary for forgiveness and mercy.</u>

   1 Jo 1:9 If we confess our sins, he is faithful and just to forgive us [our] sins, and to cleanse us from all unrighteousness.

   Pr 28:13 He that covereth his sins shall not prosper: but whoso confesseth and forsaketh [them] shall have mercy.

7. <u>Healing comes through confession.</u>

   Jas 5:16 Confess [your] faults one to another, and pray one for another, that ye may be healed. The effectual fervent prayer of a righteous man availeth much.

8. <u>Confession is an expression of our faith and releases the power of God.</u>

   Mr 11:23 For verily I say unto you, That whosoever shall say unto this mountain, Be thou removed, and be thou cast into the sea; and shall not doubt in his heart, but shall believe that those things which he saith shall come to pass; he shall have whatsoever he saith.

9. Our confession about our future has the power to destroy or bless us.

    Pr 18:21 Death and life [are] in the power of the tongue: and they that love it shall eat the fruit thereof.

10. Confessing what we believe is part of our fight of faith.

    1Ti 6:12 Fight the good fight of faith, lay hold on eternal life, whereunto thou art also called, and hast professed a good profession before many witnesses.

11. We must speak the truth in love.

    Eph 4:15 But speaking the truth in love, may grow up into him in all things, which is the head, even Christ.

Counseling Methods and Techniques

1. We need to be careful not to confess doubt and unbelief. To do so works against the power of faith in our lives. Nevertheless, sometimes clients, who have been taught on positive confession, take it to such an extreme that they are unwilling to confess that they have had or are now experiencing anything negative in their lives. This can make counseling difficult because the clients feel they cannot be honest about how they feel with their counselor or they are making a negative confession. In these cases, the counselor must help the client understand that it is not a negative confession to state that we have symptoms of a sickness or that we feel bad, even though we know that according to the Bible "by His stripes we were healed" 2000 years ago. The fact is that our healing has not yet manifested in the physical realm. It is also not negative confession to state what has happened in the past or present. It is a negative confession to state that we believe negative things will happen in the future.

2. We are to edify one-another in everything we do. That does not mean speaking "white" lies to make someone else feel better, but it does mean focusing on and speaking the positive things that we do see and believe. If we will start making this a habit by doing it daily, it will eventually become a part of our personality.

3. In our confession, we must not contradict God's positive word for us. To do so is to call God a liar, and He cannot lie. The Bible makes it clear that He has positive plans for our future. Jeremiah 29:11 states, " For I know the thoughts that I think toward you, saith the LORD, thoughts of peace, and not of evil, to give you an expected end."

The Principles of Communication

Communication is also a specific type or mode of acting. It is different from confession in that communication always involves at least two persons and perceptions and filtering can play a major part. Good communication is when what the first individual tried to express is sent and received without distortion or misinterpretation by the second person. I estimate that fifty percent of perceived offences in most marriages are the result of poor communication between men and women and were not intended to offend the other spouse. Of course, communication can be used for both good and evil purposes.

1. Anything is possible with good communication, but poor communication brings conflict and separation. Our language problems began at Babel.

Ge 11:6 And the LORD said, Behold, the people *is* one, and they have all one language; and this they begin to do: and now nothing will be restrained from them, which they have imagined to do.

7 Go to, let us go down, and there confound their language, that they may not understand one another's speech.

8 So the LORD scattered them abroad from thence upon the face of all the earth: and they left off to build the city.

9 Therefore is the name of it called Babel; because the LORD did there confound the language of all the earth: and from thence did the LORD scatter them abroad upon the face of all the earth.

2. We cannot use the excuse that we cannot communicate adequately since God made our mouth and will help us with our communication. God is eager to give us wisdom if we ask Him for it.

Ex 4:10 And Moses said unto the LORD, O my Lord, I *am* not eloquent, neither heretofore, nor since thou hast spoken unto thy servant: but I *am* slow of speech, and of a slow tongue.

11 And the LORD said unto him, Who hath made man's mouth? or who maketh the dumb, or deaf, or the seeing, or the blind? have not I the LORD?

12 Now therefore go, and I will be with thy mouth, and teach thee what thou shalt say.

3. We must really try to listen in order to understand another person. The uniform complaint of women is that "Men do not listen."

Job 13:17 Hear diligently my speech, and my declaration with your ears.

4. The object of communication is that the person listening receives what the speaker intended to communicate. Therefore, we need to speak clearly and plainly.

2 Co 3:12 Seeing then that we have such hope, we use great plainness of speech:

Tit 2:8 Sound speech, that cannot be condemned; that he that is of the contrary part may be ashamed, having no evil thing to say of you.

5. Men and women must learn to understand the other's method of communication and honor their spouse as different but equal.

1 Pe 3:7 Likewise, ye husbands, dwell with them according to knowledge, giving honour unto the wife, as unto the weaker vessel, and as being heirs together of the grace of life; that your prayers be not hindered.

10 For he that will love life, and see good days, let him refrain his tongue from evil, and his lips that they speak no guile:

6. Sometimes we cannot hear, because we do not want to hear or believe the truth.

Jo 8:43 Why do ye not understand my speech? even because ye cannot hear my word.

44 Ye are of your father the devil, and the lusts of your father ye will do. He was a murderer from the beginning, and abode not in the truth, because there is no truth in him. When he speaketh a lie, he speaketh of his own: for he is a liar, and the father of it.

45 And because I tell *you* the truth, ye believe me not.

7. <u>Our actions can speak louder than what we say.</u>

    1 Co 2:1 And I, brethren, when I came to you, came not with excellency of speech or of wisdom, declaring unto you the testimony of God.

    4 And my speech and my preaching *was* not with enticing words of man's wisdom, but in demonstration of the Spirit and of power:

    4:19 But I will come to you shortly, if the Lord will, and will know, not the speech of them which are puffed up, but the power.

8. <u>How we say our words has a lot to do with how they are accepted.</u>

    Col 4:6 Let your speech [be] alway with grace, seasoned with salt, that ye may know how ye ought to answer every man.

9. <u>What we communicate to others non-verbally is important.</u>

    Pr 6:13 He winketh with his eyes, he speaketh with his feet, he teacheth with his fingers;

    14 Frowardness is in his heart, he deviseth mischief continually; he soweth discord. Therefore shall his calamity come suddenly; suddenly shall he be broken without remedy.

10. <u>Maturity in life is found in the person who can communicate without offending the other person and can accomplish his objective.</u> This is called assertiveness.

    Jas 3:2 For in many things we offend all. If any man offend not in word, the same is a perfect man, and able also to bridle the whole body.

11. <u>We need to be able to control our tongues, or they will do a lot of damage to our relationships.</u> If we have a problem saying the wrong thing intentionally or out of anger, we will probably have a difficult time making up for what we have said.

    Jas 3:8 But the tongue can no man tame; it is an unruly evil, full of deadly poison.

    9 Therewith bless we God, even the Father; and therewith curse we men, which are made after the similitude of God.

    10 Out of the same mouth proceedeth blessing and cursing. My brethren, these things ought not so to be.

12. <u>Our communication plays a significant part in many serious sins.</u>

    Ro 1:29 Being filled with all unrighteousness, fornication, wickedness, covetousness, maliciousness; full of envy, murder, debate, deceit, malignity; whisperers,

    30 Backbiters, haters of God, despiteful, proud, boasters, inventors of evil things, disobedient to parents,

    31 Without understanding, covenantbreakers, without natural affection, implacable, unmerciful:

    32 Who knowing the judgment of God, that they which commit such things are worthy of death, not only do the same, but have pleasure in them that do them.

13. <u>To God, verbal abuse is the same as murder.</u>

    Mt 5: 21 Ye have heard that it was said by them of old time, Thou shalt not kill; and whosoever shall kill shall be in danger of the judgment:

    22 But I say unto you, That whosoever is angry with his brother without a cause shall be in danger of the judgment: and whosoever shall say to his brother, Raca, shall be in danger of the council: but whosoever shall say, Thou fool, shall be in danger of hell fire.

14. <u>Reviling or verbally abusing others can become a serious addiction, but through God, it can be overcome.</u>

    1 Co 6:10 Nor thieves, nor covetous, nor drunkards, nor <u>revilers,</u> nor extortioners, shall inherit the kingdom of God.

    11 And such were some of you: but ye are washed, but ye are sanctified, but ye are justified in the name of the Lord Jesus, and by the Spirit of our God.

15. <u>We are responsible for the control of our tongue.</u>

    Mt 12:36 But I say unto you, That every idle word that men shall speak, they shall give Account thereof in the day of judgment.

    Pr 4: 24 Put away from thee a froward mouth, and perverse lips put far from thee.

    1 Pe 3:10 For he that will love life, and see good days, let him refrain his tongue from evil, and his lips that they speak no guile:

16. <u>Our criteria must be whether our speech is acceptable unto God.</u>

    Ps 19:14 Let the words of my mouth, and the meditation of my heart, be acceptable in thy sight, O LORD, my strength, and my redeemer.

17. <u>We do not have to fear or defend ourselves from evil that is said against us, since God will provide our protection.</u>

    Isa 54:17 No weapon that is formed against thee shall prosper; and every tongue that shall rise against thee in judgment thou shalt condemn. This is the heritage of the servants of the LORD, and their righteousness is of me, saith the LORD.

Counseling Methods and Techniques

1. <u>We must learn to really listen.</u> Unfortunately, most of us are more interested in getting our point across than hearing and understanding what the other person is saying. This is not only counterproductive to good communication, but demonstrates our own self-centeredness and selfishness, which will negatively affect our relationships. We need to strive to really hear the other person first. By doing this, we earn the right to be heard. Men are many times poor listeners.

2. <u>We must learn how the other gender communicates.</u> As I said, it is my estimate that over half of all offenses in most marriages were not intended by the mate. These conflicts were caused by gender-communication errors. Numerous books have been written on this issue including *Hidden Keys to a Loving Lasting Marriage* (1988) by Gary Smalley and the secular series that started with *Men are From Mars and Women from Venus* (1992) by Dr John Gray.

3. <u>We are responsible for what we say even when provoked.</u> Many of us have a problem reacting to what others say. We seem to believe that if they said something hurtful first, that this justifies what we say back to them. This only leads to escalation, destroys relationships, and accomplishes nothing.

4. <u>We must put off cussing, swearing and all wrong communication.</u> Not only does the Bible direct this, but it only makes sense. To wrongly communicate means to do something that results in miscommunication. Miscommunication means that we do not get across what we really want to say. Cussing and swearing are usually done to try to emphasize a point. It is used by persons that feel of little worth to try to artificially communicate more powerfully. It simply tells the entire world that we have a problem with low self-worth or that in the situation we feel powerless. Putting others down is also wrong communication. When we put others down, we are assuming we are better than others. God values us all equally.

5. <u>We can teach the speaker-listener technique to help couples communicate.</u> This method was developed to stop escalation, discounting, withdrawing and excessively negative interpretations. To begin this technique, some object is selected to symbolize which person is in control of the conversation. Only the person who has the controller is allowed to initiate communication. They are to speak using "I" and "we" statements concerning any subject. The other person is to listen and paraphrase what has been said. The process proceeds a few sentences at a time. When the person with the controller wants a response, he or she asks a question and then turns the controller over to the other person. In this way, communication continues and is clarified until the conversation ends. (See *Fighting for Your Marriage* by Markman, Stanley, and Blumberg (1994) for more information.)

The Principles of Responsibility

These principles are possibly the least understood and most controversial principles in the Bible. God simply wants us to unilaterally do what is good and right without regard to how we are treated and without reacting to what others do. I will ask my clients, "When you stand before God, is He going to ask you what the other person did?" No, He will ask you what you did and how you reacted to what the other person did. God's idea of how to deal with relationships is to do good actions and think correct thoughts while always having the other person's best interest in mind (love). Many miss the fact that the principles of non-retribution are not to be blindly applied to every case. Some people are "swine" or "dogs." These methods are not to be applied to those who will attack you for being good to them.

1. <u>To God, resolving our human conflicts is more important than ministering to Him.</u> He would rather have the problem solved and have His children at peace, than have them at His side.

    Mt 5:23 Therefore if thou bring thy gift to the altar, and there rememberest that thy brother hath ought against thee;

    24 Leave there thy gift before the altar, and go thy way; first be reconciled to thy brother, and then come and offer thy gift.

2. <u>We are to do everything possible to reconcile conflicts as rapidly as possible.</u>

    Mt 5:25 Agree with thine adversary quickly, whiles thou art in the way with him; lest at any time the adversary deliver thee to the judge, and the judge deliver thee to the officer, and thou be cast into prison.

    26 Verily I say unto thee, Thou shalt by no means come out thence, till thou hast paid the uttermost farthing.

3. <u>We must not return evil for evil.</u> We should do more than expected, without regard to what has been done to us. The point of these verses is that we are to do much more than is expected for others and not retaliate for what might have been done to us. Retaliation or aggression only results in escalation. A slap on the cheek was an insult. A man's cloak could not legally be taken away since it provided warmth and protection at night. A Roman soldier had the right to make someone carry his equipment for one mile. Instead of complaining or resisting, a Christian should carry it two miles. We are to love others so much that we do not take offenses personally. We should be willing to go the "second mile" to help others and never seek the harm of those who hurt us.

Mt 5:38 Ye have heard that it hath been said, An eye for an eye, and a tooth for a tooth:

39 But I say unto you, That ye resist (set oneself against) not evil (labours, annoyances, hardships): but whosoever shall smite (slap) thee on thy right cheek, turn to him the other also.

40 And if any man will sue thee at the law, and take away thy coat, let him have thy cloke (which could not be legally taken) also.

41 And whosoever shall compel thee to go a mile, go with him twain. Give to him that asketh thee, and from him that would borrow of thee turn not thou away. (Look to his needs more than your own—no interest should be charged—be liberal and generous)

42 Give to him that asketh thee, and from him that would borrow of thee turn not thou away.

4. <u>We are to love others unconditionally and do what is right just as God does, and not react in response to what others do or do not do for us.</u> We are even to love our enemies as God does.

Mt 5:43 Ye have heard that it hath been said, Thou shalt love thy neighbour, and hate thine enemy.

44 But I say unto you, Love your enemies, bless them that curse you, do good to them that hate you, and pray for them which despitefully use you, and persecute you;

45 That ye may be the children of your Father which is in heaven: for he maketh his sun to rise on the evil and on the good, and sendeth rain on the just and on the unjust.

46 For if ye love them which love you, what reward have ye? do not even the publicans the same?

47 And if ye salute your brethren only, what do ye more than others? do not even the publicans so?

48 Be ye therefore perfect, even as your Father which is in heaven is perfect.

5. <u>We are to apply these principles with wisdom in a reasonable fashion.</u> They do not apply to depraved individuals. The Bible call them dogs or swine.

Mt 7:6 Give not that which is holy unto the dogs, neither cast ye your pearls before swine, lest they trample them under their feet, and turn again and rend you.

6. <u>This is all summed up in the Golden Rule.</u>

Mt 7:12 Therefore all things whatsoever ye would that men should do to you, do ye even so to them: for this is the law and the prophets.

7. <u>Leave justice and vengeance to God.</u>

    Ro 12:19 Dearly beloved, avenge not yourselves, but [rather] give place unto wrath: for it is written, Vengeance [is] mine; I will repay, saith the Lord.

8. <u>Passive resistance is God's method for overcoming evil with good.</u>

    Ro 12:18 If it be possible, as much as lieth in you, live peaceably with all men.

    20 Therefore if thine enemy hunger, feed him; if he thirst, give him drink: for in so doing thou shalt heap coals of fire on his head.

    21 Be not overcome of evil, but overcome evil with good.

Counseling Methods and Techniques

1. <u>We must do what is right, no matter what others do.</u> God expects us to do what is right even when provoked. When we stand before Him, He will not ask us what the other person did, but how we responded to what they did.

2. <u>We need to always respond to offenses with good instead of evil.</u> This stops escalation and keeps us from becoming perpetrators of evil. Although we are to do good to everyone, these verses do not require us to place ourselves in situations where we will be abused by truly evil people (dogs or swine).

3. <u>Passive resistance is usually God's method for overcoming evil.</u> When we continue to do what is right in spite of what others do, they may be ashamed of how they have treated us (coals on their head). Through the Christian principle of passive resistance, Gandhi (although not a Christian) ended the British colonization of India and Pakistan; and Martin Luther King successfully led the civil rights movement in the United States. Boundaries are another form of passive resistance.

The Principles of Judgment and Accountability

There is confusion in the church and in the secular world concerning when to confront others, hold others accountable, and when to judge others. Many unbelievers will quote the verse "Judge not or you will be judged" (Matthew 7:1) in order to deter Christians from telling them that what they are doing is wrong. Although the Bible is quite clear on these points, a clear difference needs to be made between legal judgment or condemning someone, judging someone under our authority, and discerning whether something is right or wrong. It all depends on what relationship we have with other people.

1. <u>Legal judgment requires that we hold a position of authority over the person to be judged.</u>

    Jas 4:11 Speak not evil one of another, brethren. He that speaketh evil of his brother, and judgeth his brother, speaketh evil of the law, and judgeth the law: but if thou judge the law, thou art not a doer of the law, but a judge.

2. <u>When we have authority over someone, we have a right to rebuke them; but this must be done with wisdom.</u>

    Pr 19:18 Chasten thy son while there is hope, and let not thy soul spare for his crying.

3. <u>A person can give us the right to judge their behavior; this is called accountability.</u> We place ourselves under accountability every time we take a job, join a church or group, or move to a new area.

Lu 19:39 And some of the Pharisees from among the multitude said unto him, Master, rebuke thy disciples.

Pr 9:8 Reprove not a scorner, lest he hate thee: rebuke a wise man, and he will love thee.

4. <u>Leaders have a right to judge those within the church, but not those outside of the church.</u> This is because the leaders of the church have been given authority over church members, both by God and by the members themselves when they join the church.

1 Co 5:3 For I verily, as absent in body, but present in spirit, have judged already, as though I were present, concerning him that hath so done this deed,

12 For what have I to do to judge them also that are without? do not ye judge them that are within?

13 But them that are without God judgeth. Therefore put away from among yourselves that wicked person.

1 Ti 5:20 Them that sin rebuke before all, that others also may fear.

Tit 2:15 These things speak, and exhort, and rebuke with all authority. Let no man despise thee.

5. <u>We have a right to rebuke others who do something that offends us when we have a relationship with them.</u>

Lu 17:3 Take heed to yourselves: If thy brother trespass against thee, rebuke him; and if he repent, forgive him.

6. <u>We are not to judge anyone who is not under our authority, or who has not specifically offended us.</u> We need to stay out of other people's business.

Ro 2:1 Therefore thou art inexcusable, O man, whosoever thou art that judgest: for wherein thou judgest another, thou condemnest thyself; for thou that judgest doest the same things.

2 But we are sure that the judgment of God is according to truth against them which commit such things.

14:4 Who art thou that judgest another man's servant? to his own master he standeth or falleth. Yea, he shall be holden up: for God is able to make him stand.

10 But why dost thou judge thy brother? or why dost thou set at nought thy brother? for we shall all stand before the judgment seat of Christ.

7. <u>We shall be judged by the same criteria that we use to judge others.</u>

Mt 7:1 Judge not, that ye be not judged.

2 For with what judgment ye judge, ye shall be judged: and with what measure ye mete, it shall be measured to you again.

Jas 2:13 For he shall have judgment without mercy, that hath shewed no mercy; and mercy rejoiceth against judgment.

8. <u>We are not to judge according to how things seem, but take the heart and intentions of the other individual into account.</u>

   Jo 7:24 Judge not according to the appearance, but judge righteous judgment.

9. <u>We should not even judge ourselves, but leave that up to God.</u>

   1 Co 4:3 But with me it is a very small thing that I should be judged of you, or of man's judgment: yea, I judge not mine own self.

   4 For I know nothing by myself; yet am I not hereby justified: but he that judgeth me is the Lord.

   5 Therefore judge nothing before the time, until the Lord come, who both will bring to light the hidden things of darkness, and will make manifest the counsels of the hearts: and then shall every man have praise of God.

10. <u>God is the only One Who has authority over everyone and has a right to hold them accountable, chastise and rebuke them.</u>

    Re 3:19 As many as I love, I rebuke and chasten: be zealous therefore, and repent.

    2 Sa 7:14 I will be his father, and he shall be my son. If he commit iniquity, I will chasten him with the rod of men, and with the stripes of the children of men:

11. <u>If we will judge ourselves and repent, we will not come under the judgment of God.</u>

    1 Co 11:31 For if we would judge ourselves, we should not be judged.

    32 But when we are judged, we are chastened of the Lord, that we should not be condemned with the world.

12. <u>God judges us according to the amount of knowledge that we have.</u> This should be a sobering thought to us who have studied and know the Word of God. However, it would not be acceptable to learn less so we would be accountable for less.

    Mt 11:22 But I say unto you, It shall be more tolerable for Tyre and Sidon at the day of judgment, than for you.

    23 And thou, Capernaum, which art exalted unto heaven, shalt be brought down to hell: for if the mighty works, which have been done in thee, had been done in Sodom, it would have remained until this day.

    24 But I say unto you, That it shall be more tolerable for the land of Sodom in the day of judgment, than for thee.

Counseling Methods and Techniques

1. <u>We are tempted to judge others because we feel inferior to or threatened by them.</u> The root cause of inappropriately judging or being critical of other people is that we are trying to bring them down to our own level or we feel threatened by them. Dealing with judgmental clients can be difficult because the real issue is a problem with low self-worth or insecurity. If we have fallen into the trap of comparing ourselves with others, we will try to make ourselves feel superior by putting them down. Of course, each of us will find some way to "justify" our own actions.

2. <u>We will be judged by the same measure that we use to judge others.</u> If we are critical and give no mercy, we should not expect to receive mercy from God and others. We need to ask ourselves, "Is that the way we want to be judged and treated?" Even though God Himself judges perfectly, He still mediates His judgment with abundant mercy.

3. <u>Do not condemn or judge others, but discern actions and sins.</u> In the Bible, the word to judge is used in two ways: to judge people and to judge actions or sins. Judgment implies a superior position of authority over the one being judged and condemnation implies a judicial action against a person. Discernment, which has previously been discussed, is an evaluation of the sin, not the person. We, as counselors, need to remember that, "For all have sinned, and come short of the glory of God" (Romans 3:23), that we are saved by grace and not by works, and that we are all of equal worth in God's eyes. It is the Holy Spirit's job to bring conviction, not ours. With these thoughts in mind, we fully love and respect every client, but hate the sin that is destroying them. We need to find the "scared little boy or girl" in every client, so that we can love them just like they are and help them "work out their own salvation with fear and trembling." (Philippians 2:12)

4. <u>We are to judge our own actions, but not condemn ourselves.</u> We are to evaluate our own sins and turn from them so that God will not have to convict and discipline us. According to Romans 8:1, God will not condemn a Christian because the blood of Christ covers us. Most persons that fall into self-condemnation either are really trying to manipulate others by telling them that they are really not that bad or justify a pity party, so they can withdraw from life or lick their wounds.

5. <u>Accountability can help us control our actions.</u> Accountability is inviting others to hold us responsible for our actions. It is one of the first steps in dealing with addictive and compulsive habits. Because most clients respect what others think of them and would be ashamed to admit that they are continuing to do things that they know are wrong, a daily or weekly accounting for their behavior can be an effective part of therapy. Of course, the issues underlying the problem must be dealt with during this period of accountability, or the behavior might easily re-occur when the accountability has ended.

6. <u>Confrontation should be used in the context of a caring relationship.</u> As mentioned in *Transformation!*, it was the confrontation with the gods of Egypt that led to the deliverance of Israel from the bondage of Egypt. However, the counselor needs to be careful to first earn the right to confront by establishing a caring relationship with the client or the result could easily be a termination of the counseling process by the client.

The Principles of Justice

To be just means to be "1. Upright; honest. 2. Fair; impartial." (The New International Webster's Concise Dictionary of the English Language, edited by Sidney Landau, 1997) It is being fair and equitable in all of our dealings and wanting what is best for everyone, not just ourselves. To do this, we must eliminate selfishness or self-bias in our lives. This requires believing that God will meet all of our needs. If our needs are met, then we are free to unselfishly meet the needs of other people. God's goal is for us to have the good of everyone in mind in all that we do. This is the very essence of love. In counseling, this is called a win-win solution. Instead of wanting to get the very best deal for ourselves, we should desire that everyone get a fair deal.

To adequately discuss this subject, we must understand the meaning of several words in the original language: justice, justification, righteousness and sanctification. Justice in the Hebrew is *tsaddiyq*. It means "rendering to every one that which is his due." Righteousness in the Hebrew, *tsadaqah*, is doing what is ethically right. In the Greek, *dikaios*, which is sometimes translated as just or righteous, deals primarily with "passing just judgment, observing divine laws, and those whose way of thinking, feeling, and acting are wholly conformed to the will of God." *Dikaiosune*, which is always interpreted as righteousness means "in a broad sense: the state of him who is as he ought to be, righteousness, the condition acceptable to God...integrity, virtue, purity of life, rightness, correctness of thinking, feeling, and acting." *Dikaioo,* which is translated as to justify, means "to either exhibit to be righteous or to declare to be righteous." A common definition of justify or justification is to declare one to be as if he had never sinned. *Hagiasmos* is translated as holiness or sanctification. It means "either the consecration of a life to God or the effect of that consecration—holiness in heart, actions and life." (Vine, 1985)

Because these words are closely associated, we must be careful to observe how they are used when discussing these basic principles. God's goal is an unbiased person who acts in accordance with what is right. We must first become just or unbiased, before we can act in a just manner. God declares us to be in right relationship with Him (imputed righteousness or justification) in order to allow us to have an intimate relationship with Him so that He can sanctify us (impart experiential righteousness to us). The ultimate goal is for us to apply right thinking and acting in our relationship with Him and others.

1. <u>God is more just than any man.</u>

    Job 4:17 Shall mortal man be more just than God? shall a man be more pure than his maker?

    Ps 71:19 Thy righteousness also, O God, is very high, who hast done great things: O God, who is like unto thee!

2. <u>God wants us to be just and act righteously.</u>

    Pr 11:1 A false balance is abomination to the LORD: but a just weight is his delight.

    21:3 To do justice and judgment is more acceptable to the LORD than sacrifice.

    Ro 14:17 For the kingdom of God is not meat and drink; but righteousness, and peace, and joy in the Holy Ghost.

3. <u>To be just means to be unbiased and follow God's laws.</u>

    Jo 5:30 I can of mine own self do nothing: as I hear, I judge: and my judgment is just; because I seek not mine own will, but the will of the Father which hath sent me.

    Eze 18:9 Hath walked in my statutes, and hath kept my judgments, to deal truly; he is just, he shall surely live, saith the Lord GOD.

4. <u>To be righteous means to think and do what is truly right.</u>

    Pr 12:5 The thoughts of the righteous are right: but the counsels of the wicked are deceit.

    1 Jo 3:7 Little children, let no man deceive you: he that doeth righteousness is righteous, even as he is righteous.

5. <u>All of us have difficulty being unselfish and impartial.</u>

    Ec 7:20 For there is not a just man upon earth, that doeth good, and sinneth not.

6. <u>Becoming just is a progressive movement toward wholeness.</u>

    Pr 4:18 But the path of the just is as the shining light, that shineth more and more unto the perfect day.

    9:9 Give instruction to a wise man, and he will be yet wiser: teach a just man, and he will increase in learning.

7. <u>We are to seek after righteousness and do justice.</u>

   Mt 5:6 Blessed are they which do hunger and thirst after righteousness: for they shall be filled.

   1 Ti 6:11 But thou, O man of God, flee these things; and follow after righteousness, godliness, faith, love, patience, meekness.

   Hos 10:12 Sow to yourselves in righteousness, reap in mercy; break up your fallow ground: for it is time to seek the LORD, till he come and rain righteousness upon you.

8. <u>We cannot become just or righteous in our own strength, deeds, or works.</u>

   Isa 64:6 But we are all as an unclean thing, and all our righteousnesses are as filthy rags; and we all do fade as a leaf; and our iniquities, like the wind, have taken us away.

   Ro 10:3 For they being ignorant of God's righteousness, and going about to establish their own righteousness, have not submitted themselves unto the righteousness of God.

   Ga 3:11 But that no man is justified by the law in the sight of God, it is evident: for, The just shall live by faith.

9. <u>Imputed righteousness or justification is based on faith in what God has promised.</u>

   Ro 3:28 Therefore we conclude that a man is justified by faith without the deeds of the law.

   4:3 For what saith the scripture? Abraham believed God, and it was counted unto him for righteousness.

   5:1 Therefore being justified by faith, we have peace with God through our Lord Jesus Christ:

10. <u>Imparted righteousness or sanctification also comes by faith.</u>

    Ro 1:17 For therein is the righteousness of God revealed from faith to faith: as it is written, The just shall live by faith.

    1 Co 1:30 But of him are ye in Christ Jesus, who of God is made unto us wisdom, and righteousness, and sanctification, and redemption:

    Php 3:9 And be found in him, not having mine own righteousness, which is of the law, but that which is through the faith of Christ, the righteousness which is of God by faith:

11. <u>We will be judged by whether our actions and words are unselfish and right, or self-serving.</u> Through faith God transforms us so that we will do good works with the right motivation. We cannot truly do good, unselfish works on our own. Consequently, God can judge whether we truly have faith in Him by the actions that result from our faith.

    Mt 25:34 Then shall the King say unto them on his right hand, Come, ye blessed of my Father, inherit the kingdom prepared for you from the foundation of the world:

    35 For I was an hungred, and ye gave me meat: I was thirsty, and ye gave me drink: I was a stranger, and ye took me in:

    36 Naked, and ye clothed me: I was sick, and ye visited me: I was in prison, and ye came unto me.

    37 Then shall the righteous answer him, saying, Lord, when saw we thee an hungred, and fed thee? or thirsty, and gave thee drink?

38 When saw we thee a stranger, and took thee in? or naked, and clothed thee?

39 Or when saw we thee sick, or in prison, and came unto thee?

40 And the King shall answer and say unto them, Verily I say unto you, Inasmuch as ye have done it unto one of the least of these my brethren, ye have done it unto me.

Counseling Methods and Techniques

1. <u>To be just and fair requires that everything be resolved with win-win solutions.</u> The first step to becoming just in our relationships is to decide that we will not agree to anything that is not a win-win solution. Win-win solutions stop competition, stop feelings of being taken advantage of or used and produce long-term friendships. To want to desire win-win solutions, we must realize that short-term wins never result in long-term victories and usually require that we lose the next time. Having everyone win is God's way and the only way to have healthy relationships. It is based on love, which is having the other person's best interest in mind. Working together or being a "team player" will increase the benefits for everyone involved.

2. <u>True justice or righteousness comes only through God.</u> To become truly righteous, we must first accept God's imputed righteousness provided by Christ so that we can have an intimate relationship with God. It is through faith (trust), which comes from this relationship that we realize that God will meet all our needs. This is what delivers us from our selfishness. As long as we are self-centered, we can never be righteous.

3. <u>We need to realize that sanctification takes time.</u> We must give ourselves a break and not condemn ourselves. God is not through with us yet. Putting ourselves down and having a pity party only provides openings for depression and further satanic assault. All God asks is that we trust Him and do our best. He is the one who will transform us from glory to glory. The Bible makes this clear in Micah 6:8, "He hath shewed thee, O man, what is good; and what doth the LORD require of thee, but to do justly, and to love mercy, and to walk humbly with thy God?"

4. <u>We need to quit trying to fix ourselves and get out of the religious rat race.</u> We cannot make ourselves more holy by our own strength, will-power, or actions. This is the subject of the entire book of Galatians. Unfortunately, many of us that have escaped the rat race of the world are now competing to become someone by our own efforts in the church. This is called legalism. (For more on this subject see my book *Revelations That Will Set You Free*.)

5. <u>In order to find true justice in the world, we must trust God.</u> All governments, even democracies, are based on selfishness and, therefore, can never be completely just. We need to do our part to support our government and seek justice in all that we do. After we have done everything we can do, we need to turn the situation over to God, confident that He will bring true justice in His time. In the end, He will make everything just. "God keeps good books." (For more on this subject see the chapter on justice in *Transformation!*)

The Principles of Covenants

When chaos exists, it is either because there are no boundaries, laws, rules or agreements; or because people have refused to follow those boundaries. This problem is typified in the Bible in Judges 17:6 through Judges 21:25 where it states, "In those days there was no king in Israel, but every man did that which was right in his own eyes." In this situation people control and manipulate each other in order to get their needs met. Whoever is strongest wins. When people feel controlled, they are offended and rebel, making more control necessary. When these kinds of problems exist, the Bible resorts to a solution called a covenant. God's laws are the boundary lines of His covenants with Abraham, Noah, Israel, and with us. If we obey them, we will be blessed. If we violate them, we will suffer consequences. Boundaries or covenants provide external control for our lives. (For more on this subject see boundaries in *Transformation!*)

In relationships, the term "personal boundary" means a declaration or agreement about what will and will not be allowed in that relationship. It usually includes a clear line of what is allowed and the natural or agreed-upon consequences if the line is crossed. Boundaries are not the same as control in that they respect the other person's free will to cross the line as long as they are willing to suffer the consequences. Boundaries attempt to ensure that the person making the decision is the one who gets the consequences of that decision. Laws are good examples of boundaries in public life. The covenant method for resolving disputes in the Bible uses boundaries in a very specific manner. Both parties agreed to establish a covenant, and some physical monument was usually built as a reminder of the covenant. Furthermore, positive as well as negative consequences were specified, and the agreement was sworn before God, calling on Him to bring vengeance if the agreement was violated. In ancient times, the covenant was the strongest of all agreements and was usually commemorated with a feast of celebration. Today, man's covenant with God and marriage are the two primary examples of covenant agreements.

1. <u>Laws or covenants are for our good.</u> The first law was for the good of Adam and Eve.

   Ge 2:16 And the LORD God commanded the man, saying, Of every tree of the garden thou mayest freely eat:

   17 But of the tree of the knowledge of good and evil, thou shalt not eat of it: for in the day that thou eatest thereof thou shalt surely die.

   De 10:13 To keep the commandments of the LORD, and his statutes, which I command thee this day for thy good?

2. <u>Sometimes covenants are primarily a one-sided promise.</u> God promised Noah and all mankind that He would never again destroy the earth by water. He placed a reminder of this covenant in the sky—the rainbow.

   Ge 9:11 And I will establish my covenant with you; neither shall all flesh be cut off any more by the waters of a flood; neither shall there any more be a flood to destroy the earth.

   12 And God said, This is the token of the covenant which I make between me and you and every living creature that is with you, for perpetual generations:

   13 I do set my bow in the cloud, and it shall be for a token of a covenant between me and the earth.

3. <u>Many blessings can come as part of a covenant, and the loss of the blessing can serve as the consequence.</u> God promised Abram (later Abraham) that he would become the father of many nations; He would bless him, and give the land of Canaan to his children as an inheritance. To receive this blessing, he would have to circumcise the flesh of each male. If he did not, that male would be cut off from the blessings for violating the covenant. Circumcision symbolizes cutting off the power of the flesh in our lives and living according to the Spirit.

   Ge 17:2 And I will make my covenant between me and thee, and will multiply thee exceedingly.

   7 And I will establish my covenant between me and thee and thy seed after thee in their generations for an everlasting covenant, to be a God unto thee, and to thy seed after thee.

   10 This is my covenant, which ye shall keep, between me and you and thy seed after thee; Every man child among you shall be circumcised.

14 And the uncircumcised man child whose flesh of his foreskin is not circumcised, that soul shall be cut off from his people; he hath broken my covenant.

4. <u>Even disputes with a long history of abuse can be resolved through a covenant.</u>

Ge 31:26 And Laban said to Jacob, What hast thou done, that thou hast stolen away unawares to me, and carried away my daughters, as captives taken with the sword?

28 And hast not suffered me to kiss my sons and my daughters? thou hast now done foolishly in so doing.

36 And Jacob was wroth, and chode with Laban: and Jacob answered and said to Laban, What is my trespass? what is my sin, that thou hast so hotly pursued after me?

41 Thus have I been twenty years in thy house; I served thee fourteen years for thy two daughters, and six years for thy cattle: and thou hast changed my wages ten times.

42 Except the God of my father, the God of Abraham, and the fear of Isaac, had been with me, surely thou hadst sent me away now empty. God hath seen mine affliction and the labour of my hands, and rebuked thee yesternight.

5. <u>The first step is to agree to make a covenant and provide a witness of the agreement.</u> In counseling, this is many times done by recording it in the notes of the counseling session. This is done so that any time in the future if there is any question as to what was agreed upon, the permanent record can be consulted. If both are Christians, God can be called upon to be the witness of the agreement as is the case in the marriage vow.

Ge 31:44 Now therefore come thou, let us make a covenant, I and thou; and let it be for a witness between me and thee.

45 And Jacob took a stone, and set it up for a pillar.

48 And Laban said, This heap is a witness between me and thee this day. Therefore was the name of it called Galeed;

49 And Mizpah; for he said, The LORD watch between me and thee, when we are absent one from another.

6. <u>The provisions of the agreement must be spelled out in very exact and quantifiable terms.</u> If the line is not exactly specified, confusion and conflict can result from different interpretations of the agreement. As an example, if a time is included, the source of the time, such as a specific clock or international atomic time needs to be specified so that it is clear to both parties exactly when a violation of that time has occurred.

Ge 31:50 If thou shalt afflict my daughters, or if thou shalt take other wives beside my daughters, no man is with us; see, God is witness betwixt me and thee.

51 And Laban said to Jacob, Behold this heap, and behold this pillar, which I have cast betwixt me and thee;

52 This heap be witness, and this pillar be witness, that I will not pass over this heap to thee, and that thou shalt not pass over this heap and this pillar unto me, for harm.

7. <u>The punishment or consequences of any transgression must be specified in advance.</u> In this case, any violation could be appealed to Jacob's father Isaac, who was still alive.

Ge 31:53 The God of Abraham, and the God of Nahor, the God of their father, judge betwixt us. And Jacob sware by the fear of his father Isaac.

8. It is good to mark the agreement with a celebration as a sign of reconciliation. Although, in this case, we are not told that all the issues from the past were forgiven, the fact that they ate together strongly implies that they were reconciled. It is much easier to forgive the past when provisions have been made to avoid future repetition of the problems.

Ge 31:54 Then Jacob offered sacrifice upon the mount, and called his brethren to eat bread: and they did eat bread, and tarried all night in the mount.

55 And early in the morning Laban rose up, and kissed his sons and his daughters, and blessed them: and Laban departed, and returned unto his place.

9. Jesus, Himself, demonstrated the use of good boundaries when He dealt with Judas' betrayal.

   a. He identified the boundary line that was not to be violated. A disciple to whom Jesus had given three years of his life, friendship and training should not betray Him to His enemies.

      Lu 22:21 But, behold, the hand of him that betrayeth me is with me on the table.

      22 And truly the Son of man goeth, as it was determined: but woe unto that man by whom he is betrayed!

   b. Jesus let Judas know the consequences of betraying him would be catastrophic.

      Mt 26:24 The Son of man goeth as it is written of him: but woe unto that man by whom the Son of man is betrayed! it had been good for that man if he had not been born.

   c. Jesus tried one last time to reach out to Judas in love. As a sign of love and honor, Jesus gave Judas a piece of meat on a stick called a sop.

      Jo 13:25 He then lying on Jesus' breast saith unto him, Lord, who is it?

      26 Jesus answered, He it is, to whom I shall give a sop, when I have dipped it. And when he had dipped the sop, he gave it to Judas Iscariot, the son of Simon.

   d. Then Jesus challenged Judas to make up his mind and repent, or go ahead and violate the boundary that Jesus had set, and receive the horrible consequences. Unfortunately, Judas chose to violate the boundary. He later hanged himself.

      Jo 13:27 And after the sop Satan entered into him. Then said Jesus unto him, That thou doest, do quickly.

      28 Now no man at the table knew for what intent he spake this unto him.

      29 For some of them thought, because Judas had the bag, that Jesus had said unto him, Buy those things that we have need of against the feast; or, that he should give something to the poor.

      30 He then having received the sop went immediately out: and it was night.

      Mt 27:5 And he cast down the pieces of silver in the temple, and departed, and went and hanged himself.

10. <u>Covenants imply a personal relationship and union with the other party.</u> Therefore, we are not to make covenants with God's enemies or those involved with false gods or religions.

Ex 23:32 Thou shalt make no covenant with them, nor with their gods.

34:12 Take heed to thyself, lest thou make a covenant with the inhabitants of the land whither thou goest, lest it be for a snare in the midst of thee:

2 Co 6:14 Be ye not unequally yoked together with unbelievers: for what fellowship hath righteousness with unrighteousness? and what communion hath light with darkness?

11. <u>Covenants can be the basis of great blessing if they are followed or they can make it abundantly clear that intentional violations have occurred.</u>

De 8:18 But thou shalt remember the LORD thy God: for it is he that giveth thee power to get wealth, that he may establish his covenant which he sware unto thy fathers, as it is this day.

1 Ki 11:11 Wherefore the LORD said unto Solomon, Forasmuch as this is done of thee, and thou hast not kept my covenant and my statutes, which I have commanded thee, I will surely rend the kingdom from thee, and will give it to thy servant.

12. <u>Covenants can be used to cement powerful friendships.</u> When we make a personal covenant with another person, all that we have is made available to them if they need it and all that they have is available to us. What a wonderful revelation it is to realize that because of our covenant with God, all that He owns (everything) is ours if we need it. Of course, in return we are expected to be willing to sacrifice all that we have for Him.

1 Sa 23:18 And they two made a covenant before the LORD: and David abode in the wood, and Jonathan went to his house.

2 Ki 13:23 And the LORD was gracious unto them, and had compassion on them, and had respect unto them, because of his covenant with Abraham, Isaac, and Jacob, and would not destroy them, neither cast he them from his presence as yet.

13. <u>We can also make self-covenants or self-boundaries.</u> Covenants can be agreements with ourselves to do or refrain from specific things. Self-boundaries are critical for having peace in our lives.

Job 31:1 I made a covenant with mine eyes; why then should I think upon a maid?

14. <u>We need to be fully committed with all our heart to fulfilling our covenants, especially our covenant with God.</u>

2 Ki 23:3 And the king stood by a pillar, and made a covenant before the LORD, to walk after the LORD, and to keep his commandments and his testimonies and his statutes with all their heart and all their soul, to perform the words of this covenant that were written in this book. And all the people stood to the covenant.

2 Chr 15:12 And they entered into a covenant to seek the LORD God of their fathers with all their heart and with all their soul;

15. <u>Covenants are forever, so they are not to be taken lightly.</u>

1 Chr 16:15 Be ye mindful always of his covenant; the word which he commanded to a thousand generations;

16 Even of the covenant which he made with Abraham, and of his oath unto Isaac;

17 And hath confirmed the same to Jacob for a law, and to Israel for an everlasting covenant,

Jer 33:20 Thus saith the LORD; If ye can break my covenant of the day, and my covenant of the night, and that there should not be day and night in their season;

21 Then may also my covenant be broken with David my servant, that he should not have a son to reign upon his throne; and with the Levites the priests, my ministers.

Ps 89:34 My covenant will I not break, nor alter the thing that is gone out of my lips.

16. Because we humans failed to keep the old covenant (in the Old Testament), God replaced it with the new covenant (in the New Testament) in which He, through the Spirit, placed the laws of the covenant into our hearts through His Spirit and forgave all of our sins.

Heb 8:10 For this is the covenant that I will make with the house of Israel after those days, saith the Lord; I will put my laws into their mind, and write them in their hearts: and I will be to them a God, and they shall be to me a people:

Ro 11:27 For this is my covenant unto them, when I shall take away their sins.

17. Jesus, Himself, established the New Testament covenant with His disciples prior to His crucifixion. The "last supper" was the celebration of the new covenant meal. When we accept Him, we become one of His disciples.

Lu 22:17 And he took the cup, and gave thanks, and said, Take this, and divide it among yourselves:

18 For I say unto you, I will not drink of the fruit of the vine, until the kingdom of God shall come.

19 And he took bread, and gave thanks, and brake it, and gave unto them, saying, This is my body which is given for you: this do in remembrance of me.

20 Likewise also the cup after supper, saying, This cup is the new testament (or covenant) in my blood, which is shed for you.

18. Jesus is the mediator and guarantor of the new covenant. In the ancient world, it was the job of the witness of the covenant to enforce and punish any violations of the covenant. (Kenyon, 1969)

Heb 8:6 But now hath he obtained a more excellent ministry, by how much also he is the mediator of a better covenant, which was established upon better promises.

19. Because God established the new covenant through the death of Jesus and has made greater provision for us, if we chose to violate or ignore it, the punishment will be greater than under the old covenant.

Heb 10:29 Of how much sorer punishment, suppose ye, shall he be thought worthy, who hath trodden under foot the Son of God, and hath counted the blood of the covenant, wherewith he was sanctified, an unholy thing, and hath done despite unto the Spirit of grace?

Counseling Methods and Techniques

1. <u>We can teach boundaries using the illustration of a neighbor's dog chewing up our client's newspaper.</u> After describing a situation in which the neighbor's dog chewed up their newspaper, I ask the client what boundaries were violated. The answer is that the dog is in the client's yard and the dog was eating the newspaper that the client had paid for. Secondly, I ask what he would do about it? His answer shows whether he is passive, passive-aggressive, assertive, or aggressive. I use the client's answer to discuss what would be the likely outcome of his actions. I then explain the steps for establishing boundary agreements. The first step would be to let the neighbor know that the client does not want the neighbor's dog in the client's yard, eating the client's paper. It might even be necessary to establish where the physical boundary line is between their yards. I continue the illustration, asking what they would do if the next day the dog chews on his paper again? The answer is that he would have to let the neighbor know what consequences would occur if the problem continued. Possibly, the neighbor should either pay for the client's newspaper or exchange his good newspaper for the chewed up one. If he is not willing to agree to this, the client might warn his neighbor that if he refuses to restrain his dog, he will have to call animal control when he sees the dog loose and the neighbor will then have to pay a fine to get the dog back after it is taken to the pound. I then explain that boundaries attempt to align the one who makes the decision with the one who gets the consequences. In this case, he is offended because the neighbor has made the decision to not adequately confine his dog and the client is getting the consequences. If our neighbor robs a bank (decides to do something), we should not have to go to jail (get his consequences) for his crime.

2. <u>Mutual boundaries are the heart of any relationship recovery process.</u> They are especially useful in resolving marital conflict, family relationships, and codependency. The first step is the establishment of boundaries that are acceptable to all of the persons involved. When a marriage is based on win-win boundary agreements, most of the conflicts are easily resolved. When a family, including the older children, sets family rules; the children can only blame themselves if they get the agreed-upon consequences. In codependent relationships, it is the boundary agreements that help the people involved find the balance between being too dependent or too independent.

3. <u>Tripwires are needed in cases of extreme abuse.</u> The concept of tripwires suggests that we can have multiple sets of boundaries against angry behavior so that the behavior can be stopped at the earliest opportunity. For example, in a domestically violent family, if one person raises their voice, they may be required to leave the room for thirty minutes; if they cuss or verbally attack someone, they have to leave for a day; and if they throw, break something or threaten someone, they must leave for a week. The idea is to stop even the lower level behaviors before they are able to escalate into violence.

Chapter 11

Principles of Experience

Some of the most powerful influences in our lives are our past and present experiences. How we perceive these experiences affects every aspect of our heart, our future choices and our actions. Experiences are determined primarily by our actions, and our actions are determined by the dictates of our hearts. Our experiences affect what we are willing to do in the future, what we believe is true, how we perceive our environment, how desperate we are to fulfill our needs, whether we are dominated by our fears, how we act, and how we feel. It is important that we do not allow our past experiences to become the table of contents for our future actions.

The Principles of the Heart

In order to understand our heart, we must first understand how the Bible uses this term. Although we have previously discussed this issue in more general terms, here we need to investigate this somewhat confusing issue in more depth. In general, it refers to the center of our being. Although some authors have interpreted it to mean only our spirit, I believe when the Bible refers to the heart it can include our mind, will, emotions or spirit. The heart might also include our attitudes, needs, past experiences, desires and how we perceive things. Our heart initiates our actions and interprets our experiences. To understand more clearly how the Bible uses this term, let us investigate the meaning of the word heart in its original language.

The primary word for heart in the Greek is *kardia*. It means "The heart, that organ in the animal body which is the centre of the circulation of the blood, and hence was regarded as the seat of physical life. It denotes the centre of all physical and spiritual life, the vigour and sense of physical life, the centre and seat of spiritual life, the soul or mind, as it is the fountain and seat of the thoughts, passions, desires, appetites, affections, purposes, endeavours, of the understanding, the faculty and seat of the intelligence, of the will and character, of the soul so far as it is affected and stirred in a bad way or good, or of the soul as the seat of the sensibilities, affections, emotions, desires, appetites, and passions. It can also mean the middle or central or inmost part of anything, even though inanimate." In the Bible, the soul is also used to refer to the inner-man, the force of life or the self of the person. The mind usually refers to the understanding but can also include the emotions and will. The spirit is usually used as the vital principle of man but sometimes includes the soul, especially when it is no longer in the body. (Pierce, 1996)

Consequently, although each word, which describes a component of the heart, is used primarily to express a particular purpose, they are generally used inclusively, rather than exclusively, and what is meant must be derived from the context. Therefore, we are a person who lives in a body, who has a center of control called the heart, which consists of a soul, which is influenced by the desires of the self-life, which has a mind that includes a will and emotions, at the center of which there is a vital principle or spirit. Although this is possibly a more-accurate understanding of the usage of these words, especially when represented by concentric circles; yet it is difficult to discuss, since they are somewhat inclusive of one another, instead of exclusive. Consequently, for clarity in this book, I have followed a more exclusive use of these terms.

From this definition, we can see that the subject of the heart is an all encompassing one. It is, without any doubt, critical to the well being of every person and is the means by which we interpret our experiences. The heart provides the foundation for both our dysfunction and our healing and in fact, is the entire realm of psychology and mental health. It is also clear from this complex definition that the realms of the heart, soul, and spirit can overlap. Let us examine what the Bible actually has to teach about this very important subject.

1. <u>Our heart determines the outcome of our life.</u> In the following verses, we see that whether the heart referred to here is the entire heart, or just the mind; the truth is that our heart determines the outcome of our lives.

    Pr 4:23 Keep thy heart with all diligence; for out of it are the issues of life.

    23:7 For as he thinketh in his heart, so is he: Eat and drink, saith he to thee; but his heart is not with thee.

2. <u>Our heart can be united or fragmented.</u> If our will, mind, emotions, and spirit are not in agreement, the conflict between them can be debilitating; and the struggle will continue until they are united.

    Ps 86:11 Teach me thy way, O LORD; I will walk in thy truth: unite my heart to fear thy name.

    Hos 10:2 Their heart is divided; now shall they be found faulty: he shall break down their altars, he shall spoil their images.

3. <u>The overall condition of our heart can influence our spirit.</u>

    Pr 15:13 A merry heart maketh a cheerful countenance: but by sorrow of the heart the spirit is broken.

    17:22 A merry heart doeth good like a medicine: but a broken spirit drieth the bones.

4. <u>God commands us to love Him and others with all of our heart.</u> These verses make it abundantly clear that no matter how we choose to translate the words, God means all aspects of our heart: mind, soul, spirit, and being.

    Mt 22:37 Jesus said unto him, Thou shalt love the Lord thy God with all thy heart, and with all thy soul, and with all thy mind.

    Mr 12:30 And thou shalt love the Lord thy God with all thy heart, and with all thy soul, and with all thy mind, and with all thy strength: this is the first commandment.

5. <u>A pure heart is necessary for a close relationship with God.</u>

    Mt 5:8 Blessed are the pure in heart: for they shall see God.

6. <u>Faith is a matter of the heart.</u>

    Mr 11:23 For verily I say unto you, That whosoever shall say unto this mountain, Be thou removed, and be thou cast into the sea; and shall not doubt in his heart, but shall believe that those things which he saith shall come to pass; he shall have whatsoever he saith.

7. <u>We must believe with all of our heart to be saved.</u>

    Ac 8:37 And Philip said, If thou believest with all thine heart, thou mayest. And he answered and said, I believe that Jesus Christ is the Son of God.

    Ro 10:8 But what saith it? The word is nigh thee, even in thy mouth, and in thy heart: that is, the word of faith, which we preach;

    9 That if thou shalt confess with thy mouth the Lord Jesus, and shalt believe in thine heart that God hath raised him from the dead, thou shalt be saved.

    10 For with the heart man believeth unto righteousness; and with the mouth confession is made unto salvation.

8. <u>To be a man after God's heart means to want what God wants, to see things the way He does, and to desire to do His will.</u> I remember a Bible teacher once saying that the ultimate in God was to never have to do anything we did not want to do—because we always want to do what God wants us to do.

    1 Sa 13:14 But now thy kingdom shall not continue: the LORD hath sought him a man after his own heart, and the LORD hath commanded him to be captain over his people, because thou hast not kept that which the LORD commanded thee.

    Ac 13:22 And when he had removed him, he raised up unto them David to be their king; to whom also he gave testimony, and said, I have found David the son of Jesse, a man after mine own heart, which shall fulfill all my will.

9. <u>We can choose to establish our hearts in a given fixed direction.</u> When we do, it will provide a basis for how we interpret our experiences.

    Ps 57:7 My heart is fixed, O God, my heart is fixed: I will sing and give praise.

    62:10 Trust not in oppression, and become not vain in robbery: if riches increase, set not your heart upon them.

    4:7 Thou hast put gladness in my heart, more than in the time that their corn and their wine increased.

10. <u>We can backslide in our hearts.</u>

    Pr 14:14 The backslider in heart shall be filled with his own ways: and a good man shall be satisfied from himself.

11. <u>Satan can attempt to fill our heart with lies.</u> If we believe those lies, it can result in sin.

    Ac 5:3 But Peter said, Ananias, why hath Satan filled thine heart to lie to the Holy Ghost, and to keep back part of the price of the land?

12. <u>If we wait on God, He can give us courage and strength in our heart.</u>

    Ps 27:14 Wait on the LORD: be of good courage, and he shall strengthen thine heart: wait, I say, on the LORD.

    31:24 Be of good courage, and he shall strengthen your heart, all ye that hope in the LORD.

13. <u>A person with a good heart is the soil in which the Word of God can flourish.</u>

Lu 8:15 But that on the good ground are they, which in an honest and good heart, having heard the word, keep it, and bring forth fruit with patience.

Counseling Methods and Techniques

1. <u>The train of psychological wholeness provides a basic understanding of the heart.</u> As I have already explained, each function of our heart interacts with the other functions. Therefore, if we wish to change one component, we can influence it by changing the others that interact with that component of the train.

2. <u>The heart can be analyzed using layer caking.</u> How we interpret our experiences and our resulting emotions is not based on how we originally perceive an event, but on a string of perceptions—what we think about it, what we have concluded about our previous evaluation of the event, and what we now believe about our most recent conclusion. For example, a wife may conclude from her husband's statement at dinner that the "peas are cold and pulpy" to mean that he does not like her peas, which means that he does not like her cooking, which means that he does not like her, which means that he does not love her, which means she is worthless." Although this example might seem somewhat excessive, our emotional reactions are generally based on our last conclusion in the layer cake. Asking the client how he perceives the event, what this perception means to him and how it affects him, eventually leads to significant conclusions concerning how he views himself and his basic needs. (See my book *Faith Therapy* for a more detailed explanation.)

3. <u>We can unite our heart by finding agreement between our will, mind, emotions, and spirit.</u> A united heart is not easily shaken.

The Principles of the Defenses of the Heart

In psychology, the defenses of the heart are called "ego defenses." They are simply our conscious and unconscious attempts to defend our heart from being hurt in some way. Morris (1973, page 499) lists them as follows:

1. Denial—not acknowledging threat, pain or hurt.

2. Displacement—shifting the blame, that cannot be expressed, to another person

3. Identification—taking on another's characteristics to avoid discomfort.

4. Intellectualism—abstracting stressful situations in order to distance emotionally.

5. Projection—transferring one's own repressed motive, feelings, and wishes to others.

6. Reaction formation—expressing exaggerated ideas or emotions that are the opposite of one's repressed beliefs, feelings, or actions.

7. Regression—reverting to childlike behavior as a defense.

8. Repression—excluding hurtful thoughts from consciousness.

9. Sublimation—re-directing repressed motives and feelings to more acceptable pursuits.

Although the Bible does not specifically address each one of these, it does warn us that our heart can be deceptive and devious as it tries to defend itself.

1. <u>Our heart can easily deceive us and is difficult to analyze.</u> Because we have a vested interest to convince ourselves we are right and true in all we do and to protect ourselves emotionally, we tend to deceive ourselves.

   Jer 17:9 The heart is deceitful above all things, and desperately wicked: who can know it?

   10 I the LORD search the heart, I try the reins, even to give every man according to his ways, and according to the fruit of his doings.

   Pr 21:2 Every way of a man is right in his own eyes: but the LORD pondereth the hearts.

2. <u>We can evaluate the condition of our heart by what comes out of it.</u>

   Mt 12:34 O generation of vipers, how can ye, being evil, speak good things? for out of the abundance of the heart the mouth speaketh.

   35 A good man out of the good treasure of the heart bringeth forth good things: and an evil man out of the evil treasure bringeth forth evil things.

3. <u>The defenses of our heart are motivated by self-protection and unbelief.</u>

   Heb 3:10 Wherefore I was grieved with that generation, and said, They do alway err in their heart; and they have not known my ways.

   12 Take heed, brethren, lest there be in any of you an evil heart of unbelief, in departing from the living God.

4. <u>We can harden our hearts by refusing to trust and follow God's directions for our lives.</u>

   Ps 95:8 Harden not your heart, as in the provocation, and as in the day of temptation in the wilderness:

   Ac 7:51 Ye stiffnecked and uncircumcised in heart and ears, ye do always resist the Holy Ghost: as your fathers did, so do ye.

5. <u>God will try our heart to help us see what is really in it.</u>

   Ps 17:3 Thou hast proved mine heart; thou hast visited me in the night; thou hast tried me, and shalt find nothing; I am purposed that my mouth shall not transgress.

   44:21 Shall not God search this out? for he knoweth the secrets of the heart.

   139:23 Search me, O God, and know my heart: try me, and know my thoughts:

6. <u>God will help us deal with and purify our hearts.</u>

   Ps 51:10 Create in me a clean heart, O God; and renew a right spirit within me.

   61:2 From the end of the earth will I cry unto thee, when my heart is overwhelmed: lead me to the rock that is higher than I.

   119:32 I will run the way of thy commandments, when thou shalt enlarge my heart.

7. <u>The Word of God can help us determine our thoughts and intents as well as the difference between what originates from our soul or our spirit.</u>

Heb 4:12 For the word of God is quick, and powerful, and sharper than any twoedged sword, piercing even to the dividing asunder of soul and spirit, and of the joints and marrow, and is a discerner of the thoughts and intents of the heart.

8. <u>Through the gifts of the Spirit, the heart can be made manifest or clearly understood.</u>

1 Co 14:25 And thus are the secrets of his heart made manifest; and so falling down on his face he will worship God, and report that God is in you of a truth.

Counseling Methods and Techniques

1. <u>We can overcome the defenses of the heart through faith.</u> When hurt, our heart will defend itself from further hurt. Sometimes these defenses become more of a problem than the original trauma. Psychological defenses are developed in response to fear. Our fears can be overcome through faith in God.

2. <u>We can analyze the heart by observing its defenses.</u> If a person is wearing a full suit of bullet-proof body armor or driving around in a tank, we can be pretty sure he is afraid of someone shooting at him. In the same way, if someone is using one of the ego defenses just discussed, we can be reasonably sure that he is afraid of something.

3. <u>We can soften our hard heart by "eroding" it with the Word of God.</u> In the parable of the sower, it was not the quality of the seed, but the quality of the ground (the heart) that determined how much the plants produced. (Luke 8:5-15) When we study, memorize and meditate on the Word of God, we renew our minds and soften our hearts, so that they can become productive in the things of God.

The Principles of Experience

Our past and present experiences can and do greatly affect our future decisions and how we view ourselves. Dealing with these past experiences is many times critical in the process of recovery. We react strongly in the present, based on the experiences of the past even when in our minds we know that the situations are not the same. How we have perceived our past experiences affects the feelings associated with them. It is these feelings, when they are brought into the present, that make the current situation excessively emotionally charged and our reactions inappropriate for the situation. This is especially the case when a person has been badly abused or suffered severe trauma.

1. <u>We can gain in wisdom and knowledge from our experiences.</u> We can use our past experiences to make better decisions in the future. Even things that have happened to other people in the past are examples for us to learn from and should be used to make us wiser.

Ec 1:16 I communed with mine own heart, saying, Lo, I am come to great estate, and have gotten more wisdom than all they that have been before me in Jerusalem: yea, my heart had great experience of wisdom and knowledge.

1 Co 10:11 Now all these things happened unto them for ensamples: and they are written for our admonition, upon whom the ends of the world are come.

2. <u>Even our bad experiences can help us develop our character and build a hope for the future, especially if we have learned to trust God through those experiences.</u>

Ro 5:3 And not only so, but we glory in tribulations also: knowing that tribulation worketh patience;

4 And patience, experience; and experience, hope:

5 And hope maketh not ashamed; because the love of God is shed abroad in our hearts by the Holy Ghost which is given unto us.

3. <u>Without God, we are at the mercy of chance or fate.</u> In the world without God, we are on our own and every day is simply left to chance.

Ec 9:11 I returned, and saw under the sun, that the race is not to the swift, nor the battle to the strong, neither yet bread to the wise, nor yet riches to men of understanding, nor yet favour to men of skill; but time and chance happeneth to them all.

4. <u>We cannot predict the future, and it is even difficult to correctly interpret the past.</u>

Isa 41:22 Let them bring them forth, and shew us what shall happen: let them shew the former things, what they be, that we may consider them, and know the latter end of them; or declare us things for to come.

5. <u>Our misinterpretation or confusion about the past can make us feel sad and disheartened with life.</u>

Lu 24:14 And they talked together of all these things which had happened.

17 And he said unto them, What manner of communications are these that ye have one to another, as ye walk, and are sad?

18 And the one of them, whose name was Cleopas, answering said unto him, Art thou only a stranger in Jerusalem, and hast not known the things which are come to pass there in these days?

19 And he said unto them, What things? And they said unto him, Concerning Jesus of Nazareth, which was a prophet mighty in deed and word before God and all the people:

20 And how the chief priests and our rulers delivered him to be condemned to death, and have crucified him.

6. <u>When we perceive things from God's perspective and understand His plans for us, our entire viewpoint can change.</u>

Lu 24:25 Then he said unto them, O fools, and slow of heart to believe all that the prophets have spoken:

26 Ought not Christ to have suffered these things, and to enter into his glory?

2 Ki 6:17 And Elisha prayed, and said, LORD, I pray thee, open his eyes, that he may see. And the LORD opened the eyes of the young man; and he saw: and, behold, the mountain was full of horses and chariots of fire round about Elisha.

Isa 55:8 For my thoughts are not your thoughts, neither are your ways my ways, saith the LORD.

9 For as the heavens are higher than the earth, so are my ways higher than your ways, and my thoughts than your thoughts.

7. <u>Nothing truly evil happens to us as long as we are living under the protection of God and obeying His direction.</u> This is the entire theme of the classic book *A Christian's Secret of a Happy Life* (1983) by Hannah Whitall Smith.

    Pr 12:21 There shall no evil happen to the just: but the wicked shall be filled with mischief.

    Ro 8:28 And we know that all things work together for good to them that love God, to them who are the called according to his purpose.

    35 Who shall separate us from the love of Christ? shall tribulation, or distress, or persecution, or famine, or nakedness, or peril, or sword?

    37 Nay, in all these things we are more than conquerors through him that loved us.

8. <u>However, when things happen, we do not always perceive them as good or understand how God will use them for our good in the future.</u> In these situations, we are simply to trust God to do what He has promised—to work everything for our good.

    Php 1:12 But I would ye should understand, brethren, that the things which happened unto me have fallen out rather unto the furtherance of the gospel;

    1 Pe 4:12 Beloved, think it not strange concerning the fiery trial which is to try you, as though some strange thing happened unto you:

    13 But rejoice, inasmuch as ye are partakers of Christ's sufferings; that, when his glory shall be revealed, ye may be glad also with exceeding joy.

    14 If ye be reproached for the name of Christ, happy are ye; for the spirit of glory and of God resteth upon you: on their part he is evil spoken of, but on your part he is glorified.

9. <u>What we are today is a combination of what we have been, the experiences that we have had, and what we have learned from them.</u>

    Mt 13:52 Then said he unto them, Therefore every scribe which is instructed unto the kingdom of heaven is like unto a man that is an householder, which bringeth forth out of his treasure things new and old.

10. <u>God will forgive our sins so that we can go forward in life.</u> He is more interested in what we will become than what we have been or done in the past. When we are saved, we are born again of the Spirit of God and have the power of His Spirit available, so that we can change and overcome our past.

    Isa 38:17 Behold, for peace I had great bitterness: but thou hast in love to my soul delivered it from the pit of corruption: for thou hast cast all my sins behind thy back.

    2 Co 5:17 Therefore if any man be in Christ, he is a new creature: old things are passed away; behold, all things are become new.

Counseling Methods and Techniques

1. <u>We can heal our past with Theophostic Ministry.</u> Theophostic Ministry is based on the fact that it is not the event, but our perception of the experience that determines our feelings associated with the event. Not only are children good recorders and poor interpreters of experiences, but most of the time they have failed to see or recognize God in their experiences. Theophostic Ministry, originated by Dr. Ed Smith in his book *Beyond Tolerable Recovery* (1996), attempts to change the perceptions and, consequently, the emotions connected to an experience by asking the Holy Spirit to reveal the truth

concerning it. Because the most effective way to change an experience is with another experience, we must go back into the memory of the experience, identify the lies we believed about it, and let the Holy Spirit reveal the truth as He sees fit. Although some have concerns with the imagery involved, in our experience, the presence of the Holy Spirit is truly involved and traumatic memories can be healed and filled with the peace that only God can bring.

2. <u>We can change our perceptions of our past and present events by reframing them.</u> Reframing means looking at them and perceiving their meaning differently. As examples, a child acting out can be seen as a child trying to keep his parents from fighting; and marriage conflicts can be seen as attachment alarms and a desperate cry for love. Since our emotions, including our anger, are primarily controlled by how we perceive our experiences, this is a powerful tool for change. One of the most powerful reframes of all is seeing our experiences from God's standpoint of eternity.

3. <u>We can process our past using Monday Morning Quarterbacking (MMQ).</u> In order to deal with past hurts and prepare the way for forgiveness and possible reconciliation, I use the analogy of what has been called Monday Morning Quarterbacking. When a team loses the Sunday night football game, they will meet on Monday to try to determine what needs to be done to ensure that they will win the next game. They replay the videotapes of the game in an attempt to learn from their mistakes, to develop new plays for the next game, and to rebuild team unity. Therefore, no one is allowed to make accusations or try to place blame for the mistakes that have been made. In this way, no one will be defensive and arguments can be avoided. Everyone will be open and honest about what really happened, how they saw things at the time, and what mistakes they made. I apply these same rules in the counseling setting. In doing so, we try to discover what the real issues are that created the past negative experiences and develop plans to insure that they do not re-occur. I have found that it is much easier for clients to forgive when they have a reasonable reassurance that what happened in the past will not happen again in the future.

The Principles of Relationships

Most of our important experiences in life involve relationships. God wants to have a personal relationship with us. People need healthy relationships in order to enjoy life. Relationships offer one of the greatest areas of potential for healthy change. They are also the source of most of our emotional pain. Healthy people can edify and strengthen others. Hurting people tend to take out their emotional pain on others. Marriages and friendships can be heaven on earth or hell on earth. Relationship problems are the subject of a large majority of counseling sessions. Whole areas of counseling such as marriage and family counseling, abuse recovery, domestic violence, and codependency focus on relationship problems.

1. <u>God wants to have a personal relationship with us.</u> Building such a relationship takes faith and time with God. This is a wonderful opportunity to develop relationship skills with someone Who knows everything, understands us perfectly, and loves us completely as we are.

   Isa 41:8 But thou, Israel, art my servant, Jacob whom I have chosen, the seed of Abraham my friend.

   Jas 2:23 And the scripture was fulfilled which saith, Abraham believed God, and it was imputed unto him for righteousness: and he was called the Friend of God.

2. <u>God wants us to seek a relationship with Him with all of our hearts.</u>

   De 4:29 But if from thence thou shalt seek the LORD thy God, thou shalt find him, if thou seek him with all thy heart and with all thy soul.

   Jer 29:13 And ye shall seek me, and find me, when ye shall search for me with all your heart.

3. <u>Friends are those who have our best interests in mind and show it by their actions.</u>

Pr 18:24 A man that hath friends must shew himself friendly: and there is a friend that sticketh closer than a brother.

Lu 15:6 And when he cometh home, he calleth together his friends and neighbours, saying unto them, Rejoice with me; for I have found my sheep which was lost.

Pr 27:17 Iron sharpeneth iron; so a man sharpeneth the countenance of his friend.

4. <u>Building friendships or relationships takes time, communication and sacrifice.</u>

Jo 15:13 Greater love hath no man than this, that a man lay down his life for his friends.

14 Ye are my friends, if ye do whatsoever I command you.

15 Henceforth I call you not servants; for the servant knoweth not what his lord doeth: but I have called you friends; for all things that I have heard of my Father I have made known unto you.

5. <u>When someone does not have our best interests in mind, we see them as enemies.</u>

La 1:2 She weepeth sore in the night, and her tears are on her cheeks: among all her lovers she hath none to comfort her: all her friends have dealt treacherously with her, they are become her enemies.

Jas 4:4 Ye adulterers and adulteresses, know ye not that the friendship of the world is enmity with God? whosoever therefore will be a friend of the world is the enemy of God.

Php 3:18 (For many walk, of whom I have told you often, and now tell you even weeping, that they are the enemies of the cross of Christ:

6. <u>Even though it is hard, God wants us to even love and do good to our enemies.</u> If we please God in this way, He can even make our enemies be at peace with us.

Pr 25:21 If thine enemy be hungry, give him bread to eat; and if he be thirsty, give him water to drink:

Mt 5:44 But I say unto you, Love your enemies, bless them that curse you, do good to them that hate you, and pray for them which despitefully use you, and persecute you;

Pr 16:7 When a man's ways please the LORD, he maketh even his enemies to be at peace with him.

7. <u>God desires that we all come into unity and love for each other in the same way that God loves us.</u>

Jo 13:34 A new commandment I give unto you, That ye love one another; as I have loved you, that ye also love one another.

17:21 That they all may be one; as thou, Father, art in me, and I in thee, that they also may be one in us: that the world may believe that thou hast sent me.

22 And the glory which thou gavest me I have given them; that they may be one, even as we are one:

23 I in them, and thou in me, that they may be made perfect in one; and that the world may know that thou hast sent me, and hast loved them, as thou hast loved me.

8. <u>In marriage, the closest of relationships, we are to become one flesh, not one identity.</u> Becoming one identity, or losing one's identity in a relationship with another, is a characteristic of codependency.

    Mt 19:5 And said, For this cause shall a man leave father and mother, and shall cleave to his wife: and they twain shall be one flesh?

9. <u>The ultimate healthy relationship is modeled by the Trinity.</u> The Father, Son and Holy Ghost have separate identities, yet they cooperate and work together in perfect unity. In marriage, the husband, wife, and God are to form a team similar to that of the Trinity. God's job in this relationship is to meet the needs in the marriage that the mate cannot or will not meet.

    1 Jo 5:7 For there are three that bear record in heaven, the Father, the Word, and the Holy Ghost: and these three are one.

    Mt 3:16 And Jesus, when he was baptized, went up straightway out of the water: and, lo, the heavens were opened unto him, and he saw the Spirit of God descending like a dove, and lighting upon him:

    17 And lo a voice from heaven, saying, This is my beloved Son, in whom I am well pleased.

10. <u>The wife is to cooperate with the husband's leadership as if she was submitting to Christ Himself, as long as he submits to the direction of God.</u> This is known as spiritual authority. The wife is not obligated to follow directions from her husband that violate the commands of his higher authority, God.

    Eph 5:21 Submitting yourselves one to another in the fear of God.

    22 Wives, submit yourselves unto your own husbands, as unto the Lord.

11. <u>The husband is to be responsible to ensure that his wife and children reach their fullest potential, just as Christ was responsible for the development of the church.</u>

    Eph 5:23 For the husband is the head of the wife, even as Christ is the head of the church: and he is the saviour of the body.

    24 Therefore as the church is subject unto Christ, so let the wives be to their own husbands in every thing.

12. <u>Husbands are to love their wives and be willing to sacrifice and die for them if necessary.</u>

    Eph 5:25 Husbands, love your wives, even as Christ also loved the church, and gave himself for it;

13. <u>They are to ensure that the family is sanctified through training in the Word of God.</u>

    Eph 5:26 That he might sanctify and cleanse it with the washing of water by the word,

    27 That he might present it to himself a glorious church, not having spot, or wrinkle, or any such thing; but that it should be holy and without blemish.

14. <u>Men should have the best interests of the family in mind at least as much as they look out for themselves.</u>

    Eph 5:28 So ought men to love their wives as their own bodies. He that loveth his wife loveth himself.

    29 For no man ever yet hated his own flesh; but nourisheth and cherisheth it, even as the Lord the church:

15. <u>Families are to have good boundaries that will protect them from the detrimental influences of relatives and friends, so that they can form a strong team.</u>

    Eph 5:31 For this cause shall a man leave his father and mother, and shall be joined unto his wife, and they two shall be one flesh.

    32 This is a great mystery: but I speak concerning Christ and the church.

16. <u>Men are to love their wives as much as they love themselves; and women are to honor, respect, and appreciate their husbands.</u> This is the theme of the new book, *Love and Respect* (2004), by Eggerichs.

    Eph 5:33 Nevertheless let every one of you in particular so love his wife even as himself; and the wife see that she reverence her husband.

17. <u>Children are to obey and honor their parents, since a good relationship with their parents is a key to a successful life.</u> Numerous problems in later years result from unresolved conflicts with our parents.

    Eph 6:1 Children, obey your parents in the Lord: for this is right.

    2 Honour thy father and mother; (which is the first commandment with promise;)

    3 That it may be well with thee, and thou mayest live long on the earth.

18. <u>Fathers need to be careful to control their anger, to effectively discipline, and to teach their children about God.</u>

    Eph 6:4 And, ye fathers, provoke not your children to wrath: but bring them up in the nurture and admonition of the Lord.

19. <u>Marriage is a permanent institution of God and is not to be broken except in situations where one mate is involved in ongoing fornication or adultery, or if an unbelieving mate chooses to divorce the believer.</u>

    Mt 19:9 And I say unto you, Whosoever shall put away his wife, except [it be] for fornication, and shall marry another, committeth adultery: and whoso marrieth her which is put away doth commit adultery.

    1 Co 7:10. And unto the married I command, [yet] not I, but the Lord, Let not the wife depart from [her] husband:

    11 But and if she depart, let her remain unmarried, or be reconciled to her husband: and let not the husband put away his wife.

15 But if the unbelieving depart, let him depart. A brother or a sister is not under bondage in such [cases]: but God hath called us to peace.

20. <u>After a divorce, remarriage is permitted only when the divorce was based on biblical grounds, or the divorced spouse has died or remarried.</u> Otherwise, by remarrying, the couple is committing adultery. God wants everyone to do everything possible to reconcile because He knows the damage and the emotional pain of divorce. A spouse is free to remarry if their previous spouse dies, remarries or has sex with someone else, because by doing so that spouse has committed adultery. Consequently, the grounds for a biblical divorce have been fulfilled.

Mt 5:32 But I say unto you, That whosoever shall put away his wife, saving for the cause of fornication, causeth her to commit adultery: and whosoever shall marry her that is divorced committeth adultery.

Counseling Methods and Techniques

1. <u>We can do a quick relationship analysis with four questions.</u> The first question I ask is, "Does the spouse believe that the other person has their best interest in mind?" This question determines whether they perceive their spouse's actions as being for them or against them. If they believe that the other is for them, they will act as friends and if they believe they are against them, they will act like enemies. Secondly, I ask if the wife feels that she is loved. This question has more to do with emotional support and affection, than actions. A woman will do almost anything for a man if she feels loved. I ask the husband if he feels respected and appreciated. A man will do almost anything for a woman if he feels respected and appreciated. (This difference in questions for the husband and wife reflects Ephesians Chapter 5.) Finally, I ask them to rate their marriage and their "love life" or sexual relationship on a scale from 1 (the worst marriage or sexual relationship they know) to 10 (the best marriage or sexual relationship they know). I particularly ask the question about the physical relationship, because this area many times mirrors other problems in the relationship or deep unresolved issues. At other times, their physical relationship may be the strongest part of the marriage.

2. <u>We can evaluate intimacy using the five types of love.</u> Conducting an intimacy analysis is very useful in helping a person investigate his or her love relationship. Because the word love in the English language can mean anything from having a taste for ice cream to a sexual relationship, we must clarify exactly how love is defined. Many times one spouse will say that they love their spouse but they are not "in love" with them. This usually means that they have lost the romantic feeling of love for the spouse. I use five biblical Greek or Hebrew words and their English counterparts to evaluate the levels of intimacy experienced by the couple. I ask the clients to rate on a scale of one to ten how strong each type of love is in their relationship.

   a. **Agape** (Biblical Greek) which is the unconditional **commitment** in the relationship. This may or may not include strong feelings of caring. This is "having the other's best interest in mind."

   b. **Phileo** (Biblical Greek) which is the friendship or **companionship** in the relationship. This usually reflects whether they are friends and like to spend time and do things together.

   c. **Eros** (Greek) which is the **romantic love** in the relationship. These are the connection or feelings of affection, excitement, and pleasure expressed in the relationship.

   d. **Theleo** (Greek) which is spiritual love including **beliefs, goals, and worldview.** This question tells me how united the couple is in their vision and direction for life.

e. **Yada`** (Hebrew) which means "to know" or have physical love with someone. Because men and women are so different in this area, many conflicts from other areas of their relationship are manifested in the couple's "**love life**."

3. <u>Use intersecting circles to diagram healthy and unhealthy relationships.</u> In order to explain what dysfunctional and ideal relationships or marriages looks like, I use circles to represent each of the persons involved. In marriage, we are not to become one identity or two circles on top of each other (codependent dependence) or two separate circles where there is not relationship (codependent independence). Not even the two intersecting circles that describes a healthy worldly relationship are ultimate, but three intersecting circles identical to the Trinity which consist of ourselves, our spouses, and God. I point out that these circles represent seven different relationships that must remain sound to have a healthy marriage. These relationships consist of: 1. How I relate to myself. 2. How my spouse relates to herself. 3. The Trinity. 4. Our marriage. 5. My relationship with God. 6. My spouse's relationship with God. 7. Our joint relationship with God. God's place in the marriage is to direct it and to meet the needs that our mate cannot meet or fails to meet.

4. <u>The blood covenant of marriage emphasizes the seriousness of marriage.</u> Because marriage is taken so lightly in our society, I show clients that marriages are blood covenants, the most binding and irrevocable type of agreement on earth. I usually start by telling them the story of Stanley's search for Dr. Livingstone told in *The Blood Covenant* by Kenyon (1969). The blood covenant at that time required the shedding of blood, the drinking of wine, curses or oaths before God, gifts and a witness. I show them that God made a covenant with Noah, Abraham, Israel, and us. In fact, the division of the Bible, between the Old and New Testament, is really the old and new blood covenant. Jesus clearly stated that the last supper was a covenant supper and that the blood He was to shed was the blood of the new covenant of salvation that He made with us. I then show them that their marriage vows were the oath, the rings they exchanged were the gifts, the grape juice they drank was the wine of the covenant and when the woman's hymen was broken as they consummated the marriage, the blood was shed. The final point I make is that it was the witness' job to insure that the vows of the covenant were kept and to punish any violation of the covenant. I then have them turn to the book of Malachi and read Malachi 2:14. "Yet ye say, Wherefore? Because the <u>LORD hath been witness</u> between thee and the wife of thy youth, against whom thou hast dealt treacherously: yet is she thy companion, and the <u>wife of thy covenant.</u>" It is, therefore, clearly God's job to punish any violation of our marriage vows. In ancient days, the penalty for violation of a blood covenant was death.

5. <u>We can use analogies to emphasize the need for teamwork.</u> I try to get those in any relationship to realize that it is in all of their interests to work together as a team instead of competing or attacking each other. I use three analogies.

   a. <u>The football team analogy.</u> If they seem to be competing and not working together in their marriage, I suggest that it is like they are on a football team; and they have just lost the last game because they have been tackling each other and have been helping the other team. I ask what they would do if they were on such a team? The answer, of course, is that they need to quit competing and make some plans of how they can work together to win the game. I suggest that mutual boundary agreements are like plays, and their marriage agreement is like their team contract. They are committed until the end of the season (life) so they might as well start working together to win the Super Bowl.

   b. <u>The sinking ship analogy.</u> If the couple is in a major power struggle or a "love fight," I suggest that it is like they are on a sinking ship. They are complaining that the other is not bailing water fast enough while they are drilling holes in the bottom of the boat. If they do not start working together as a crew, they are both going to drown; and their entire family is going down with them!

c. <u>The rats in the cage analogy.</u> If they are constantly verbally attacking each other, I suggest they are just like two rats in a cage. The cage is outfitted with an electric shock pad on the bottom that can be turned off if one of the rats pushes a button. The experimenter has turned off the button so that no matter how hard they try they cannot stop the shocks. I ask them what they think the rats did in actual experiments? The answer is that the rats attacked each other! This analogy is like some marriages. In a marriage, they expect that their mate will at least attempt to shield them from the problems or shocks of life. They are okay as long as they are able to cope effectively with the stress in their lives, but when they are no longer able to stop the shocks, the clients, just like the rats, are attacking each other. Problems, circumstances and possibly Satan have conspired to try to split up their marriage and make them fight each other. So far, Satan seems to be winning. At least one rat could climb on the back of the other and they could take turns so only one would be shocked at a time, or they could try to work together to escape from the cage at the next feeding. Attacking each other makes no sense and gains nothing.

6. <u>We can use tennis as an example of healthy relationships.</u> When discussing how to build a healthy relationship, especially with somebody who is codependent, I will say that "you must learn to play tennis." The analogy is this. In a healthy relationship, one person initiates and waits for the other to respond. If the other chooses not to respond, they go on their way and may try again another day. Because a codependent is so desperate for a relationship, they will keep initiating until they drive the other person away. It is almost as if they are a tennis serving machine, and the other person thinks they are "shooting" tennis balls at them. Trying to demand attention or manipulate someone into a relationship never works for long.

7. <u>A chariot race analogy can teach healthy dating relationships.</u> The goal of this chariot race is to keep all of the horses abreast of each other and to have both chariots finish the race together. Each chariot has five horses representing the five types of love discussed above. If some of the horses, pulling one of the chariots, get way ahead of the others, the chariot will be upset. For example, if physical love gets way ahead of commitment, as is sometimes the case, the woman may feel used; or if spiritual love gets way ahead of romantic love, the relationship will feel dry. Of course, it is also a problem if one member of the dating couple gets way ahead of the other and is ready to marry, while the other is still not ready to commit to the relationship. The point is that any horses that are getting ahead need to be reigned in until the remaining horses can get caught up, or an unbalanced, unstable relationship will develop. Solid relationships take time and require a foundation in all five areas of intimacy.

8. <u>God expects us to be under submission to His spiritual authority.</u> This means we ultimately work for Him, but we do so by cooperating with those He has set over us. This is analogous to the situation in the United States Armed Forces where a senior master sergeant salutes and works for the brand new second lieutenant, not because he believes the new lieutenant knows more; but because he respects the authority of those above him; and ultimately he works for his country. He also feels protected since he is not expected to follow his superior's orders if they violate the directions of those having authority above them. As an example, a wife can more easily follow her husband, even if she disagrees with him, knowing that she is following and serving Christ. This submission is much easier when she understands that she is not expected to follow any directions that violate either God's specific direction or the Bible. This is called spiritual authority. (For more information read *Spiritual Authority* (1972) by Watchman Nee.)

9. <u>All marriage problems can be eventually resolved using consistent, effective boundaries.</u> Because of the strict biblical limits on divorce and remarriage, sometimes one of the members of a difficult marriage may feel trapped; but there is an effective way out. Especially in marriages where one spouse is saved and has not committed adultery, yet still is abusive or addicted, the other spouse might feel they have no choice but to violate biblical principles and divorce. In my experience, this is not

ever necessary. Although the Bible does not recommend separation, it is sometimes necessary when abuse or addictions are involved. If the non-offending spouses will choose to deal with their own problems, get healthy themselves, and learn to set effective boundaries, eventually their spouses will either have to deal with their own problems, will crash and have to get help, or will divorce them to marry somebody else. According to biblical principles, if the offending spouse remarries, they have committed adultery, thus providing the grounds for a biblical divorce. In this case, the spouse is free. In my own experience, this type of resolution has occurred in every case, but sometimes, it has taken as long as two years to complete. The length of time involved is usually dependent on how long it takes the non-offending spouse to recover themselves and start exercising loving, healthy boundaries.

10. <u>A decrease in sexual intimacy may result from the "cycle of sexuality."</u> A significant decrease or the cessation of sexual intimacy is not uncommon in many marriages. Although many factors may be involved, this problem is many times due to what I call the "cycle of sex." Women and men function sexually as mirror images. Women need affection and emotional support in order to feel sexual, while men need sex to feel affectionate and emotionally supporting. Consequently, if a man becomes busy and does not give his wife affection or emotional support, over a period of time she will not be as interested in sex and the frequency of love making will decrease. Because he has not been sexual, he will not feel as affectionate and emotionally supportive, etc. and the sexual relationship will wind down. Of course, the opposite is true. If he will again become affectionate, she will feel more sexually responsive; he will receive more sexual intimacy and will, therefore, feel more affectionate toward his wife, etc.

11. <u>Men build relationships primarily by working together.</u> Consequently, while women tend to use communication, songs, and worship to develop their relationship with God, men can develop intimacy with God by working for and with Him. The book *Experiencing God* (1990) provides principles for building a strong relationship with God through action. Whatever works in human relationships also works in building relationships with God and what works in building a relationship with God also works with people.

12. <u>Feelings depend on our perceptions of how others meet our needs.</u> Dr. Harley's Love Bank Theory suggests that the more we perceive another person as meeting our need, the more we fall in love with them; and the more we perceive them as against us, the more we hate them. (See *His Needs, Her Needs* and *Love Busters*.) As long as we are insecure, we will be limited to loving those who love us and hating those who we perceive are against us. This is the natural state of affairs for those who see themselves as needy. It will not change until we have a revelation of God's love and care for us, which is not based on our works.

13. <u>Emotional problems in relationships are usually the result of attachment wounds.</u> Attachment wounds occur when we feel our attachment needs threatened. Often, when we try to address them, the attachment figure is defensive, insensitive or rejecting. We, as counselors, need to help those involved address these wounds in a more sensitive way. Can we help each of them to see these wounds as attachment alarms and coping mechanisms, and help them to understand the deep hurt that they have caused? The counseling of attachment alarms goes well beyond forgiveness and usually requires the training of each spouse to do a better, more sensitive job in handling emotional issues. (For steps to heal attachment wounds see Chapter 9 of *Safe Haven Marriage* (Hart, 2003))

The Principles of Forgiveness, Reconciliation and Restitution

Almost everyone has heard about forgiveness, but it is my experience that few people really understand or know how to effectively do it. When I suggested that a client, who had been repeatedly sexually abused over her lifetime, forgive her abusers, she turned to me and asked "How?" In another situation, a Christian woman that I knew heard a sermon on forgiveness and, trying to be obedient, forgave and re-married her ex-husband. A few days later, he asked her to leave because he liked his current girlfriend better! She did not understand that although we are required to forgive, according to Matthew Chapter 18 we are not required to be reconciled with someone who has not truly repented. In another situation, I was witnessing to an alcoholic who said that he had become addicted after someone killed his wife and children. The killer had never been caught. I asked if he had forgiven the killer. He said no. I then explained to him that until he forgave and gave up his right to avenge himself, God would not get involved in bringing justice to the situation.

Forgiveness means, "To grant pardon for or remission of (something). 2. To cease of blame or feel resentment against. 3. To remit, as a debt." (The New International Webster's Concise Dictionary of the English Language edited by Sidney Landau, 1997) I define it as "giving up our right for revenge or payment from the other person." Forgiveness must be done from all of our heart—the mind, will, emotions, and spirit—before the process is complete. The Bible discusses three situational types of forgiveness: 1. When a person repents and we forgive and reconcile the relationship. 2. When a person does not repent. We are to forgive them but are not obligated to reconcile the relationship. 3. When forgiveness is unilaterally granted and rights for justice are waived out of concern for the abuser.

1. <u>In the Old Testament offenses by men were punished with harsh judgment equal to the wrong done to others.</u> This is what most of us want for those who offend us. This method of justice has become known as "an eye for an eye and a tooth for a tooth" or legalism. Unfortunately, because we humans tend to want even more done to others than was done to us, this type of legalism results in escalating violence. The results are a world full of blind and toothless people. The Israelis and the Palestinians are a perfect example of this type of "justice" since both Judaism and Islam ascribe to it. It has resulted in thousands of deaths and no end to the conflict between them.

   Lev 24:19 And if a man cause a blemish in his neighbour; as he hath done, so shall it be done to him;

   20 Breach for breach, eye for eye, tooth for tooth: as he hath caused a blemish in a man, so shall it be done to him again.

2. <u>The Old Testament method of forgiveness was atonement, the covering up of sin.</u> This was a kind of restitution to God. Restitution was also required to make things right when people were offended.

   Le 4:20 And he shall do with the bullock as he did with the bullock for a sin offering, so shall he do with this: and the priest shall make an atonement for them, and it shall be forgiven them.

   Ex 21:35 And if one man's ox hurt another's, that he die; then they shall sell the live ox, and divide the money of it; and the dead ox also they shall divide.

3. <u>Forgiveness in the New Testament is based on the shed blood of Jesus that takes away all of our sin.</u>

   Col 1:14 In whom we have redemption through his blood, even the forgiveness of sins:

   Ps 103:12 As far as the east is from the west, so far hath he removed our transgressions from us.

4. <u>Because we all sin, we all need forgiveness.</u> A British General said to John Wesley, "I never forgive." Wesley responded, "I hope then, that you never sin." (Tan, #1985)

   Ro 3:23 For all have sinned, and come short of the glory of God;

   Ps 32:1 Blessed is he whose transgression is forgiven, whose sin is covered.

5. <u>We are required to forgive all the offenses of other people, because God has forgiven us for our sins.</u>

    Mt 6:14 For if ye forgive men their trespasses, your heavenly Father will also forgive you:

    15 But if ye forgive not men their trespasses, neither will your Father forgive your trespasses.

6. <u>The only sin that cannot be forgiven is the blasphemy of the Holy Spirit because it drives away the very Spirit that must draw us unto salvation.</u> If we continually reject the wooing of the Holy Spirit, we cannot be saved and without salvation, we cannot be forgiven. Many psychotic clients fear that they have committed the unforgivable sin. I believe that this is because spirits take advantage of their psychosis in an attempt to overwhelm them with fear. From these clients point of view, if they have committed the unpardonable sin, it means that they are hopelessly doomed to hell and nothing can be done about it. In order to refute this belief, I usually explain that if they are already saved or if they still want to do what is right, it is clear evidence that the Holy Spirit still dwells within them. If this is true then, since they have not driven the Holy Spirit away, they have not committed the unforgivable sin.

    Mt 12:31 Wherefore I say unto you, All manner of sin and blasphemy shall be forgiven unto men: but the blasphemy against the Holy Ghost shall not be forgiven unto men.

    32 And whosoever speaketh a word against the Son of man, it shall be forgiven him: but whosoever speaketh against the Holy Ghost, it shall not be forgiven him, neither in this world, neither in the world to come.

7. <u>Forgiveness is giving up a debt that we perceive is owed to us when we are unjustly treated.</u> To forgive, we must give up our right for vengeance. Unforgiveness is an affront to God and a lack of understanding of the gravity of our own debt (sin). One reason why people do not forgive is because they see their own sins as less evil than the offense done against them. God sees all sins as rebellion and the consequence of even one sin is the fire of hell. The following parable makes it clear that the debt of the first man (us) was huge (millions of dollars) compared to the debt of the second (one day's wages).

    Mt 18:23 Therefore is the kingdom of heaven likened unto a certain king, which would take account of his servants.

    24 And when he had begun to reckon, one was brought unto him, which owed him ten thousand talents.

    26 The servant therefore fell down, and worshipped him, saying, Lord, have patience with me, and I will pay thee all.

    27 Then the lord of that servant was moved with compassion, and loosed him, and forgave him the debt.

8. <u>We cannot expect to have God forgive us and not forgive others.</u> God has a right to be angry with us when we refuse to forgive because He paid the price of His Son to redeem us.

    Mt 18:28 But the same servant went out, and found one of his fellowservants, which owed him an hundred pence: and he laid hands on him, and took him by the throat, saying, Pay me that thou owest.

    29 And his fellowservant fell down at his feet, and besought him, saying, Have patience with me, and I will pay thee all.

    30 And he would not: but went and cast him into prison, till he should pay the debt.

32 Then his lord, after that he had called him, said unto him, O thou wicked servant, I forgave thee all that debt, because thou desiredst me:

33 Shouldest not thou also have had compassion on thy fellowservant, even as I had pity on thee?

9. Refusing to forgive brings internal torment onto ourselves. Our psychological tormentors are bitterness, the mental torment of obsession, being preoccupied with the past, not being able to forgive ourselves, and stuffed anger which results in angry blowups and physical health problems. We are the only ones who are hurt by the situation. By not forgiving, we must realize that we are the ones who are turning ourselves over to the tormenters. By our actions, we choose the world in which we will live: judgment or grace.

    Mt 18:34 And his lord was wroth, and delivered him to the tormentors, till he should pay all that was due unto him.

    35 So likewise shall my heavenly Father do also unto you, if ye from your hearts forgive not every one his brother their trespasses.

10. Unforgiveness gives Satan an advantage over us.

    2 Co 2:10 To whom ye forgive any thing, I [forgive] also: for if I forgave any thing, to whom I forgave [it], for your sakes [forgave I it] in the person of Christ;

    11 Lest Satan should get an advantage of us: for we are not ignorant of his devices.

11. When another person admits their fault and changes their behavior, we are not only to forgive them, but to do what we can to be reconciled in our relationship with them. This is the first type of forgiveness.

    Lu 17:3 Take heed to yourselves: If thy brother trespass against thee, rebuke him; and if he repent, forgive him.

    Mt 18:15 Moreover if thy brother shall trespass against thee, go and tell him his fault between thee and him alone: if he shall hear thee, thou hast gained thy brother.

12. Although we are still required to forgive someone who refuses to repent, we are not required to be reconciled with them. This second type of forgiveness is, in effect, turning the situation over to God for justice. In doing so, we have still given up our rights for vengeance. However, forgiveness does not mean we have to put ourselves back into the same situation to be abused again.

    Mt 18:16 But if he will not hear thee, then take with thee one or two more, that in the mouth of two or three witnesses every word may be established.

    17 And if he shall neglect to hear them, tell it unto the church: but if he neglect to hear the church, let him be unto thee as an heathen man and a publican.

13. If we do not forgive, God does not get involved in bringing justice to the situation. If we choose to hold on to our right for vengeance, God is not released to bring justice or vengeance.

    Mt 18:18 Verily I say unto you, Whatsoever ye shall bind on earth shall be bound in heaven: and whatsoever ye shall loose on earth shall be loosed in heaven.

19 Again I say unto you, That if two of you shall agree on earth as touching any thing that they shall ask, it shall be done for them of my Father which is in heaven.

14. <u>The third type of forgiveness involves dropping the matter as an act of mercy to an evil and unrepentant offender.</u> Both Jesus and Stephen chose to do this as they were dying.

Lu 23:34 Then said Jesus, Father, forgive them; for they know not what they do. And they parted his raiment, and cast lots.

Ac 7:60 And he (Stephen) kneeled down, and cried with a loud voice, Lord, lay not this sin to their charge. And when he had said this, he fell asleep.

15. <u>Sometimes, people do not forgive; because they do not believe that forgiveness is fair.</u> God disagrees! He forgave a much greater debt (all of our sins) because He is more interested in what we will become in the future than what we have done in the past. It is only fair that we do the same. We are all supposed to be growing in maturity and righteousness. He sent Jesus to forgive us, so that we could have a relationship with Him and become more progressively whole.

Eze 18:25 Yet ye say, The way of the Lord is not equal. Hear now, O house of Israel; Is not my way equal? are not your ways unequal?

27 Again, when the wicked [man] turneth away from his wickedness that he hath committed, and doeth that which is lawful and right, he shall save his soul alive.

28 Because he considereth, and turneth away from all his transgressions that he hath committed, he shall surely live, he shall not die.

16. <u>Because forgiveness seems to cost us something, some people are not willing to pay the price.</u> We need to ask ourselves how much do we value the other person? God paid the price of His Son Jesus for each of us so that we could have another chance to become all He designed us to be! We must also remember that the price of not forgiving is much higher. If we will not forgive God will not forgive us.

Mt 18:14 Even so it is not the will of your Father which is in heaven, that one of these little ones should perish.

17. <u>When we have been wrong in offending someone, restitution is appropriate.</u> Jacob gave presents to Esau to make restitution for stealing his birthright and blessing.

Ge 33:10 And Jacob said, Nay, I pray thee, if now I have found grace in thy sight, then receive my present at my hand: for therefore I have seen thy face, as though I had seen the face of God, and thou wast pleased with me.

Counseling Methods and Techniques

1. <u>We must forgive, but reconciliation is required only if the offender truly repents.</u> Forgiveness is giving up our right for vengeance and is not the same as reconciliation. If the other refuses to repent or does not show the fruit of repentance, we are required to forgive, but not to reconcile.

2. <u>We need to learn how to biblically forgive others.</u> Some clients need to be taught how to forgive. The first step is to choose to forgive as an act of the will, because God commands it. We will not be forgiven without it. When we forgive, we are delivered from the internal torment that unforgiveness perpetuates. Next, we must try to see the situation from the viewpoint of the other person

and value them as God does—a person of infinite worth. Then, we should try to find compassion and empathy for them. Remembering our own sins and our need for forgiveness can help. After attempting to resolve the offense according to Matthew Chapter 18, we must choose the type of forgiveness appropriate to the situation: forgive and reconcile if they have truly repented, forgive by turning the situation over to God if they have not, or ask God to not hold this sin against them as Jesus and Stephen did when they were murdered. Once the decision is made, either reconcile the relationship, if they have repented, or treat the offender as a "heathen man and a publican"—that is, you keep your distance, but pray for their salvation and a change of heart. Realize that forgiveness is an act of faith. When you act according to your faith and pray for the offender, your emotions will eventually follow.

3. <u>We must identify and overcome any resistance to forgiveness.</u> Using these principles, we need to determine why the client is unwilling to forgive and help them to overcome this problem. Usually people do not forgive because they feel forgiveness is not fair, that the abuser will get away with the offense if they forgive, or that if they forgive they will be abused again. They need to realize that the opposite is true. If they refuse to forgive, God will not forgive them for their sins, and they will be the one hurt by the inner torment and rumination caused by the unforgiveness. By not forgiving, they are holding onto their rights for vengeance, and God does not get involved in bringing justice. Most of the time, when the client realizes that they can forgive an unrepentant offender by giving up their rights for vengeance to God and that God will take up their cause, they are willing to do so. Finally, forgiveness does not imply that they should reconcile and again put themselves in a vulnerable position. Reconciliation is only required if the other person truly repents and changes his behavior.

4. <u>Reconciliation in abuse cases should be done slowly and step-by-step.</u> The first step is testing that true repentance has occurred. In fact, sometimes waiting helps solidify the repentance and results in restitution or the fruit of repentance. Even if the other person has truly repented, that does not necessarily insure that all issues have been adequately resolved. In addition, many times trust has been destroyed and fear is present. Starting the new relationship at a safe distance and closing that distance only after any conflicts and abusive behavior have been resolved can slowly rebuild trust. Systematic desensitization is used in an incremental fashion to rebuild the relationship as fear is faced. This is especially true when domestic violence or abuse has been a pattern. (For more on this subject see the story of Joseph as a model for abuse recovery in my book *Transformation!*)

5. <u>Direct or indirect restitution is the fruit of repentance.</u> If the offending person is not willing to make restitution, we should question whether full repentance has occurred. Although no one can ever completely rectify a wrong, the offender can at least demonstrate a change of heart through his actions. It also helps an offender to feel that the perpetrator has done all that he can do to make up for the wrong. Direct restitution is repaying a debt or doing something for the one offended. Sometimes this is impossible. In cases where the person has died or when revisiting the offense could bring further damage or hurt, indirect restitution should be made. The offender should do something symbolic. An example would be making a donation to the family of the victim or to a charity that assists in helping victims of this type of offense.

Chapter 12

Principles of the Emotions

Most people would agree that their emotions are their most unruly member. It is not unusual for clients to believe that they cannot control their emotions or that they are not responsible for them. If they believe this, they may allow their emotions to rule their lives.

The Principles of Emotions

As I have already stated, our emotions operate much like a thermometer. The type of emotion, the strength of the emotion, and the subject of the current emotion are all controlled by how we perceive our current situation. In addition to our perceptions, what we desire to do, what we are thinking about, our actions, our experiences, how we have dealt with our emotions in the past, stress, hormones, physical activity and other physical and psychological problems can all effect our emotions.

1. <u>Our emotions are not a valid indicator of how we are doing because they can come and go rapidly.</u>

   Ps 30:5 For his anger endureth but a moment; in his favour is life: weeping may endure for a night, but joy cometh in the morning.

2. <u>How we perceive things has a very great impact on our emotions.</u>

   Lu 10:17 And the seventy returned again with joy, saying, Lord, even the devils are subject unto us through thy name.

   15:7 I say unto you, that likewise joy shall be in heaven over one sinner that repenteth, more than over ninety and nine just persons, which need no repentance.

   Jo 16:22 And ye now therefore have sorrow: but I will see you again, and your heart shall rejoice, and your joy no man taketh from you.

3. <u>What we say, especially to ourselves and others, has a significant effect on how we feel.</u> Our self-talk is a reflection of our perceptions.

   Pr 15:23 A man hath joy by the answer of his mouth: and a word spoken in due season, how good is it!

4. <u>Generally, doing what is right leads to positive emotions and doing evil produces negative ones.</u>

   Ec 2:26 For God giveth to a man that is good in his sight wisdom, and knowledge, and joy: but to the sinner he giveth travail, to gather and to heap up, that he may give to him that is good before God. This also is vanity and vexation of spirit.

5. <u>Our emotions are connected to our prosperity and to receiving what we desire.</u> Consequently, our perceived circumstances have an effect on our emotions.

    Ps 35:27 Let them shout for joy, and be glad, that favour my righteous cause: yea, let them say continually, Let the LORD be magnified, which hath pleasure in the prosperity of his servant.

    Jo 16:24 Hitherto have ye asked nothing in my name: ask, and ye shall receive, that your joy may be full.

6. <u>What others say about us can affect our emotions.</u> However, we should value the opinion of God more then the opinion of man.

    Lu 6:23 Rejoice ye in that day, and leap for joy: for, behold, your reward is great in heaven: for in the like manner did their fathers unto the prophets.

    Jo 5:44 How can ye believe, which receive honour one of another, and seek not the honour that cometh from God only?

7. <u>Having healthy positive emotions like joy and peace are automatic by-products of following Christ, being in His presence, and serving in the Kingdom of God.</u>

    Ro 14:17 For the kingdom of God is not meat and drink; but righteousness, and peace, and joy in the Holy Ghost.

    Ps 16:11 Thou wilt shew me the path of life: in thy presence is fulness of joy; at thy right hand there are pleasures for evermore.

8. <u>Even in disastrous circumstances, we can experience positive emotions by looking forward to the rewards to come and the end results.</u>

    1 Pe 4:13 But rejoice, inasmuch as ye are partakers of Christ's sufferings; that, when his glory shall be revealed, ye may be glad also with exceeding joy.

    Jas 1:2 My brethren, count it all joy when ye fall into divers temptations;

    3 Knowing this, that the trying of your faith worketh patience.

    4 But let patience have her perfect work, that ye may be perfect and entire, wanting nothing.

9. <u>We can face even the worst worldly circumstances and maintain our joy.</u> Jesus made the following statement just before His arrest and crucifixion.

    Jo 16:33 These things I have spoken unto you, that in me ye might have peace. In the world ye shall have tribulation: but be of good cheer; I have overcome the world.

10. <u>God promises to help us heal our emotions.</u>

    Ps 147:3 He healeth the broken in heart, and bindeth up their wounds.

    37:24 Though he fall, he shall not be utterly cast down: for the LORD upholdeth him with his hand.

11. <u>Jesus cares how we feel since He experienced the same kind of feelings when He lived among us.</u>

    Heb 4:15 For we have not an high priest which cannot be touched with the feeling of our infirmities; but was in all points tempted like as we are, yet without sin.

12. <u>Through God, we can overcome even deep depression by hoping and trusting in Him.</u> Although Elijah was deeply depressed when he ran from Jezabel, God sent angels to him and led him step-by-step out of his depression. (1 Kings Chapter 19) (See the model for overcoming depression in my book *Transformation!*)

Ps 42:5 Why art thou cast down, O my soul? and why art thou disquieted in me? hope thou in God: for I shall yet praise him for the help of his countenance.

11 Why art thou cast down, O my soul? and why art thou disquieted within me? hope thou in God: for I shall yet praise him, who is the health of my countenance, and my God.

13. <u>We do not have to allow our emotions to destroy us.</u>

2 Co 4:9 Persecuted, but not forsaken; cast down, but not destroyed;

14. <u>After our own emotions have been healed through Christ, we can encourage others, through what we say, and even lead them to salvation.</u>

Job 22:29 When men are cast down, then thou shalt say, There is lifting up; and he shall save the humble person.

2 Co 1:4 Who comforteth us in all our tribulation, that we may be able to comfort them which are in any trouble, by the comfort wherewith we ourselves are comforted of God.

Counseling Methods and Techniques

1. <u>A grocery store analogy can be used to demonstrate emotional control.</u> I learned this technique in a seminar many years ago and have since adapted it for use in a counseling setting. In this seminar, given at St. Joseph Hospital in Wichita, Kansas, the presenter asked how we would react emotionally if we were in a grocery store on a hot day, the checkout lines were long and barely moving, and the person behind us was running his cart into our back. I ask my clients to tell me what emotion they would be feeling, how strong it would be and who would it be directed at? I am usually surprised at the varied answers that this question elicits. Most of the time, the emotion is anger. The presenter then changed the perception of the situation by saying that after we turned around to say something, we noticed that the person has a red and white cane similar to those carried by a blind person. Again I ask the client what emotion they would feel, how strong it would be, and who it would be directed at? At this point, the emotion usually changes to pity. Finally, the situation is again changed. This time we overhear a conversation between the person behind us and a friend. From the conversation, we learn that the person is not blind at all, but that the entire situation is a joke and that the people behind us are trying to make us look stupid. Usually, this last perception elicits strong anger; because the client takes the situation personally. I then show them that the overall situation has not really changed, but, because our perception of the situation has changed, the type, strength, and direction of the emotion has changed drastically. I then ask them how their emotional response would be different if they simply said to themselves in each case, "They have a problem. I will pray for them." Most agree that this simple change in the way they perceive the problem would calm their emotional responses.

2. <u>The emotional train analogy provides a method for changing emotions.</u> As we have discussed before and from the verses above, we can see that our emotions are affected primarily by our will, what we think and our actions. These form an emotional train. Although I have alluded to this emotional train before, I will discuss it here in more detail. The engine is our will, and it is supposed to direct our lives. The first car in the train is our mind, which is closely associated with our will and our

actions. The next car is our actions; and finally, the caboose is our emotions. From this we can draw two important conclusions:

a. <u>Clients who attempt to direct their lives by following their emotions are going to be in trouble.</u> This is like trying to heat a house using a thermometer instead of a thermostat. In the case of the train analogy, if you try to direct and pull the train with the caboose, the only direction it can go is downhill; because it only has weight and momentum. It has no engine to pull you uphill. In this scenario, the person's emotions affect his actions which affect his thinking which affect his will. The direction of the train is now subject to the momentary fickleness of the person's emotions and only chaos can result.

b. <u>Emotions must be changed through indirect means.</u> First, we must decide to do what is right in spite of how we are feeling and use our will to direct the train onto the right track going in the right direction. Next, we must convince our mind to look at the situation in a way that will create the correct emotions. Then, we must act in accordance with our will and our mind. Eventually, our emotions will follow. Of course, we must truly believe what we are doing is right and that our perceptions are correct; or the cars in the front of the train will have no effect on those behind them. Faith is the hitch between the cars.

3. <u>Getting in and out of depression is like getting in and out of a cellar.</u> We begin to get depressed if, when we get up in the morning, we allow ourselves to act in ways we know are wrong, because we feel badly. As an example, we call in to work sick. Now because we have just lied, we feel worse so we watch the TV soaps. Since we are now wasting time, we feel worse so we just pull the covers over our head and stay in bed all morning. Every time when we feel badly, if we allow it to influence us to make bad decisions, these actions, in turn, will cause us to feel more depressed. Our thoughts are, of course, also involved. They are the basis of how we perceive each step as we descend further into the cellar and each step into the cellar leads to greater and greater depression. However, this chain of events is also the key for getting out of the cellar. If we will use our will and decide to do what is right, and make our minds and actions follow, we will feel a little better. Because we feel better, we can do something else right, like wash the dishes. Because we have done this, we will feel better and possibly call in to work to tell them that we will be in after lunch. This, of course, is another application of the emotional train discussed above.

4. <u>We can encourage our heart in God by what we say to ourselves.</u> We saw this in the example of David in 1 Samuel 30:6 "And David was greatly distressed; for the people spake of stoning him, because the soul of all the people was grieved, every man for his sons and for his daughters: but David encouraged himself in the LORD his God." What we say to ourselves is critical.

PART III

Application

Chapter 13

How to Build a Counseling Plan Using Bible Principles

Now that we have examined the principles of change, discussed many of the significant sets of biblical principles for application, and proposed a model for applying biblical principles to effect change in each area of intervention, we are ready to integrate this information into a complete plan for counseling, using biblical principles. Building such a plan in each case is like putting together an a la carte meal at a cafeteria. Using counseling models is like ordering a complete meal from a menu. Both ways of obtaining a meal can satisfy our hunger, but coming up with an a la carte meal that meets all of our needs is the greater challenge. Again, I will use the train of psychological wholeness analogy as a backdrop for this method.

Building a Counseling Plan from Biblical Principles

Although there are probably numerous ways to develop a counseling plan using biblical principles, I suggest the following steps.

1. <u>What is the problem?</u> Using a basic counseling interview method, we start by asking, "What can I do to help you," attempt to connect with the client, assess the client's goals for the therapy and gather information. From this information, we "put the puzzle together" and construct a hypothesis concerning the problem to be addressed. (See the assessment form in the appendix for a listing of the information required to assess most problems effectively.)

2. <u>What is the primary component of the train of psychological wholeness that is affected by the problem?</u> Once the pieces of the problem have been analyzed and put together in a way that makes sense to us, we must determine where the major impact of the dysfunction resides. This will be one of the nine components of the heart: will, spirit, experience, mind, perceptions, needs, motivation, actions or emotions.

3. <u>What other members or functions of the heart have been affected by it or affect it?</u> In almost all cases, more than one function will be impacted; and a large number of other components will either affect or be affected by the problem. Of course, in complex problems all of the components or members of the heart will usually be affected.

4. <u>Where is the root cause of the problem?</u> In order to effect long-term change, the root cause or faith problem must be identified. Usually the very root of the problem is a lack of faith that an unmet need for love, security, worth, or significance will be met. Questioning what the function of the dysfunctional behavior is that led to the problem many times can easily identify this. The client will usually be trying, in his own strength in the flesh, to meet that need.

5. <u>Determine the order of the components that are creating the problem.</u> This can be a fairly complex step because it is important to determine which components are the most critical ones and how they are affected by other components in order to create the presenting problem. This information is important

because we need to understand what is creating the problem before we can couple the train together in the next step to resolve the problem. To determine the problem train we begin by asking what component initially caused this problem to occur. We then attempt to determine what effect it had on the next component and logically sequence the cars that led from this initial component to the one most effected by the problem (already identified in step 2). All the affected cars identified in step 3 should either be part of the train from the initial car to the most affected component or one of the cars that were subsequently affected by the problem. The problem train should completely and logically explain how this problem occurred and what affect it had on the person. Our goal is to eventually construct a train to produce an ever-increasing chain of healing that will affect the cars behind it until complete wholeness is achieved.

6. <u>Couple the cars to build a train to resolve this problem.</u> In this step, we attempt to sequence the cars (components) in such a way as to resolve the deeper issues successfully until overall healing is achieved. This is an inside-to-outside strategy of healing rather than the usual outside-in or more superficial method used in classical biblical counseling. Of course, most trains, no matter how simple, will have to include at least an engine (our will), some important cars (our mind, needs, actions, and experiences) and the caboose (our emotions). I suggest actually listing the components of the train in the order necessary to resolve the problem in this step.

7. <u>What principles apply to each component?</u> Once the area of intervention is identified, the specific principles to be applied to each component can be selected from those presented in Part II of this book or by reviewing the Index of Counseling Methods and Techniques in the appendix. What are the lies that the client believes? What is he doing that violates biblical principles? What is the motivation behind those actions?

8. <u>What counseling methods or techniques are needed?</u> In this book, I have presented two sources of methods and techniques to be applied in actual counseling. The first is the list of classical biblical counseling principles of change already discussed in the first chapter of this book. The second is found in the section following each set of principles in Part II of this book. This second set goes beyond the methods discussed under the principles of change and is specifically designed to deal with common problems in that subject area. The Index of Counseling Methods and Techniques in the appendix is extremely helpful in identifying which methods are appropriate for each principle. Of course, the direct application of any basic truths, which make up each of these principles, can also be used as effective change agents.

9. <u>What is the faith component?</u> We need to remember that the entire train is coupled together with faith, that without faith it will not be possible to deal with the deeper issues of life, and that faith in God is the most effective of all change agents. These faith techniques are found at the end of the study of the Principles of Faith in Chapter 3.

10. <u>Load the train cars.</u> At this step, we use the information gathered above to specifically assign the principles to be taught and methods to be used for each component of the train as it has been coupled together.

11. <u>What are the goals and how will the outcome be measured in order to determine if progress is being made?</u> Based on the presenting problem, we need to determine our overall goal and how to quantifiably assess progress as we move toward this goal. Goals can be as diverse as preventing a divorce, stopping an addiction or alleviating emotional pain.

12. <u>Define the route for the train.</u> Now that the train has been coupled and the cars loaded, we need to determine the route of the counseling process. Although in simple cases, counseling might be as simple as starting with the engine and having each car follow in succession, others will be rather complex involving repeated use of the same cars, using a number of cars at the same time, or dropping off cars when their purpose has been fulfilled. An example of this latter case exists after past

traumatic experiences have been resolved. Another example of a complex route is what I call, "Fix the future, fix the present, fix the past." Sometimes, this pattern is required to give the client a vision for the future, so that they will have the motivation to deal with past trauma and offenses.

13. <u>What is the plan for intervention in the whole person?</u> In this step, the entire plan needs to be constructed to attack the overall problem through a series of interventions throughout all aspects of the heart of the client. This will usually include at least the motivation, perceptions, thought-life, actions and, finally, emotions. At this point, we need to ask, "How does this plan fit with the principles of Proverbs 3:5?" If it does not, something might be missing from the train. In our train analogy, this step occurs when the switchman is checking the entire train prior to departure.

14. <u>How does this plan fit into The Biblical Plan for Christian Counseling?</u> Final implementation requires integrating this new plan for counseling within the Biblical Plan for Christian Counseling developed from the story of the exodus of the children of Israel in *Transformation!* I have listed those steps in bold print so that they will not be confused with the steps for building a counseling plan. I will discuss this integration below:

1. **Determine the problem.** In the process of developing the counseling plan, this step has already been completed.

2. **Demonstrate that what the client is doing will not meet his needs and build hope that his problems can be overcome through Christ.** Note that building hope is the second step in the method of change used by The Biblical Counseling Foundation listed under the principles of change. Building hope is a function of building faith and is part of the process of motivation.

3. **Use the biblical principles and models to help the client perceive and understand the problem from a biblical perspective.** First, the counselor explains how he perceives the problem from a biblical perspective. He then explains the counseling plan using the train analogy including the principles and methods to be used. Explaining the problem and presenting the plan for overcoming it continues the process of building hope that the problem can be resolved (as begun in the previous step).

4. **Determine where the client is in the process of salvation and, if appropriate, lead him to accept Christ, be baptized, yield the control of his life to God, and help him get established in a church.** This step of faith is required in order to couple the cars to the train; because without accepting and building on the spiritual foundation of salvation, the needs of the flesh will predominate and spiritual influence will not be available to direct the train. Although the client can be helped to some extent, without the power of the Spirit in his life, any progress will be limited to attempting to socialize the flesh.

5. **Help the client take responsibility for his own actions, not blame others or react to what they do, and do everything as unto God.** This step is an application of the principle of responsibility and is required in the resolution of almost every problem.

6. **Help the client grow in his personal relationship with Christ and build faith that, with God's help, he can overcome the problem.** The goal of this step is to transform the hope that we have attempted to build in the client (in steps two and three) into faith that they will recover. It is this faith that couples the entire train together and provides the basis for believing that all of the client's needs will be met.

7. **Assist the client in receiving the empowerment of the baptism of the Holy Spirit if he chooses to do so.** This step requires teaching the client the principles of the baptism of the Holy Spirit so that he can receive the baptism. It is especially important in overcoming the problems associated with the lust of the flesh or in dealing with spiritual oppression.

8. **Help the client apply the Biblical principles or model to overcome the identified psychological problem.** Now that the client understands his problem from a biblical perspective, it is time to directly apply the counseling plan based on biblical principles or models. This is the point when the train is scheduled to leave the station to follow the route specified for it.

9. **Determine the root cause of the difficulty and assist the client in developing and applying faith to overcome this root problem.** This is where the root of the problem is addressed through faith. Without addressing the root issue underlying the problem, it may resurface in some other form. (For more information on dealing with deeply rooted problems, see my book *Faith Therapy*.)

10. **Release the client again to the care of the Holy Spirit, to continue orchestrating this growth process of salvation in his life.** At this step, the entire counseling process has been completed and the client is again released to the care of the Holy Spirit. At this time, the train has completed its scheduled run and returns to the station for future use. Ideally, this step should not occur until the established goals have been reached.

15. Schedule the train. With the completion of the counseling plan, it is now necessary to execute its implementation. Many times this includes assigning workbooks, as well as scheduling support groups and individual counseling sessions. In most cases, I schedule weekly sessions until significant progress has been made toward the major goals, and the majority of the problem has been resolved. Then I will reduce sessions to bi-weekly ones as I monitor the client's progress and he is able to take on more and more responsibility for his own recovery.

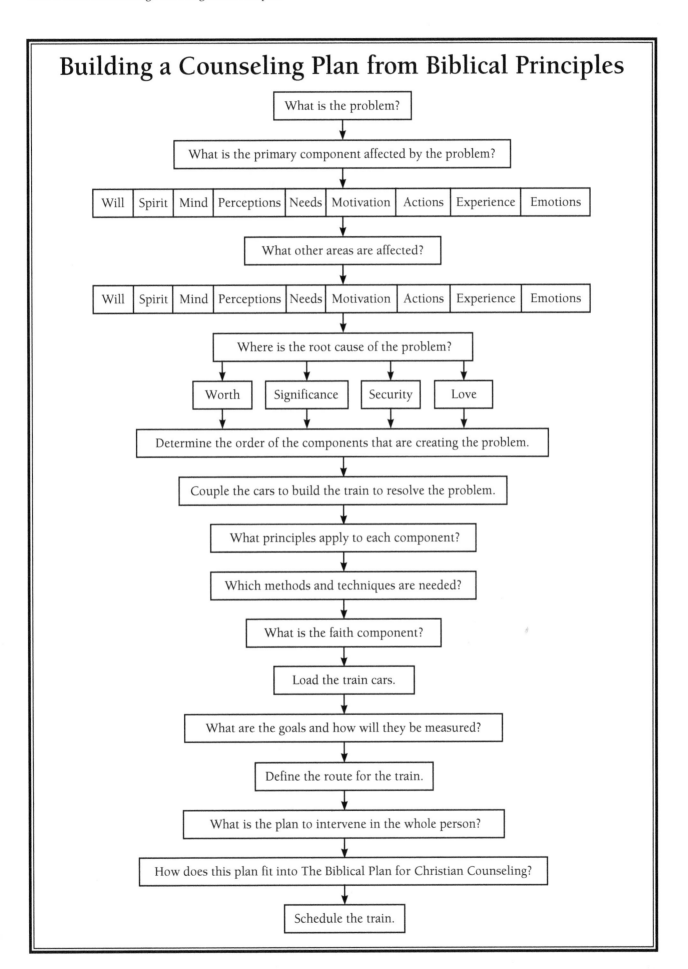

Chapter 14

Biblical Counseling Plans for Common Problems

In this chapter, I will develop and present examples of counseling plans built from biblical principles. I will emphasize common problems seen in the church, especially those for which biblical models have not been presented in my previous books, *Transformation!* and *Faith Therapy*. I will start with simple examples and progress to more complex ones. The names of the clients and some of the details of these cases have been changed to protect the identities of the clients. Some are composites of several cases. After giving a very detailed development of the first model, I will present only the problem and solution trains, and the completed counseling plan in order to save space and avoid repeating the detailed work commonly carried out on the Quick Form for Building a Counseling Plan.

Although this method is designed to develop plans for problems for which we do not yet have biblical counseling models directly from the Bible, in reality four different types of plans are needed. 1. Those that are adequately resolved by models directly addressed in the Bible. 2. Those built exclusively from biblical principles. 3. Those that are a combination of principles and models. 4. Those that are not specifically addressed in the Bible and require a more in-depth understanding, through further research and investigation. This fourth type many times includes physical malfunctions of mental or emotional processing or mental disorders that are not directly addressed in the Bible. Counseling plans, in these cases, become a blend of research that attempts to understand the problem through experientially developed techniques and biblical principles. Consequently, this last type is usually the most difficult to develop.

Building a Counseling Plan for Anxiety using Biblical Principles

In order to clarify the processes of developing counseling plans based on biblical principles, let us follow the step-by-step process discussed in the previous chapter, as we develop a plan for resolving a problem with anxiety. In this example, I will explain this process in detail and demonstrate the use of the Quick Form for Building a Counseling Plan from Biblical Principles. (See the appendix for a copy of this form.) Later in this book, I will present the application of this same example in more detail, from the initial intake through the conclusion of the entire counseling process.

Mary was sent to me by her insurance company after she had had a serious, life-threatening automobile accident when she was forced off the road by a semi-truck. She was now afraid to drive. She was a Christian and felt that because she was, something like this should not have happened to her. She was now not sure how much she could rely on God for protection. She became anxious if she even thought about driving. During my initial assessment, I learned that she had had a normal childhood without abuse, although she did have some dependency issues with her mother and siblings. She was divorced after a marriage to an alcoholic husband. She had developed an ambivalent attachment style, which resulted in attempts to perform and please others in order to be accepted.

Using the method just described in the previous chapter, I would develop a counseling plan based on biblical principles as follows:

1. <u>What is the problem?</u> The problem outlined above is anxiety resulting from the automobile accident. Otherwise, Mary is functional in life and is in the psychologically normal range. She does have some codependency issues that are based on insecurity and may contribute to the underlying anxiety. Therefore, although this case would probably fall into the simple problem category, the codependency issue is a complex one. Her progress in the process of salvation or wholeness is blocked by her fear of driving and possibly her codependency.

2. <u>What is the primary component affected by the problem?</u> If we scan the nine components of the Train of Psychological Wholeness, the primary one affected is her emotions due to the fear of driving. If we were using the quick form in the appendix, we would place a star in the box representing the train car of emotions, the caboose.

3. <u>What other members or functions of the heart have been affected by it or affect it?</u> As I again scan the nine components, I would select: 1. Her will since she will not drive. 2. Her spirit because her faith in God is shaken. 3. Her mind because she does not know the truth of God concerning protection. 4. Her perceptions because she is viewing life differently. 5. Her needs because it is her security that is under attack. 6. Her motivation because she is no longer motivated enough to drive. 7. Her actions because she refuses to act. 8. Her experience because she had a traumatic experience. 9. Her emotions because she is dominated by her fear of driving. This emotional part of her heart was already starred as the primary part affected. Consequently, if we were using the quick form, we would place an X in all of the component boxes except the emotions since it was already selected. In many, but not all cases, most of the Train of Psychological Wholeness will be affected in some fashion.

4. <u>Where is the root cause or psychological need or needs underlying the problem?</u> The primary need affected is that of security, since Mary is afraid to drive. Due to the accident, her world has become a very insecure place. On the quick form, we could place an X on the Security box.

5. <u>Determine the order of the components that are creating the problem.</u> We have concluded that all of the heart is involved in this problem. However, we need to understand and determine how each component is affecting the others in sequence to create the presenting problem. We need this information in order to take the next step in determining the sequence of the train cars to resolve the problem. I hypothesize that this problem has been created by the experience of the accident, which affected what she believed about her security in life, which changed how she perceived things, which affected her faith in God, which increased her insecurity, which led to the emotion of fear, which de-motivated her to want to drive, which kept her from driving.

Experience	Mind	Perceptions	Spirit	Needs	Emotions	Motivation	Will	Actions

6. <u>Couple the cars to build the train to resolve this problem.</u> When we recognize that the critical factors in the problem train above are precipitated by the experience that affected Mary's faith and led to the emotion of fear which keeps her from driving, we can construct a train to overcome these factors. First, we need the client to be willing to address the problem. In this case, Mary was willing since without driving she could not keep her job. In order to overcome the fear, we will need to change her thinking, which will change her perception of her experience. This change of perception will help her view her spiritual relationship with God differently, which will change her perception of her needs, which will change her motivation allowing her to act to confront her fear until it is overcome. As she confronts her fear, it will diminish.

Will	Mind	Perceptions	Experience	Spirit	Needs	Motivation	Actions	Emotions

7. <u>Which principles apply in each component?</u> When we review the principles in this book described under each component, we find that we need to apply the following principles. On the Quick Form these would be listed by letter under each of the boxes above below the word "Principles."

Will—Principles of free choice—to teach that she can choose in God's strength to face her fear.

Mind—Principles of truth—to teach her the truth about God's protection.

Perceptions—Principles of grace—to learn that her protection is based on God's grace, not her works.

Experience—Principles of experiences—to learn that her response is based not on the actual experience, but on her perception of the experience.

Spirit—Principles of faith—to truly change, she must build her faith and get it into her spirit by revelation.

Needs—Principles of security—to learn what God will and will not do to protect her.

Motivation—The Principles of motivation and fear—to learn that the fear is de-motivating her, that she can use systematic desensitization to overcome it, that she can conquer anxiety by praising God for the good He will bring from the accident, and that she can overcome her fear with faith.

Actions—The Principles of action and confession—to learn that she must act on her faith and confess what the Word of God says in order for her faith to become a reality.

Emotions—The Principles of Emotions—to learn that her emotions are the caboose of the train and will come into line as she acts on her faith and faces her fear.

8. <u>What methods and techniques are needed?</u> When we review the "counseling methods and techniques" under each of these principles, we can identify those that are needed. On the Quick Form, we would list these by number under the boxes above below the word "Methods." The Index of Counseling Methods and Techniques in the appendix is extremely helpful in completing this step.

Principles of Free Choice—If she will yield to God and ask Him, He will help her to want to face her fear.

Principles of Truth—She can rely on the Word of God, knowing that He cannot lie.

Principles of Grace—Since she is in Christ, she has the protection of God without works.

Principles of Experience—Theophostic Ministry can be used to change Mary's perception of the accident and bring peace.

Principles of Revelation—We can use "If it is true…" to move the truth from her mind to her spirit.

Principles of Faith—Help her present evidence to herself that her fears can be overcome.

Principles of Security—We can use the Protection from Catastrophe Chart from *Faith Therapy* to teach her what God provides in the way of protection, and that pride, direct disobedience, and tempting God removes her protection.

Principles of Motivation—We can analyze her motivation by listing motivators and de-motivators to help Mary understand why she will not drive.

Principles of Fear—We can use Systematic Desensitization to alleviate the fear.

Principles of Fear—Praising God in everything allows her to express her faith that God will work even this for her good. It is an effective tool for overcoming anxiety.

Principles of Fear—She must be willing to face her fear with her faith.

Principles of Action—We can help Mary realize that she needs to confess her faith to help her face her fear.

Principles of Confession—We can help her build her faith by confessing the Word of God and not her fears.

Principles of Emotions—We can use the "Emotional Train" to help her overcome her fears.

9. <u>What is the faith component?</u> In this case, we need to build faith that God has and will protect her from catastrophe, if she will rely on Him, even though she might still have to face a certain amount

of tribulation in her life. This faith needs to be built in her spirit. On the Quick Form, we would list Faith as a principle under the Spirit box above.

10. <u>Load the train cars.</u> At this point, we need to prioritize the principles and techniques for each car, including the Bible truth from the principles involved and the techniques to be used with each. On the Quick Form, this is done by reordering them.

11. <u>What are the goals and how will they be measured?</u> The goal in this case is to overcome the fear so that Mary can drive again. We can measure our progress in counseling by evaluating Mary's progress as she drives without fear in previously fearful circumstances. Secondary goals include overcoming her generalized anxiety as well as recovery from codependency.

12. <u>Define the route of the train.</u> In this case, we need to recognize that the motivation, actions, and emotions phase of this plan needs to be executed again and again until the fear is removed from previously fearful circumstances. Using the Quick Form, we would add an arrow back from the emotions to the motivations car in order to show that her emotions then affect her motivation, so that the cycle is repeated.

13. <u>What is the plan to intervene in the whole person?</u> At this step we would gather together all the information, principles, and techniques in order to write out the entire plan. We must remember that we have a second underlying issue of codependency that, up until now, we have not addressed. Consequently, it must be included at this point. The method for dealing with the codependency will be the model for this type of codependency developed in *Transformation!* Using the Quick Form, it would appear like this:

Step	Component	Principle	Intervention
1.	Will	Free Choice	Convince her to trust God to face her fears.
2.	Mind	Truth	Convince her she can rely on God's Word.
3.	Perceptions	Grace	Convince her protection depends on grace.
4.	Experience	Experience	Theophostic Ministry to heal experience.
5.	Spirit	Revelation	Use "If it is true…" to make truth real.
6.	Spirit	Faith	Present evidence that fear can be overcome.
7	Needs	Security	Teach Protection from Catastrophe Chart.
8	Motivation	Motivation	List motivators and de-motivators to drive.
9.	Motivation	Fear	Use Systematic Desensitization to face fear.
10.	Motivation	Fear	Praise God the accident will work for good.
11.	Motivation	Fear	In her fear, help her to rely on God.
12.	Action	Confession	In her fear, help her to confess the Word.
13.	Emotions	Emotions	Use the Emotional Train to alleviate fear.
14.	Repeat	Steps 9-12	Complete the desensitization process.
15.	Codependency	Model of Abigail	Treat the underlying codependency issue.
16.	Evaluate	Progress	Determine when goals are reached.

14. <u>How does this plan fit into The Biblical Plan for Christian Counseling?</u> We still need to integrate this plan within the ten steps of The Biblical Plan for Christian Counseling before it can be implemented. In this case, we find that our specific plan Step 1 becomes part of the biblical plan step 2. Steps 2-3 become part of biblical plan step 2. Step 4 becomes part of biblical plan step 3. Steps 5-7 become part of biblical plan step 6. The remainder of the steps then become part of biblical plan step 8. Additional work to deal with the root problem of insecurity and codependency may be required in biblical plan step 9.

15. Schedule the train. In order to implement the overall plan that we have just devised, we would schedule weekly individual sessions until Mary is able to adequately drive with minimum anxiety

in all circumstances and then reduce the counseling to bi-weekly sessions until her confidence is fully restored. In order to provide additional support during the process, we would assign her to our Codependency Support Group because of the dependence issues identified during the assessment. To help her to understand codependency from a biblical perspective, we might also give her the assignment to complete the 12-step *Conquering Codependency* workbook, by Springle. Using the Quick Plan, we would assign the following:

Individual weekly sessions: One/week

Support Groups: Codependency

Books/workbooks: 12-step Codependency workbook

In learning how to put together counseling plans, I suggest that the student initially start with simple problems and progress toward more complex ones. Initially, this may seem very complicated and time consuming but as more of these plans are developed and implemented the process and results become easier and more successful.

A Biblical Counseling Plan for Panic Attacks

Phyllis was rushed to the emergency room three times during the last week, when she experienced panic attacks. She believed she was having a heart attack and was afraid that she was dying. She came to counseling after her doctor diagnosed that she was perfectly healthy, but was experiencing panic attacks. She had a heightened sensitivity to the suggestions of others and was now so afraid of having another attack that she was afraid to drive by herself. She said that when she had an attack, she felt dizzy and was afraid that she would pass out while driving and have an accident. She seemed to only have the panic attacks when she was alone and especially after a fight with her husband or when she felt overwhelmed with life.

The Problem Train

Panic attacks occur when a person's past experiences of a fearful situation result in a physical response, and the person interprets it to mean that there is something physically wrong with them. Because they believe something is physically wrong, they become more afraid, and the physical response increases. If they believe the lie that if their heart beats too fast they will die or that they are having a heart attack, the fear and the resulting physical response increases until they start to hyperventilate which makes them feel dizzy. The person eventually believes that something catastrophic is happening, and they enter a panic phase. This usually leads to an emergency room visit, but by the time he or she arrives, the panic has subsided. It seldom lasts for more than 10 minutes. Consequently, this problem is diagramed showing that the problem begins with an emotional response, which causes a physical experience, which is perceived incorrectly in the mind, which results in false perceptions, which leads to feeling insecure. This cycle is repeated until the person avoids certain activities or actions that might place them in a vulnerable position if another attack might occur.

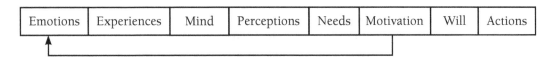

Emotions	Experiences	Mind	Perceptions	Needs	Motivation	Will	Actions

The Solution Train

To resolve this problem, Phyllis will have to decide to face her fear. She will have to displace any lies that she believes, trust God, and perceive the problem for what it is—just a mistaken perception. She will have to find her security in Christ and motivate herself to face her fears as soon as they occur. She will have to take actions to stop the cycle of panic. When she does, she will experience victory over her panic attacks; and in her emotions, she will eventually find peace.

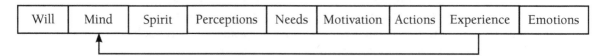

| Will | Mind | Spirit | Perceptions | Needs | Motivation | Actions | Experience | Emotions |

The Counseling Plan for Panic Attacks

Step	Component	Principle	Intervention
1.	Will	Free Choice	Convince her to face her fears trusting God.
2.	Mind	Truth	Convince her that panic attacks cannot hurt her.
3.	Spirit	Revelation	Use "If it is true…" to move the truth to the spirit.
4.	Spirit	Faith	Present evidence that problem can be overcome.
5.	Perceptions	Discernment	Show that panic attack perceptions are wrong.
6.	Needs	Security	God will take care of her no matter what happens.
7.	Motivation	Fear	Act on faith by praising God for the problem.
8.	Motivation	Fear	Use Systematic Desensitization to deal with fear.
9.	Actions	Action	Teach breathing and relaxation techniques.
10.	Actions	Confession	Teach self-talk techniques.
11.	Actions	Action	Have her drive or go out in public to face fear.
12.	Experience	Heart	Layer cake experience to find any remaining lies.
13.	Repeat	Steps 2-11	Until panic attacks subside.
14.	Emotions	Emotions	Use emotional train to eliminate fear
15.	Evaluate	Progress	Determine that panic attacks no longer happen.

A Biblical Counseling Plan for Obsessions

Margery believed that her husband was having an affair with her best friend and that he had had affairs throughout their marriage. All these problems had begun about the time she lost her executive job, her children left home, and he began serving as a soccer coach for their son's soccer team. Intuitively, she felt him distancing himself from her and that "could only mean one thing—he was involved with someone else." She got to the point that nothing could convince her of his innocence and everything he said or did just became more proof that she was right. All she wanted was for him to "tell her everything." When he attempted to do this, she would not believe him and just used it against him. Because he felt he could not win, he told her less and less and became more and more angry. She interpreted this as a sign that he did not love her. All she wanted was for him to show his love by talking to her.

The Problem Train

Obsessions are an attempt to make ourselves feel in control when we feel powerless. Another term for mild cases of obsession is worry. The more we focus on our problem, the larger it gets and the more concerned we become. Consequently, we feel we have to focus more on the problem. If we are confronted, we resist by gathering evidence to prove that we are right and soon we become so convinced that no amount of opposing evidence can dissuade us from our opinion. In this case, it was a deep need to feel loved and valued by her husband and was precipitated when she felt he was emotionally distancing himself from her. In her mind, she feared that this meant that he was involved with someone else and that led her to evaluate everything he had done and would do, suspiciously. As she did this, she gathered evidence that what she feared was true; and the more she gathered evidence the more convinced she became that she was right. Her emotions eventually overcame her logic, and in order to alleviate her feelings of anxiety, she accused him of having affairs in an effort to make him prove his love to her. Of course, her unfounded accusations only drove him further away and the cycle continued.

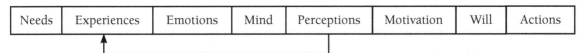

Needs	Experiences	Emotions	Mind	Perceptions	Motivation	Will	Actions

The Solution Train

To resolve this problem, Margery is going to have to take responsibility for her actions and decide to face her obsessions that are the result of her deep need to be loved. She will have to learn to trust God to meet her needs so that she is not so overly dependent on her husband, displace any lies that she believes, relearn discernment, and perceive the problem for what it is—a mistaken perception. If there is any truth in her fears, she can set boundaries to protect her marriage. Getting her to accept the fact that she could be wrong about her emotionally based perceptions will be the greatest challenge. Finally, she will have to face her anxious feelings and learn to cope with them in more effective ways.

Mind	Perceptions	Will	Actions	Spirit	Needs	Motivations	Experience	Emotions

The Counseling Plan for Obsessions

Step	Component	Principle	Intervention
1.	Mind	Truth	Convince her that what she is doing is not working.
2.	Perceptions	Position in Christ	Understand how much Christ loves her.
3.	Perceptions	Discernment	Help her deal with the underlying fear problem.
4.	Perceptions	Discernment	Help her to learn how to discern life events again.
5.	Will	Repentance	Convince her to change her actions.
6.	Action	Responsibility	Take responsibility for her obsessions and fear.
7.	Action	Covenants	Set mutual boundaries concerning adultery.
8.	Actions	Judgment	Convince her she should not judge her husband.
9.	Spirit	Revelation	Use "If it is true..." to turn knowledge to revelation.
10.	Needs	Security	Use the Word and Theophostic Ministry to convince her that God will always take care of her.
11.	Motivation	Fear	Use Systematic Desensitization to deal with fear of her husband emotionally abandoning her.
12.	Experience	Relationships	Develop a strong, loving relationship with God.
13.	Experience	Forgiveness	She needs to forgive and be forgiven.
14.	Experience	Heart	Move her faith that God loves her to her heart.
15.	Repeat	Steps 2-12	Until she feels loved by God and her husband.
16.	Emotions	Emotions	Use the emotional train to eliminate fear.
17.	Evaluate	Progress	Determine that her obsessions and attacks stop.

A Biblical Counseling Plan for Compulsions

Compulsions are so closely associated with obsessions that in The Diagnostic and Statistical Manual for Mental Disorders (DSM IV) they are categorized as an Obsessive Compulsive Disorder (OCD). Julie was afraid that she might lose her job if she did not stop what she was doing. She was spending almost an hour of her time each day at work washing her hands in the bathroom because she was afraid she had become contaminated by the germs on her computer keyboard. At home when washing the dishes she would have to wipe each one seven times with a clean towel before she could put it away. She came from a very legalistic home and feared what God would do to her if she did not do everything exactly perfect.

The Problem Train

Compulsions are again an attempt to feel in control when in fact we feel powerless and out of control. They also serve to alleviate the anxiety caused by obsessions. By focusing on a specific area and getting it just right, we try to make ourselves feel in control of our lives. Many times this is associated with Christian legalism, because it is an attempt to feel secure by perfectly obeying the law of God. The problem is that all these actions do not work! We just have to do more and more to try to feel in control. The problem begins with a deep need to feel secure that has been triggered by the experiences of life which we perceive as threatening. Therefore, we feel insecure. In attempting to cope with this insecurity, the lies in our mind tell us that if we were just perfect and performed better in some area, we would feel better. Thus, we are motivated and decide to act to make ourselves feel secure. Just like an addiction, we initially feel somewhat better, but in the long run feel ashamed and less secure, so we are motivated to repeat the action over and over again.

Needs	Experiences	Perceptions	Emotions	Mind	Motivation	Will	Actions

The Solution Train

To resolve this problem, Julie is going to have to decide to face her deep feelings of insecurity, realize that she believes a lie, and change her legalistic perceptions about life. She will have to learn to trust God to meet her needs so that no matter what experiences she has; she will feel secure in Him. To walk this out, she will have to face her fears with her actions. As an example, if she fears her husband will die if she turns off the computer, she must turn off the computer. When she does and he does not die, she will see that her fears were wrong and will be more willing to face the next fear. This experience will reinforce her faith in the truth in her mind, she will perceive life as more secure, which will make her more confident to face the next fear in her life.

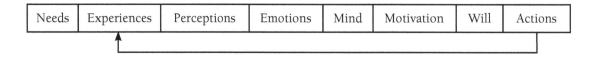

Will	Mind	Perceptions	Spirit	Needs	Motivation	Actions	Experience	Emotions

The Counseling Plan for Compulsions

Step	Component	Principle	Intervention
1.	Will	Free Choice	Decide to face the compulsions in her life.
2.	Mind	Truth	Convince her that what she is doing is not working.
3.	Perceptions	The law	Teach her she is no longer under the law but grace.
4.	Spirit	Faith	Help her develop a trusting relationship with God.
5	Needs	Security	Teach her security in God using Catastrophe Chart.
6.	Motivation	Fear	Understand that we overcome fear by facing it.
7.	Motivation	Fear	Praise God for the good He will do with this.
8.	Motivation	Fear	Use Systematic Desensitization for strong fears.
9.	Action	Action	Do what the compulsion says not to do.
10.	Experience	Experiences	Evidence that the fears are not true.
11.	Emotions	Emotions	Feelings of fear reduced by experience.
12.	Repeat	Steps 1-10	Repeat until all fears are faced.
13.	Emotions	Emotions	Use emotional train to eliminate fear.
14.	Evaluate	Progress	Determine that she no longer acts on her compulsions, is not legalistic, and is feeling secure.

A Biblical Counseling Plan for Sexual Abuse

Mandy's mother called me because she had some concerns about the relationship between her daughter by a previous marriage and her new husband. She had found a hole through which a person could view someone taking a shower. Recently, she caught him with some of Mandy's underclothing. He gave Mandy money and anything else she wanted. It turned out that Mandy's new step–father had been abusing her for some time.

The Problem Train

Sexual abuse is all too common in our society. Most clients come to counseling after the effects of the abuse become apparent in adulthood. Others are brought soon after the abuse has been discovered. In both cases, the damage is already apparent. To some degree they blame themselves either for being naïve or needy, and for not doing what they should have to stop the abuse sooner. In cases of childhood abuse, the victimized child usually believes it was their fault, because children during the concrete period of development see most things as the result of their own actions. They feel dirty and perceive life as no longer safe. Consequently, they build emotional defenses to insure that their needs are met and that the abuse does not happen again. Many times these defenses result in either a promiscuous life-style or sexual frigidity. Sometimes, in extreme cases, the memory of the abuse is hidden from the conscious mind. If the clients remember the abuse, they almost always have strong feelings against the perpetrator and even stronger feelings against those that did not protect them. Many times, they cannot understand why their parents or God did not stop the abuse.

In constructing the problem train, her need for love makes her vulnerable to being abused. The experience of the abuse changes how she thinks about loving relationships, her perceptions about herself, and about life itself. Her emotions, which are based on these perceptions, motivate her to take "defensive" actions that exasperate the problem, and many times lead to more abuse.

Needs	Experiences	Mind	Perceptions	Emotions	Motivation	Will	Actions

The Solution Train

To resolve this problem, Mandy is going to have to decide to face the lies that she believes about the abuse, shame and the emotional pain that she feels. She is going to have to sort the false shame from any real shame based on allowing the abuse to continue in order to meet her own needs. She will need to accept the forgiveness and grace of God to meet her need for love, acceptance and worth. In order to deal with her defenses, she will have to choose to act according to the Word of God, again learn to trust people, lower her defenses and choose to forgive the perpetrator and those who failed to defend her. Only after she does these things as an act of her will is there hope that her emotions will eventually follow.

Will	Mind	Perceptions	Experience	Spirit	Needs	Motivation	Actions	Emotions

The Counseling Plan for Sexual Abuse

Step	Component	Principle	Intervention
1.	Will	Free Choice	Decide to face the damage of the abuse.
2.	Mind	Truth	Know that she is not responsible for the abuse.
3.	Perceptions	Position in Christ	Understand that God still loves and values her.
4.	Perceptions	The law	Understand God is not judging her but gives grace.
5.	Experience	Experiences	Theophostic Ministry to see the abuse as God does.
6.	Experience	Forgiveness	Help her to forgive herself and others involved.
7.	Spirit	Conscience	Help her to teach her conscience she is not dirty.
8	Needs	Security	Teach her security in God using Catastrophe Chart.
9.	Motivation	Fear	Understand that we overcome fear by facing it.
10.	Motivation	Fear	Praise God for how He will use this for good.
11.	Motivation	Fear	Use Systematic Desensitization for strong fears.
12.	Action	Action	When safe, do what the defenses say not to do.
13.	Action	Judgment	Confront the abuser's actions, when appropriate.
14.	Action	Judgment	Turn judgment of the abusers over to God.
15.	Emotions	Emotions	Use the emotional train to change her feelings.
16.	Emotions	Emotions	Understand that the abusers are hurting people.
17.	Repeat	Steps 1-16	Until emotions of the abuse are healed.
18.	Evaluate	Progress	Determine that she can again love and be loved in a healthy way.

A Biblical Counseling Plan for Domestic Violence

James was a classical domestic violence perpetrator. He was a Gulf War veteran whose entire view of life had been changed by his war experiences. To him "life was a sea of sharks and if you showed any vulnerability you would be devoured." He was married and went faithfully to church, but he had failed again and again to stop the abusive and violent episodes, that seemed to have a cyclical pattern of their own. After an episode, he would be repentant and declare that it would never happen again. However, as time went by, tension would build again until he was convinced that the women in his life were just using him and that everyone was against him. His rage was sometimes so strong other people could feel it in the air.

The Problem Train

Classical domestic violence is rooted in a need to feel secure in life, a strong fear of abandonment and an attempt to be self-sufficient. This insecurity and fear result in a strong desire to be in control of what others, especially the abuser's mate, do in order to ensure that they do not leave him. The abuser usually has a low opinion of himself and is convinced that if he lets his mate out of his sight, she will find someone better and will abandon him. Consequently, he will do everything possible, including suggesting that she is so inadequate that she could not get along without him, convincing her that she cannot trust her own judgment, making her feel so insecure that she needs his protection, isolating her from her friends so that she has nowhere to turn to for help or to get a reality check on life, and causing her to be so afraid that she does not even have her own opinion. He will, in effect, attempt to "turn her into a sniffling idiot." Because, when the abuser tries to control or take away another's free will, the person being abused eventually rebels, more and more effort and force is required to keep the spouse under control until the abuser has to resort to violence. The resulting cycle of violence is based on the belief that the abuser is supposed to be able to be in control of his life. Initially, as the abuser attempts to control his circumstances, he fails, blames himself for being inadequate and tries harder. As he fails over and over, his frustration and tension increases. At some point, he begins to blame others for interfering with his attempts to succeed, and the tension escalates. The cycle continues until he explodes in rage at anything or anyone whom he cannot control.

In building the problem train, we see that it is his past experiences, lies about life, and perceptions concerning his needs that underlie the problem. His deep needs result in fear of abandonment, which provide the motivation to try to control his circumstances, which result in escalating frustration that eventually explodes in violent behavior.

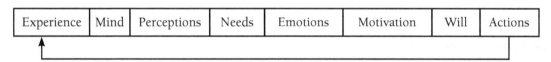

The Solution Train

To resolve this problem, we are going to have to convince James that what he is doing is not working and that it will result in the destruction of his family. He will have to turn his life over to God and quit trying to be the lord of his own life. Many times the abuser is strongly obsessed by his need to control and, therefore, it may be difficult to get him to change. We need to deal with the lies he believes in his mind, change how he perceives life, teach him anger management, and help him meet his needs for security and love through God. When this is accomplished, he will be motivated to bring his actions under control and through the use of boundaries or covenants; he will experience an ever-improving quality of life.

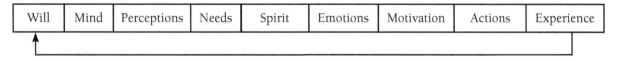

The Counseling Plan for Domestic Violence Abuse

Step	Component	Principle	Intervention
1.	Will	Free Choice	Understand his actions are destroying his family.
2.	Will	Lordship	Help him to make God, Lord and ruler of his life.
3.	Mind	Truth	Understand that by controlling, he loses control.
4.	Perceptions	Position in Christ	Understand that God still loves and values him.
5.	Perceptions	Discernment	Help him see life differently.
6.	Needs	Security	Teach him how to feel secure through God.
7.	Needs	Self-worth	Help him find his worth without performance.
8.	Spirit	Revelation	Use "If it is true…" to get God's view of life.
9.	Spirit	Prayer	Help him learn to pray when tempted to explode.
10.	Spirit	Fasting	Use fasting to break the power of the flesh.
11	Spirit	Spirit	Cast out the spirit of anger when it manifests.
12.	Spirit	Walking	Teach him to walk according to the Spirit.
13.	Emotions	Emotions	Help him learn to calm his emotions when upset.
14.	Motivation	Fear	Understand that he will overcome fear by facing it.
15.	Motivation	Fear	Praise God for how He will use this for good.
16.	Motivation	Fear	Use systematic desensitization for fear and trust.
17.	Motivation	Anger	Teach him anger management techniques.
18.	Action	Covenants	Establish and enforce tripwire boundaries.
19.	Action	Action	Teach him to act differently to break the dance.
20.	Experience	Experiences	Theophostic Ministry to see the abuse as God does.
21.	Experience	Forgiveness	Help him to be forgiven and to forgive himself.
22.	Experience	Forgiveness	Abuse reconciliation done one step at a time.
23	Repeat	Steps 1-22	Until abuse stops, control ends, trust is rebuilt.
24.	Evaluate	Progress	Determine that God is in control.

A Biblical Counseling Plan for Marital Therapy

One of the most frequent forms of counseling is marital therapy. It comes in numerous varieties and forms and represents a wide variety of problems. However, marital problems are usually based on unmet needs, poor communication and the inability to resolve problems. In fact, sometimes I will say to a couple that if they could just learn to communicate and resolve their problems they would not need a counselor.

John and Martha came to me because they were in constant conflict. They had separated and returned to each other numerous times. He felt that no matter what he did, it would not be good enough for her, and she felt unloved in the marriage. It seemed that they were in a love fight. They each wanted the other to prove their love by their actions. They were also in a power struggle wanting the other one to meet their needs first and they believed that if they could just fix their mate everything would be okay. Of course, there were also the usual issues of poor communication, inadequate problem solving skills and gender differences.

The Problem Train

After asking them to each tell me how they saw the problem, I would gather the pieces of the puzzle to determine the whole picture of what was happening in their relationship. (See the form in the appendix for the data that I would collect.) I would then make a list of the major issues to be resolved, so that I would not miss anything when I wrote up the counseling plan.

From the information above, I would be suspicious that the underlying problem is one of codependency because codependency most often results in ongoing conflict with multiple separations. Codependents also usually believe that "if they could just fix their mate everything would be okay." Consequently, they are critical of each other and try to fix their mates instead of focusing on their own issues. This leads to a power struggle to make the mate change so that their needs will be met. I would use a codependency test or inventory to determine if this was true and, if it was, try to identify the sub-type of codependency that each of them typified. I would then list codependency as one of the items to be addressed. (See *Transformation!* for models of codependency and a codependency assessment.) Because conflict is the presenting problem, I would ask them to give me an example and layer cake (see Principles of Experience, Heart, Method #2) their perceptions of the problem to determine the unmet needs that underlie the conflict. From this I would determine the particular issues that prevent them from effectively resolving their problems, so that these issues could be addressed later. I would also evaluate their communication, gender and attachment issues.

From this information, we can construct the problem train. Codependency usually results from growing up in a dysfunctional or codependent family. The past experience, lies, and perceptions of life result in unmet needs. The resulting fear that these needs will not be met motivates the client to try to meet these needs through the flesh. Since needs can never be fully met by relying on other people, these attempts in the flesh will result in frequent criticizing, manipulating and controlling of the other person, which will result in greater dysfunction and conflict. Of course, the underlying problem is that they are trying to meet these needs through the flesh instead of God. The problem is accentuated by the fact that they lack communication and problem solving skills, and, most likely, have insecure attachment styles.

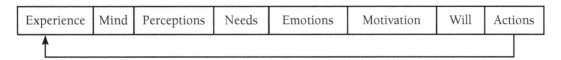

The Solution Train

To resolve this problem, we are going to have to convince John and Mary to face their own problems and to quit trying to fix their mate. They will have to turn their lives over to God and quit trying to be the lord of their own lives. We are going to have to teach them about marriage, codependency, boundaries, communication, problem solving, gender issues and attachment. We will have to try to get them to perceive their problem and themselves differently. Possibly, the most difficult change will be to help them to rely primarily on God to meet their needs. When they do, it will provide the motivation to start changing how they act and it will help them to focus on actually loving and meeting their mate's needs. They will have to implement boundaries or covenants to de-conflict their relationship and practice their new communication, gender and problem solving skills. When they do, these new relationship methods will stop the dance of anger and they will experience what a Christian marriage is supposed to be like.

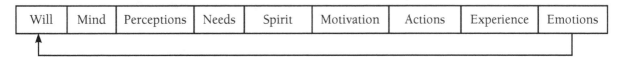

The Counseling Plan for Marital Therapy

Step	Component	Principle	Intervention
1.	Will	Free Choice	Choose to fix their problems and not their mates.
2.	Will	Lordship	Help them make God, Lord of their lives.
3.	Mind	Truth	Understand that by controlling they lose control.
4.	Mind	Truth	Teach them about their codependency.
5.	Mind	Truth	Teach them about boundaries.
6.	Mind	Truth	Teach them about marriage and attachment.
7.	Mind	Truth	Teach them communication and gender issues.
8.	Mind	Truth	Teach them about problem solving.
9.	Perceptions	Position in Christ	Understand that God still loves and values them.
10.	Perceptions	Discernment	Help them to see life differently.
11.	Needs	Love	Teach them to feel loved and accepted by God.
12.	Needs	Self-worth	Help them find worth and approval through God.
13.	Needs	Security	Help them believe that God will meet their needs.
14.	Spirit	Revelation	Use "If it is true…" to get God's revelation of life.
15.	Spirit	Prayer	Help them learn to pray when tempted to get angry.
16.	Spirit	Fasting	Use fasting to break the power of the flesh.
17.	Spirit	Spirit	Help them to learn to walk according to the Spirit.
18.	Motivation	Consequences	Help them learn about sowing and reaping.
19.	Motivation	Fear	Praise God for how He will use this for good.
20.	Motivation	Fear	Use systematic desensitization to alleviate fears.
21.	Motivation	Anger	Teach them anger management techniques.
22.	Action	Communication	Teach and practice speaker-listener technique.
23.	Action	Responsibility	Assume unilateral responsibility for actions.
24.	Action	Covenants	Establish and enforce boundaries or covenants.
25	Action	Action	Teach them to act differently to break the dance.
26	Action	Justice	Practice conflict resolution to win-win solutions.
27.	Experience	Experiences	Use Theophostic Ministry to alleviate past trauma.
28.	Experience	Experiences	Use MMQ (Monday Morning Quarterback) to resolve offense.
29.	Experience	Forgiveness	Help them to forgive and be forgiven.
30.	Emotions	Emotions	Help them learn to calm their emotions when upset.
31.	Emotions	Emotions	Help them to attach and fall in love again.
32.	Repeat	Steps 1-27	Determine when emotions return and trust rebuilt.
33.	Evaluate	Progress	If they believe spouse loves and appreciates them.

A Biblical Counseling Plan for Borderline Personality Disorder

Some of the most difficult problems to treat are those listed in the *Diagnostic and Statistic Manual of Mental Disorders* (DSM IV). These disorders usually require counseling plans that integrate secular research, biblical principles and models because most are not even described in any detail as specific problems in the Bible. Of these, Borderline Personality Disorder is known to be especially difficult to treat.

According to DSM IV, Borderline Personality Disorder begins in early adult life and is characterized by problems with unstable impulse control, interpersonal relationships, moods and self-image. This disorder is diagnosed if the person has five of the following: Frantic attempts to prevent abandonment, unstable relationships alternating between idealization and devaluation, severely unstable self-image, self-damaging impulses such as binge eating, reckless driving, sex, spending, or substance abuse, self-mutilation or suicidal threats or attempts, or severe reactivity of mood leading to marked instability. (American Psychiatric Association, 1994)

Jane was a very popular High School psychology teacher married to a quiet mannered computer engineer. She was usually able to confine her problem to her private life, but recently she had blown up at the school principal when he had told her he was going to retire. Even the very slightest hint that her husband might be emotionally unavailable to her would result in rage, hitting him, and breaking or throwing almost everything in sight. Once, in my office, when her husband made a innocent remark that she perceived could be a threat of abandonment, she regressed to the behaviour of a three-year-old little girl, through a temper tantrum, and started beating on him. Although he had learned to put up with it, it was clear that this was a very difficult relationship to maintain.

The Problem Train

In dealing with clients with Borderline Personality disorder, we must first admit that, although much has been written on this subject, it is a very complex and difficult problem. In my experience dealing with this problem, I have learned that the deep underlying fears must be addressed first or little progress will be made. Dealing with the self-worth, security, significance, love needs and processing childhood traumatic experiences is mandatory. Theophostic ministry and addressing these deep needs have proven to be the most effective methods available. (See Smith, 1996, and my book *Faith Therapy*.) Codependency is usually also an issue. Of course, once the trauma and needs have been addressed, the emotionality, anger and acting out must be dealt with. As always, a loving personal relationship with God is the final answer. Again, it is the childhood trauma, unmet needs, the lies that she believes, and her catastrophic perceptions of her life that fuel the strong emotions which motivate her to act in catastrophic ways.

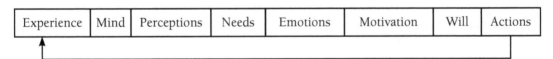

The Solution Train

To resolve this problem, we will first have to deal with the traumatic experiences that have affected her subconscious mind, her perceptions of her life, and her deep neediness within, and help her develop a dynamic relationship with God. She must turn the control of her life over to God and trust Him to meet her needs. Only He can promise "never to leave or forsake her." Because of the extreme control issues, if possible, she needs the power inherent in the baptism of the Holy Spirit. Once she realizes that because of God all her needs will be met, her perceptions of life will become more positive and her strong emotions will subside. With a diminished emotional response, she will be less motivated to want to act in catastrophic ways, and she will begin to be more in control of her actions. At this point, we can help her establish boundaries, teach her anger management techniques, and alternate ways of expressing her emotional pain. Of course, this will be a long-term process until her experiences, perceptions and emotions begin to line up with the truth of God's Word, and she has a new secure loving experience with God and her husband.

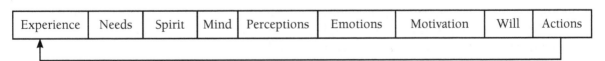

The Counseling Plan for Borderline Personality Disorder

Step	Component	Principle	Intervention
1.	Experience	Experiences	Theophostic Ministry to alleviate past trauma.
2.	Experience	Experiences	Use MMQ to process past problems.
3.	Experience	Forgiveness	Help her to forgive others as well as herself.
4.	Needs	Love	Teach her how to feel loved and accepted by God.
5.	Needs	Self-worth	Help her find her worth and approval through God.
6.	Needs	Security	Help her believe that God will meet all her needs.
7.	Needs	Significance	Help her to feel important to God without works.
8.	Spirit	Revelation	Use "If it is true…" to make this truth revelation.
9.	Spirit	Prayer	Help her learn to pray when tempted to get angry.
10.	Spirit	Fasting	Use fasting to break the power of the flesh.
11.	Spirit	Spirit	Help her to learn to walk according to the Spirit.
12.	Spirit	Baptism	If willing, help her receive the Spirit baptism.
13.	Spirit	Baptism	Suggest she edify herself with her prayer language.
14.	Mind	Truth	Understand that controllers lose everything.
15.	Mind	Truth	Teach her about codependency.
16.	Mind	Truth	Teach her about boundaries.
17.	Mind	Truth	Teach her about marriage and attachment.
18.	Mind	Truth	Teach her about communication and gender issues.
19.	Mind	Truth	Teach her about problem solving.
20.	Perceptions	Position in Christ	Understand that God still loves and accepts her.
21.	Perceptions	Law and Grace	Help her understand and accept God's grace.
22.	Perceptions	Discernment	Help her see life differently.
23.	Emotions	Emotions	Help her learn to calm her emotions when upset.
24.	Emotions	Emotions	Help her develop a secure attachment style.
25.	Motivation	Consequences	Help her learn about sowing and reaping.
26.	Motivation	Fear	Praise God that He will use everything for good.
27.	Motivation	Fear	Use systematic desensitization to overcome fears.
28.	Motivation	Anger	Teach her anger management techniques.
29.	Motivation	Accountability	Support groups and accountability are helpful.
30.	Will	Free Choice	Help her realize that she can choose how she acts.
31.	Will	Lordship	Help her to make God Lord and ruler of her life.
32.	Action	Communication	Teach and practice speaker-listener technique.
33.	Action	Responsibility	Assume unilateral responsibility for actions.
34.	Action	Covenants	Establish and enforce boundaries or covenants.
35.	Action	Action	Teach to act differently in order to break the dance.
36.	Action	Justice	Practice conflict resolution with win-win solutions.
37.	Repeat	Steps 1-37	Until emotional stability returns and trust is rebuilt.
38.	Evaluate	Progress	Achievement of stable moods and relationships.

From this example, it is apparent that counseling plans for very complex problems can become very complex in themselves. However, the more complicated the problem, the more we need an overall plan for the entire counseling process. We can then rely on the Holy Spirit to provide the day-by-day direction for its implementation.

Chapter 15

How to Counsel Using Biblical Principles

Once we have developed a counseling plan from biblical principles, we must integrate that plan within the overall counseling process. This overall process has five phases or components:

1. The assessment. This is establishing the relationship, determining the presenting problem, gathering the data and analyzing the problem to determine the structure of the problem train.

2. Develop the counseling plan for this particular problem. This phase may take the form of the process for developing plans from biblical principles that has been the main focus of this book or it can be based on one of the complex biblical models developed in *Transformation!* or one of the "deeply-rooted" models developed in *Faith Therapy*.

3. Integrate the counseling plan into the overall counseling process as outlined in "The Biblical Plan for Christian Counseling." This provides the overall biblical structure for the counseling process that was derived in *Transformation!* from the story of the exodus of the children of Israel.

4. Implement the integrated plan following the direction of the Holy Spirit. Counseling models and plans are developed to provide a direction for the overall approach to the problem. They do not direct the moment-by-moment conduct of each counseling session. As I stated earlier in this book, the counseling plan or model are the roadmap, not the written directions that tell of each turn to be taken. We, as counselors, need to submit the conduct of each counseling session to the direction of the Holy Spirit, the Chief Counselor.

5. Evaluation and termination. When the goal and objectives of the counseling process are reached, it is time for termination of the individual counseling process. For long-term problems, this will usually mean referring the client to a support group, suggesting additional books and workbooks, and inviting them to call if they encounter further difficulties. At other times, especially for more simplistic problems, we should pray for the client and release them again to the continued guidance and direction of the Holy Spirit.

In order to make this entire process clear, let us revisit the biblical plan for anxiety developed in the previous chapter. Although the two cases that make up this composite case actually occurred before much of the development of this book, I will describe it as if I conducted it using the forms and techniques that are provided in this book. The basic methods and outcomes described are authentic but some details have been changed to protect the clients' identities.

A Biblical Counseling Plan for Anxiety

Remember Mary? She was sent to me from her insurance company because, after an automobile accident, she was afraid to drive. In this chapter, I will describe her case from the initial session through termination in order to help the reader fully understand how the methods of this book fit within the overall process of Christian counseling. I will highlight the steps of The Biblical Plan for Christian Counseling that I originally developed in *Transformation!* in bold print.

1. **Determine the problem.** After meeting Mary for the first time, I asked her what brought her to counseling. I explained that it was my role as a resource to help her deal with her problem, not to fix her or to make her decisions for her. I always try at the outset to make the roles of the counselor and client clear in order to insure the client feels fully responsible for her recovery and in control of the therapeutic process. Just as God does not attempt to control us in the decisions we make, so I set the client free to make her own decisions, as long as she is willing to accept the consequences of those decisions. Of course, I will provide biblical direction and help her evaluate her alternatives, but I will never attempt to control her decisions. Except in the cases of suicide, homicide or child abuse, everything discussed in session will be held in confidence. In conducting this intake assessment, I had her fill out our standard intake form which asks for personal information, including name, address, phone numbers, family members, and presenting problem. I gave her our informed consent and confidentiality form and, after she read it, I asked her to sign it so I could place it into her records. I then began to gather the information necessary to analyze the problem. This form as I filled it out appears on the next page. (See the appendix for a blank copy of these forms.)

   As I asked the appropriate questions to gather this data, I identified the most significant items and tried to integrate them into an overall picture of my client and the presenting problem. I placed a star beside the important items in my personal notes that I took during this first session. A double star meant something very important or critical. From Mary's answers to my questions, I concluded that she was functioning normally with an underlying problem with codependency that probably led to her divorce. I hypothesized that she is a codependent dependent rescuer from her need to accomplish, as well as her failed marriage to an alcoholic. Consequently, she would need additional help and support in this area in order to help her face her fear of driving. Although her faith had been shaken by the accident, she was definitely saved and had no occult or other non-Christian background that might indicate a need for deliverance. However, she was not a strong student of the Bible and would need teaching on the subject of God's protection for Christians, in order to restore her faith. I diagnosed the main issue, as an Adjustment Disorder with Anxiety. This diagnosis was based on the fact that she did not have a problem with anxiety prior to the accident, and no other recent stressors were noted during the interview. This type of anxiety is a classical case for the use of systematic desensitization. Although I made this initial analysis from the data collected, a full counseling plan would still be required by the third step of the counseling process. In this case, the therapy would be a blend of a plan using biblical principles and the biblical model for Codependency. The Bible does not give us a specific example or model for anxiety caused by an accident, but it does provide a model for a codependent dependent rescuer. (See the model of Abigail in my book *Transformation!*)

Client Problem Assessment

Client Name <u>Mary Johnson</u>   Counselor Name <u>Troy Reiner</u>   Phone <u>652-1677</u>   Date <u>Jan 3, 2004</u>

Presenting Problem <u>Car accident, afraid to drive. Possible anxiety or adjustment disorder.</u>

_____

_____

_____

Issues involved:

[ ]   Marital/relationship conflict _____

[ ]   Parenting _____

[ ]   Blended family/family issues/unforgiveness_____

[ ]   Anger problems/verbal abuse _____

[ ]   Domestic violence Worst incident? _____How long? _____

[ ]   Drug/alcohol abuse/addictions Types? _____How long?_____ Dependent? _____

[ ]   Pornography/sexual addiction?_____

[ ]   Rape/incest/homosexuality? _____

[ ]   Sexual problems Affairs? _____ How often do they have sex? _____

[ ]   Other abuse/trauma/sicknesses/abortions? _____

[X]   Codependency How severe?_____Moderate_____ Subtype?_____Dependent Rescuer_____

[X]   Divorce/separation?_____To Alcoholic_____ When separated?_____

[ ]   Loss/grief _____

[ ]   Depression _____ Bi-polar?_____ Suicidal? _____ Plan? _____

[X]   Emotional problems? ____Anxiety____ Low Self-worth? _____ Driven?_____ Pride?_____

[ ]   Financial problems? _____

[X]   Other_____Afraid to drive due to car accident_____

Relationship Analysis

Married/Divorced/Cohabitation? _Divorced_ How long? _3 years_ #Marriages _1_ # Children _____

                                                                Client   Spouse

Perceived Best Interest in Mind?

Perceived Loved and Appreciated?

Rate Marriage 1-10

Rate Sex Life 1-10

Family of origin

Client: Child # __3__ out of __4__ children in the family _____ Adopted? __No__ Role in the family Lost Child

Describe father Disciplinarian, Christian Abuse/controller? _____No_____ Child met expectations? _____No_____

Describe mother Passive Codependent Abuse/controller? _____No_____ Child met expectations? _____Yes_____

Divorced? __No__ At what age?_____ Who did you live with? _____

Describe step father/mother _____ Abuse/controller? _____ Child met expectations? _____

Describe family life _Good Christian family with codependent tendencies_ _____

School performance _____average_____ Sports? _____No_____ Parental support _____Yes_____

Describe relationships Married alcoholic who refused to quit and divorced her after three years.

Mental/physical health problems in family? _____No_____ Suicide attempts? _____No_____

Spouse: Child # ____ out of ____ children in the family _____ Adopted? _____ Role in the family _____

Describe father _____ Abuse/controller? _____ Child met expectations? _____

Describe mother _____ Abuse/controller? _____ Child met expectations? _____

Divorced?_____ At what age?_____ Who did you live with?_____

Describe step father/mother _____ Abuse/controller? _____ Child met expectations? _____

Describe family life_____

School performance _____ Sports? _____ Parental support _____

Describe relationships_____

Mental/physical health problems in family?_____ Suicide attempts? _____

Spiritual assessment: Client

[X]   Saved? How long? __30__ Baptized? __Y__ Bible knowledge? __OK__ Spiritual disciplines? _____Y_____

[X]   Attends church? __X__ What church? _Charismatic_ How involved? _some_ Bible study? _____

[ ]   Involvement in other religion/occult/new age? __No__ Type/extent? _____

Spiritual assessment: Spouse

[ ]   Saved? How long? _____ Baptized? _____ Bible knowledge? _____ Spiritual disciplines? _____

[ ]   Attends church? ____ What church? _____ How involved? _____ Bible study? _____

[ ]   Involvement in other religion/occult/new age? _____ Type/extent?_____

Attachment analysis: Client

[ ]   Secure style—Worthy and capable of receiving love and can trust others to give love.

[ ]   Avoidant style—Worthy and capable of receiving love but can not trust others to give love.

[X]   Ambivalent style—Must perform to be loved but can trust others to give love.

[ ]   Disorganized style—Not worthy of receiving love and can not trust others to give love.

Attachment analysis: Spouse

[ ]   Secure style—Worthy and capable of receiving love and can trust others to give love.

[ ]   Avoidant style—Worthy and capable of receiving love but can not trust others to give love.

[ ]   Ambivalent style—Must perform to be loved but can trust others to give love.

[ ]   Disorganized style—Not worthy of receiving love and can not trust others to give love.

Counselor's evaluation of the problem <u>Adjustment disorder with anxiety complicated by codependency. Possibly performance and approval self-worth. Reasonably mature Christian whose faith is shaken by the accident. Believes she should have been protected by God. Does not know extent of requirements of protection. Wonders why it happened. Needs support.</u>

Recommended treatment plan

	Issues to be addressed	*Method*	*Goal*
1.	Fear	Systematic Desensitization	Able to drive again
2.	Loss of faith	Protection from catastrope chart	Trust God again
3.	Codependency	12-Step workbook	Recovery
4.	Support	Codependency Support Group	Support
5.			
6.			
7.			
8.			
9.			

Prior to moving on to step two, I needed to develop a counseling plan built from biblical principles and integrate it with the Biblical Plan for Christian Counseling. I followed the steps previously listed as they appeared on the Quick Form for Building a Counseling Plan from Biblical Principles. This form is available in the appendix and is presented on the next two pages as I filled it out. For the logic behind these selections, please refer back to the discussion of this case in the previous chapter.

Quick Form for Building a Counseling Plan from Biblical Principles

1. **What is the problem?**

<u>The problem is that Mary has developed a fear of driving as a result of an accident. The problem is accentuated by the fact that her faith has been shaken by the incident and underlying insecurity and codependency issues.</u>

2. **What is the primary component affected by the problem?** Place a star on the primary component.

| X | X | X | X | X | X | X | X | * |

Will	Spirit	Mind	Perceptions	Needs	Motivation	Actions	Experience	Emotions

3. **What other members or functions of the heart have been affected by it or affect it?** Place an X on the remainder of the blocks above that are involved in the problem.

4. **What is the root cause or psychological need or needs underlying the problem?** Place an X on the appropriate boxes below.   X

Worth		Significance		Security		Love

5. **Determine the order of the components that are creating the problem.** Fill in the train cars below in the order that you hypothesize is the sequence that is creating the problem.

Experience	Mind	Perceptions	Spirit	Needs	Emotions	Motivation	Will	Actions

6. **Couple the cars to build the train to resolve this problem.** Reconstruct the train using only the cars selected. Place the psychological need in the need car.

Will	Mind	Perceptions	Experience	Spirit	Security	Motivation	Actions	Emotions

7. **Which principles apply in each component?** Under each component list the principles by letter. Chapter numbers represent the principles of change (1) and faith (3).

Principles

a	b	c	c	g	d	a	b	a
				3		c		
						c		
						c		

Methods

3	1	3	1	3	1	3	3	2
				3		2		
						5		
						1		

8. **What methods and techniques are needed?** Under each component (below the principles), list the number of the methods or techniques for their application. See the index of methods in the appendix.

9. **What is the faith component? How is faith applied in this counseling plan?** List faith principles and methods on the appropriate lines if applicable under each component. Chapter numbers represent the principles of change (1) and faith (3). (For more on the principles of faith see *Faith Therapy*.)

10. **Load the train cars.** Determine the order and importance of each technique as they are to be applied to that component by reordering the principles and techniques.

11. **What are the goals and how will they be measured?**

Goal	*How Measured?*
1. Overcome fear of driving	Ability to drive as well as before
2. Regain faith in God for security	Lowered anxiety
3. Codependency recovery	Healthy relationships with boundaries

12. **Define the route of the train.** By placing flow diagram arrows on the train diagram above indicate any flow between the cars

13. **What is the plan to intervene in the whole person?** List the plan according to the order of steps. Both principles and methods may be used as interventions.

Step	Component	Principle	Intervention
1.	Will	Free Choice	Convince her to trust God to face her fears.
2.	Mind	Truth	Convince her she can rely on God's Word.
3.	Perceptions	Grace	Convince her protection depends on grace.
4.	Experience	Experience	Theophostic Ministry to heal experience.
5.	Spirit	Revelation	Use "If it is true…" to make truth real.
6.	Spirit	Faith	Present evidence that fears can be overcome.
7	Needs	Security	Teach Protection from Catastrophe chart.
8	Motivation	Motivation	List motivators and de-motivators to drive.
9.	Motivation	Fear	Use Systematic Desensitization to face fear.
10.	Motivation	Fear	Praising God accident will work for good.
11.	Motivation	Fear	Help her to replace fear with faith.
12.	Action	Confession	Confess God's Word, not her fears.
13.	Emotions	Emotions	Use the Emotional Train to overcome fear.
14.	Repeat	Steps 9-12	Complete the desensitization process
15.	Codependency	Model of Abigail	Treat the underlying Codependency issue.
16.	Evaluate	Progress	Determine when goals are reached.

14. **How does this plan fit into The Biblical Plan for Christian Counseling?** Step 1 becomes part of the biblical plan step 2. Steps 2-3 become part of biblical plan step 2. Step 4 becomes part of biblical plan step 3. Steps 5-7 become part of biblical plan step 6. The remainder of the steps become part of biblical plan step 8. Additional work to deal with the root problem of insecurity and codependency may be required in biblical plan step 9.

15. Schedule the train.

    [X]   Individual weekly sessions <u>1</u>

    [X]   Support Groups <u>Codependency Support Group</u>

    [X]   Books/workbooks <u>Conquering Codependency</u>

2. <u>**Demonstrate that what the client is doing will not meet his needs and build hope that his problems can be overcome through Christ.**</u> Note that step one of the specific plan is to be applied at this point in the process. After the assessment, I usually explain my conclusions concerning the problems to be addressed. In this case, I made it clear that the problem is that her faith in God's protection has been shaken by the accident. It is her fear of another accident that is causing the anxiety when she even thinks about driving again. I explained that this is not unusual for a situation of this type, but that it is probably extenuated by her past experiences growing up in an insecure, codependent family, and her lack of understanding of exactly what God promises us in the way of protection and what the biblical requirements are for receiving it. I applied step one of the specific plan by showing her that attempting to rely on herself and her flesh to force herself to drive was not working and that she needed to decide to again rely on God for her security and to overcome her problem with anxiety. I explained that because God is in total control of the universe, He, and only He, is able to provide total security for her life.

3. <u>**Use the biblical principles and models to help the client perceive and understand the problem from a biblical perspective.**</u> In this session, I explained the overall plan for recovery from a biblical perspective. I told her that to regain her faith in God, we would study God's Word to determine exactly what He did and did not promise in the way of protection in this life. Next, we would use systematic desensitization to help her to overcome her fear of driving slowly and experientially. I told her that this technique is effective 90 percent of the time, even in secular counseling, and is used to overcome anxiety and phobias such as a fear of flying. It is simply a method to slowly confront her fear and with the help of God, I saw no reason why she could not be driving again in the near future. I prepared the foundation for addressing what the Bible says about protection in a future session by teaching her the truth about the reliability of the Word of God and that what God promises us through grace does not depend on our works or performance. This last point was important because if her protection from God was dependent on her performance, she might always question her security because of her own feelings of inadequacy which underlie her codependency. Finally, we would deal with her codependency through the use of the biblical model of Abigail directly from the Bible. In the remainder of this session, I explained what Codependency is, how it was affecting her life and how it can be overcome through faith in Christ.

    The specific plan specified that at this point, I was to use Theophostic Ministry to help her see the accident as God did. In Theophostic Ministry, we attempt to alleviate traumatic emotions by changing the perception of the event. In most cases, the client has not even considered that God was involved in the experience. As she described the accident and the fear that she felt even when talking about it, I asked the Holy Spirit to reveal the truth to her. In this case, she did not see Jesus in her memory or hear God speaking to her but felt a strong feeling of peace come over her. Somehow, she just knew that she knew that God protected her in the accident. This new experience helped her to know that no matter what happened, God would be there to protect her.

4. <u>**Determine where the client is in the process of salvation and, if appropriate, lead him to accept Christ, be baptized, yield the control of his life to God, and help him get established in a church.**</u> Although Mary's faith had been shaken by the accident, it was not overcome to the degree that she was questioning her salvation. She had been baptized and she was still attending church. However, I questioned whether Jesus was still in charge of her life. When a person's faith is shaken, she will

many times revert back to attempting to rely again on herself to meet her needs. Because I had not anticipated this, I had not specified making Jesus Lord in the specific plan. Plans are made to provide the roadmap, but not always every turn, so I added this to her plan. I placed the principle of lordship under principles of her will and used the first counseling method in that section. I challenged her by questioning if she had enough information to direct her life. I used my own experience of making Jesus Lord of my life and suggested that she was not capable of effectively providing her own protection without knowledge of the future. Even with that knowledge, she was not all-powerful like God. I concluded that session by leading her again in a prayer to make Jesus Lord in her life.

5. **Help the client take responsibility for his own actions, not blame others or react to what they do, and do everything as unto God.** In this step, we sorted out the responsibility for the accident. I explained that even if it was not her fault (it clearly wasn't), she still needed to take responsibility for her feelings toward the offending party and forgive him. Because she said that she had already forgiven the other driver and felt the police and emergency personnel had done an excellent job, I did not have to add another step into the specific plan to address this under the component of experience. If required, teaching on the Principles of Forgiveness, Reconciliation, and Restitution and helping her to forgive the other driver and herself would have been appropriate at this point.

6. **Help the client grow in his personal relationship with Christ and build faith that, with God's help, he can overcome the problem.** The goal of this step is to transform the hope that we have attempted to build into the client in steps two and three, into faith that they will recover. It is faith that couples the entire train together and provides the basis for believing that all the client's needs will be met. According to the specific plan built from biblical principles, at this point, I was building her faith so that she could recover using the "If it is true…" method. To do this, I gave her a number of Bible verses that state that God will protect us if we will trust in His protection. Therefore, I asked, "If God is your rock and your fortress in time of need, and God cannot fail…how would you act?" Of course, the answer is she would at least attempt to drive, and she would be at peace. I assigned her the homework of using this method and acting as much as she could according to what she had confessed was true. The idea here was to begin the process of confronting her fears with action. Next, according to the plan, I presented evidence to rebuild her faith. I told her stories of other clients (being careful to maintain confidentiality) who overcame fearful situations, stories of Bible characters who overcame their fears, and a few personal stories of people I know who were greatly protected by God. To finally convince her that, with God's help, she could overcome this problem, I taught her what the Bible says about protection from catastrophe using the chart that I developed when I wrote *Faith Therapy*. I explained that, as long as she trusted in God for her protection and avoided pride, direct disobedience, and tempting God by purposely putting herself in dangerous situations, she could count on Him to work everything for her good from His perspective. Since God knows everything including the future, He is the only one who can truly decide what is best for her. Consequently, He asks her to trust Him even when things do happen that do not make sense to her at this moment of time. Of course, God does not promise to protect her from the tribulations of life. It is her job, relying on Him, to overcome them. That is one of the ways He builds character. I then suggested that "If it is true…"what I had just taught her…how would she act? Of course, the answer is that she would feel secure in life and see this world as a safe place. I assigned the homework of confessing this truth to herself and acting on it until it became reality in her spirit.

7. **Assist the client in receiving the empowerment of the baptism of the Holy Spirit if he chooses to do so.** This step requires teaching the client the principles of the baptism of the Holy Spirit so that she could receive it, if desired. This is especially important in overcoming the problems associated with the lust of the flesh or in dealing with spiritual oppression. In this case, Mary already had received the baptism of the Holy Spirit and attended a charismatic church.

8. **Help the client apply the biblical principles or model to overcome the identified psychological problem.** Now that Mary understood her problem from a biblical perspective, it was time to directly apply the remainder of the specific counseling plan based on biblical principles or models. This is usually the point in therapy when the majority of the specific plan is implemented to resolve the presenting problem. In Mary's case, we had already made progress helping her experience the peace of God about her accident and rebuilding her faith that she could depend on God for protection from catastrophes. However, this progress had not yet resulted in her facing her fear of driving. First, I had her list her motivators and de-motivators for facing her fear of driving. She could not expect her friends to drive her to work forever, and she liked and needed her job. Not driving also greatly limited her social life and almost everything else. Because we had already spent time rebuilding her faith, her fears or de-motivators had already diminished to some extent. Consequently, she was ready to face her fear of driving. In accordance with the process of systematic desensitization, I taught her relaxation techniques and had her develop a hierarchy of her fears from the least to the greatest. Her greatest fear was driving in heavy traffic in bad weather or near the edge of high cliffs. We began having her imagine just going out into the garage and looking at her car. If she felt anxiety, she was to rehearse what the Bible said about protection and work on relaxing. When she was able to successfully accomplish facing a certain level of fear in her mind, I gave the assignment to actually do it the next week. If she became anxious, she was to confess God's word and relax. In this way, we worked through the hierarchy of fears until she was able to drive around the block, then on back streets, then on the freeway with little traffic, and finally at rush hour. In her mind, she was finally able to face even the most dangerous situation. If she became anxious, she was encouraged to pray, confess God's protection for her, and relax again until the anxiety subsided. This process took quite a number of sessions as her motivation led to action, which affected her emotions a little at a time.

9. **Determine the root cause of the difficulty and assist the client in developing and applying faith to overcome this root problem.** The root cause of this problem was the lack of security that Mary felt in life that was due primarily to her experiences growing up in a codependent family. It had also affected most of her other relationships. The underlying problem of codependency is an over-reliance on people, rather than God, to meet the client's needs. To deal with this issue, I concurrently had Mary work through a 12-Step codependency workbook and attend one of our Codependency Support Groups. I also taught her boundaries, using the model of Abigail from the Bible, and helped her act in her relationships in non-codependent ways. She was finally able to visit her parents without relapsing into her old ways of acting and even confront her codependent siblings when they crossed her boundaries. The process of overcoming her fear of driving took several months, but her recovery from codependency is still continuing. (For more information on dealing with deeply rooted problems see *Faith Therapy*. For more on the topic of Codependency, see my book *Transformation!*)

10. **Release the client again to the care of Holy Spirit to continue orchestrating this growth process of salvation in his life.** Today, Mary has no problem driving in any conditions, feels much more secure in life and has almost completely recovered from her codependency. Of course, she still has to be careful when returning home or dealing with her codependent siblings, but she has learned to not be a people pleaser and is less stressed at work. I have not seen her in counseling for over a year as she continues to work out her own salvation under the guidance of the Holy Spirit. I have confidence that God did indeed use her accident to motivate her to face her problems and get her the help that God intended through the application of biblical principles in her life.

Chapter 16

Integrating Biblical Counseling

In this final chapter, I want to address two issues of integration: 1. How does counseling, using biblical principles, fit within the entire scope of counseling from a Christian perspective? 2. How is counseling, using biblical principles, integrated into the church?

The Role of Counseling using Biblical Principles

Once we understand how to build a biblical counseling plan to resolve a particular problem, it is important to see how this plan fits within the overall framework of bringing wholeness to the entire person from a Christian perspective. As I explained in *Faith Therapy*, the process of salvation by faith is God's method for transforming us into spiritually and psychologically whole people. Satan resists this process at numerous points and in various ways. These blocks stop the process from going forward and these blockages are to be addressed by the counselor. As I have already stated, these blockages have several levels of complexity and each level of complexity requires an increasingly more sophisticated approach to counseling.

The most basic blocks to the process of salvation are lies, feelings or actions that prevent clients from accepting and acting on God's truth for their lives. The process for addressing these simple blockages has been called biblical counseling. Either we see it as God does, build biblical hope, put off the wrong behavior and put on the new behavior, and practice the new behavior (The Biblical Counseling Foundation, 1998), or we identify and confront the sin, repent, and replace it with the truth (Adams, 1973).

The second category is that of moderately complex problems that block the client at a number of points in the process of salvation and is complicated by the interactions of the members of the heart. This is the realm of the biblical principles that help us understand how the entire person functions. Because of these more complex interactions, these blockages are not easily overcome unless all the affected parts of the heart are addressed. Except where biblical models are available to address the specific problem, a counseling plan developed from a number of biblical principles is required. This area has been the main focus of this book.

Some problems are the direct results of need deficits within the individual. This third category I call deeply rooted problems. The solution to these types of problems has been addressed in depth in my book *Faith Therapy*.

The fourth category of problems is complex ones. These pervade the entire personality and the heart of the client. Because of their complexity, they are best addressed with biblical counseling models. When models are not available, they present a significant challenge to the development of a counseling plan using biblical principles. Counseling models and a comprehensive plan for their application are presented in my book *Transformation!*

The fifth category of problems primarily requires spiritual growth. These problems occur simply because the client has not progressed far enough in his spiritual walk to have an adequate knowledge of God to move beyond the set of problems that he is encountering. For example, a person who lacks self-discipline has clearly not reached the fourth level of spiritual development called self-control. The eight steps of spiritual development are addressed in detail in my book *Revelations That Will Set You Free*.

The sixth and final category of problems is those that are caused by, or have a contributing factor resulting from a physical injury, mental chemical imbalance or disease. These problems are extremely difficult to sort out because it is hard to determine the extent of the physical problem, co-existing psychological ones and psychological problems that are the consequence of the physical malfunction. Those that support the "medical model" emphasize the physical origin of the problem, while biblical counselors emphasize the spiritual and psychological aspects. Of course, healing the physical component through faith is also a viable option for those who believe in spiritual healing for physical problems. Most of the problems in this category are very resistant to simple solutions. Sometimes psychoactive drugs are helpful and are even required to stabilize the client, so that therapy can begin to address the problem. Consequently, treatment plans are many times complex and require the integrated efforts of a number of professionals including doctors and psychiatrists. This complexity requires that the physical, psychological, and spiritual aspects of the problem be addressed in an integrated way.

Counseling with Biblical Principles in the Church

A second area of integration I wish to address is the place of counseling with biblical principles in the church. An unfortunate problem in the church today is the perception that counseling has no place in the church at all. This lack of acceptance usually is based on a feeling or past teaching that counseling is really of secular origin and that it is a substitute for preaching and teaching. Most pastors will admit that there are many problems in their congregation that they do not have the knowledge or time to handle. However, they are still resistant to referring these situations outside of the church or even to a Christian counselor, except in extreme circumstances. Unfortunately, this resistance to counseling in the church has been experienced by many of our students and it has taken years for them to finally prove themselves as valuable assets to their pastors.

Because Christian counseling using biblical principles is simply the application of the Word of God to resolve spiritual and psychological problems, this should not be the case. Pastors who fear "psycho-babble" or secular counseling methods should be more open to counseling using biblical principles. In the past, biblical counseling was of limited effectiveness simply because it relied on the simplistic methods that I listed under the principles of change. With the more robust model developed in this book based on Proverbs Chapter 3, it is my hope that we can now have both increased acceptance and improved effectiveness in Christian counseling within the church.

Too often, even in churches that believe strongly in counseling, what goes on in the church is not integrated with what goes on in the counseling center. In fact, in many cases the counseling center is seen as a separate entity. This should not be the case, since fellowship, discipleship, teaching, preaching, and small groups should all play as much of a role in the plan for recovery as biblical counsel and psychological knowledge and techniques. God has chosen salvation by faith and ministry within the church as His tools to bring psychological and spiritual wholeness to His people. (For more on this subject see *Faith Therapy*.)

Conclusion

In this book, I have attempted to provide a more comprehensive method for counseling using biblical principles. I have developed a specific systematic method for developing counseling plans from biblical principles. I have demonstrated how to integrate these plans within the overall Christian counseling process and developed counseling plans for a number of common problems. I have presented a large number of biblical principles derived directly from the Bible, provided specific counseling methods and techniques, and I have demonstrated the application of this new method in a detailed case study.

It was my intention in writing this book to fill a number of gaps that exist today in the Christian counseling arena. The first gap lies between those that call themselves biblical counselors and those that call themselves Christian counselors. Biblical counselors limit what they do in counseling, solely to Bible truth and principles. Christian counselors counsel from a Christian perspective, but integrate research, secular counseling methods that agree with the Bible, and Christian principles. The first has tended to be simplistic in their approach to counseling complex and difficult problems, while the second has sometimes tended to rely more heavily on secular methods than biblical principles. It is my hope that by providing in this book a more comprehensive method for using biblical principles, that the first can be challenged to become more effective in dealing with complex problems and the second will not be so tempted to rely heavily on secular theory and methods in order to be effective.

The second gap is between using biblical truth and biblical principles for counseling simplistic problems and the use of models as guidance for counseling more complex problems (which I developed in *Transformation!*). The problem is that we do not have, and probably will not have models for a number of very significant problems, especially the majority of those listed in DSM IV. With the comprehensive method presented in this book, I hope to eventually prepare and fully test biblical approaches for every one of these problems.

The third gap is that many of our churches still have not accepted the integration of counseling as a part of their church program. As discussed in the last chapter, I believe that it is God's will that hurting people have their needs met within the church through a combination of all of the ministries of the church, including counseling, working together in an integrated way. If counseling is not fully accepted within the church, this integration will continue to be an impossibility. It is my hope that more churches will open their doors to a type of counseling developed from and totally relying on the Bible. Christian counseling should simply be the direct application of Bible knowledge to bring healing to the whole person.

At Word of Life Counseling Center and Word of Life Institute, we are continuing to develop and to apply these concepts. I take no credit for what we are doing, because God has led me and others step-by-step, revelation by revelation, in understanding these concepts. However, I do take total responsibility for all mistakes, errors, misconceptions, and lack of insight contained in this book. We have only just begun to understand the impact of what the Lord has been trying to help us understand. As we do so, the Lord is providing greater effectiveness in our efforts to "heal the broken hearted and set the captive free." (Luke 4:18)

A Biblical Plan for Christian Counseling

1. Determine the problem.

2. Demonstrate that what the client is doing will not meet his needs and build hope that his problems can be overcome through Christ.

3. Use the biblical principles and models to help the client perceive and understand the problem from a biblical perspective.

4. Determine where the client is in the process of salvation and, if appropriate, lead him to accept Christ, be baptized, yield the control of his life to God, and help him get established in a church.

5. Help the client take responsibility for his own actions, not blame others or react to what they do, and do everything as unto God.

6. Help the client grow in his personal relationship with Christ and build faith that, with God's help, he can overcome the problem.

7. Assist the client in receiving the empowerment of the baptism of the Holy Spirit if he chooses to do so.

8. Help the client apply the biblical principles or model to overcome the identified psychological problem.

9. Determine the root cause of the difficulty and assist the client in developing and applying faith to overcome this root problem.

10. Release the client again to the care of Holy Spirit to continue orchestrating this growth process of salvation in his life.

Word of Life Counseling Center
Client Intake Form

Name of Client _____Social Security Number _____Date of Birth _____

Street Address _____ City _____State _____ ZIP_____

Employer _____ Occupation _____ Annual Income _____

Single _____ Married _____Divorced _____Widowed _____Other _____Number of years _____

Family Members:

Name	*Relationship*	*Age*	*Living at home?*

Presenting Problem

_____

_____

_____

_____

Medications:

_____

Insurance Company_____ Insurance ID_____

Insurance Mental Health Telephone Number _____ Deductible _____ Co-pay _____

Previous Counseling: _____

Previous Counselor: _____ Telephone _____

I, _____, hereby grant permission for Word of Life
Counseling to consult with my psychiatrist, medical doctor, psychologist or previous counselor and to obtain
any previous medical or counseling records.

Signed this _____ day of _____ (month), _____(year). _____
(signature)

Word of Life Counseling Center
Informed Consent and Confidentiality Form

Your Rights As A Client

1. All personal information given here is confidential and will not be released to outside persons or agencies unless we have your written consent, or that of your guardian. However, as part of the agreement, the client agrees to the release of any and all counseling information (without another written release of information) for the following reasons:
   a. As required by law or when homicide, suicide, child or elder abuse is involved, or in cases necessitated by a medical emergency.
   b. For consultation with other members of the counseling or pastoral staff (including wives), the client's pastor or guardian, or for counseling supervision purposes.
2. You will not be photographed, videotaped, or otherwise identified in any media form without your consent.
3. No research information identifying you will be released from this facility without your consent.
4. You will be informed of alternative forms of treatment should you request it.
5. You have the right to express opinions, recommendations and grievances to staff without fear of prejudice or penalty.
6. You will not be denied treatment based on race, religion, political affiliation, or gender.
7. You have the right to participate in the formulation of your treatment.
8. Bills and charges will be explained to you upon your request.
9. We respect your right to make your decisions but will attempt to help you understand the consequences of those decisions.
10. You have a right to terminate counseling at any time without additional charges unless a specific contract requiring a specific number of sessions has been agreed upon.
11. Clients may request referral to another counselor or agency if they believe that the therapeutic relationship is no longer effective.
12. Your counseling, insurance, or medical records will not be transmitted in electronic form without your specific consent.
13. Your counselor is not a medical doctor and therefore is not authorized to prescribe medication or prescription drugs.
14. Your counselor has the following degrees and/or licenses/certifications: _____

Your Responsibilities As A Client

1. Deal realistically with your problem(s).
2. Accept that there will be ups and downs in treatment.
3. Discuss any important life decisions with your therapist before a decision is made.
4. Be honest and open in your communications.
5. Respect the confidentiality of other clients with whom you come in contact.
6. Be responsible for your own growth, which means work.

I Have Read and Acknowledge My Client Rights and Responsibilities

Signed this _____ day of _____ (month), _____(year). _____
                                                                                        (signature)

Client Problem Assessment

Client Name _____ Counselor Name _____ Phone _____ Date _____

Presenting Problem_____

_____

_____

_____

Issues involved:

[ ]   Marital/relationship conflict _____

[ ]   Parenting _____

[ ]   Blended family/family issues/unforgiveness _____

[ ]   Anger problems/verbal abuse _____

[ ]   Domestic violence Worst incident? _____ How long? _____

[ ]   Drug/alcohol abuse/addictions Types? _____ How long? _____ Dependent? _____

[ ]   Pornography/sexual addiction? _____

[ ]   Rape/incest/homosexuality? _____

[ ]   Sexual problems Affairs? _____ How often do they have sex? _____

[ ]   Other abuse/trauma/sicknesses/abortions? _____

[ ]   Codependency How severe? _____ Subtype? _____

[ ]   Divorce/separation? _____ When separated? _____

[ ]   Loss/grief _____

[ ]   Depression _____ Bi-polar? _____ Suicidal? _____ Plan? _____

[ ]   Emotional problems? _____ Low Self-worth? _____ Driven? _____ Pride? _____

[ ]   Financial problems? _____

[ ]   Other _____

Relationship analysis

Married/Divorced/Cohabitation? _____ How long? _____ #Marriages ____ # Children _____

                                         Client   Spouse

Perceived Best Interest in Mind?

Perceived Loved and Appreciated?

Rate Marriage 1-10

Rate Sex Life 1-10

Family of origin

Client: Child # _____ out of _____ children in the family _____ Adopted? _____ Role in the family _____

Describe father _____ Abuse/controller? _____ Child met expectations? _____

Describe mother _____ Abuse/controller? _____ Child met expectations? _____

Divorced? _____ At what age?_____ Who did you live with? _____

Describe step father/mother _____ Abuse/controller? _____ Child met expectations? _____

Describe family life _____

School performance _____ Sports? _____ Parental support _____

Describe relationships _____

Mental/physical health problems in family? _____ Suicide attempts? _____

Spouse: Child # _____ out of _____ children in the family _____ Adopted? _____ Role in the family _____

Describe father _____ Abuse/controller? _____ Child met expectations? _____

Describe mother _____ Abuse/controller? _____ Child met expectations? _____

Divorced?_____ At what age?_____ Who did you live with?_____

Describe step father/mother _____ Abuse/controller? _____ Child met expectations? _____

Describe family life_____

School performance _____ Sports? _____ Parental support _____

Describe relationships_____

Mental/physical health problems in family? _____ Suicide attempts? _____

Spiritual assessment: Client

[ ] Saved? How long? _____ Baptized?_____ Bible knowledge? _____ Spiritual disciplines?_____

[ ] Attends church? _____ What church?_____ How involved? _____ Bible study? _____

[ ] Involvement in other religion/occult/new age? _____ Type/extent? _____

Spiritual assessment: Spouse

[ ] Saved? How long? _____ Baptized?_____ Bible knowledge? _____ Spiritual disciplines?_____

[ ] Attends church? _____ What church?_____ How involved? _____ Bible study? _____

[ ] Involvement in other religion/occult/new age? _____ Type/extent? _____

Attachment analysis: Client

[ ] Secure style—Worthy and capable of receiving love and can trust others to give love.

[ ] Avoidant style—Worthy and capable of receiving love but can not trust others to give love.

[ ] Ambivalent style—Must perform to be loved but can trust others to give love.

[ ] Disorganized style—Not worthy of receiving love and can not trust others to give love.

Attachment analysis: Spouse

[ ] Secure style—Worthy and capable of receiving love and can trust others to give love.

[ ] Avoidant style—Worthy and capable of receiving love but can not trust others to give love.

[ ] Ambivalent style—Must perform to be loved but can trust others to give love.

[ ] Disorganized style—Not worthy of receiving love and can not trust others to give love.

Counselor's evaluation of the problem _____
_____
_____
_____

Recommended treatment plan:

Issues to be addressed	*Method*	*Goal*
1.		
2.		
3.		
4.		
5.		
6.		
7.		
8.		
9.		

Quick Form for Building a Counseling Plan from Biblical Principles

1. **What is the problem?**

    _____

    _____

    _____

2. **What is the primary component affected by the problem?** Place a star on the primary component.

Will	Spirit	Mind	Perceptions	Needs	Motivation	Actions	Experience	Emotions

3. **What other members or functions of the heart have been affected by it or affect it?** Place an X on the remainder of the blocks above that are involved in the problem.

4. **Where is the root cause or psychological need or needs underlying the problem?** Place an X on the appropriate boxes below.

    | Worth | | Significance | | Security | | Love |

5. **Determine the order of the components that are creating the problem.** Fill in the train cars below in the order that you hypothesize is the sequence that is creating the problem.

6. **Couple the cars to build the train to resolve this problem.** Reconstruct the train using only the cars selected. Place the psychological need from #4 above in the need car.

7. **Which principles apply in each component?** Under each component list the principles by letter. Chapter numbers represent the principles of change (1) and faith (3).

    Principles

    ___ ___ ___ ___ ___ ___ ___ ___
    ___ ___ ___ ___ ___ ___ ___ ___
    ___ ___ ___ ___ ___ ___ ___ ___
    ___ ___ ___ ___ ___ ___ ___ ___

    Methods

    ___ ___ ___ ___ ___ ___ ___ ___
    ___ ___ ___ ___ ___ ___ ___ ___
    ___ ___ ___ ___ ___ ___ ___ ___
    ___ ___ ___ ___ ___ ___ ___ ___

8. **What methods and techniques are needed?** Under each component below the principles, list the number of the method or technique to be applied. See the index of methods in the appendix.

9. **What is the faith component? How is faith applied in this counseling plan?** List faith principles and methods on the appropriate lines if applicable under each component. Chapter numbers represent the principles of change (1) and faith (3). (For more on the principles of faith see *Faith Therapy*.)

10. **Load the train cars.** Determine the order and importance of each technique as they are to be applied to that component by reordering the principles and techniques.

11. **What are the goals and how will they be measured?**

	Goal	*How Measured?*
1.		
2.		
3.		

12. **Define the route of the train.** By placing flow diagram arrows on the train diagram above indicate any flow between the cars

13. **What is the plan to intervene in the whole person?** List the plan according to the order of steps. Both principles and methods may be used as interventions.

Step	Component	Principle	Intervention
1.			
2.			
3.			
4.			
5.			
6.			
7			
8			
9.			
10.			
11.			
12.			
13.			
14.			
15.			
16.			

14. **How does this plan fit into The Biblical Plan for Christian Counseling?**

15. **Schedule the train.**

[ ] **Individual weekly sessions**   _____

[ ] **Support Groups**   _____   _____   _____   _____

[ ] **Books/workbooks**   _____   _____   _____   _____

INDEX OF COUNSELING METHODS AND TECHNIQUES

This index provides a quick reference listing of the Counseling Methods and Techniques provided in this book. The page numbers listed are the page of the beginning of the description of the particular methods and techniques in that chapter. Each method or technique is briefly described so that it can be identified. The numbers and letters provide for identifying each method or technique on the Quick Form for Building a Counseling Plan for Biblical Principles. They are identical to those used to identify each method or technique when it was more fully described in each chapter.

PART I. Principles of Biblical Change

PART II. Biblical Principles for Application

4. Experiencing the love of God casts out all fear.
5. We can overcome anxiety by praising God in all situations.
6. Anxiety disorders are generalized fears.
7. Panic attacks result from a cycle of fear.
8. Phobias are irrational excessive fears.
9. Post Traumatic Stress Disorder is a traumatic fear response.
10. Obsessions are an attempt to feel in control.
11. Compulsions are an attempt to compensate for feeling out of control.

1. We can control the amount of anger by how we perceive the situation.
2. The first step in anger management is to realize that we are angry.
3. We need to take an "anger break" in order to have time to control our anger.
4. We need to de-anger or talk ourselves down from high levels of anger.
5. We need to use our anger to resolve the situation, give it to God or drop it.
6. We should avoid the wrong uses of anger.
7. We should not take offenses personally.
8. We can use an anger diagram to teach anger management.

10. Principles of Action

1. We are to do everything as unto God.
2. We must break the dance of anger and conflict.

1. We need to be careful not to confess doubt and unbelief.
2. We are to edify one-another in everything we do.
3. In our confession, we must not contradict God's positive Word for us.

1. We must learn to really listen.
2. We must learn how the other gender communicates.
3. We are responsible for what we say even when provoked.
4. We must put off all wrong communication including cussing and swearing.
5. We can teach Speaker-listener Technique to help couples communicate.

1. We must do what is right no matter what others do.
2. We need to always respond to offenses with good instead of evil.
3. Passive resistance is usually God's method for overcoming evil.

1. We judge others because we feel inferior to or threatened by them.
2. We will be judged by the way we judge others.
3. Do not condemn or judge others but discern actions and sins.
4. We are to judge our own actions but not condemn ourselves.
5. Accountability can help us control our actions.
6. Confrontation should be used in the context of a caring relationship.

1. To be just and fair requires that everything be resolved by win-win solutions.
2. True justice or righteousness comes only through God.
3. We need to realize that sanctification takes time.

References

Adams, Jay (1973). <u>The Christian Counselor's Manual</u>. Zondervan Publishing, Grand Rapids, Michigan.

American Psychological Association (1994). <u>Diagnostic and Statistical Manual of Mental Disorders</u> (4th ed.). Washington D.C.

Anderson, Neil T. (2000). <u>Victory Over Darkness</u>. Regal Books, Ventura, California.

Barlet, Donald L. and Steele, James B. (1997). <u>Howard Hughes: His Life and Madness</u>. W. W. Norton & Co., Inc., New York.

Biblical Counseling Foundation (1998). <u>Biblical Principles for Discipleship/Counseling</u>. Biblical Counseling Foundation, Palm Desert, California.

Blackaby, Henry T., and King, Claude V. (1990). <u>Experiencing God: Knowing and Doing the Will of God.</u> Lifeway Press, Nashville, Tennessee.

Bounds, E. M. (1997). <u>E. M. Bounds on Prayer</u>. Whitaker House, New Kensington, Pennsylvania.

Clinton, Tim, and Sibcy, Gary (2002). <u>Attachments.</u> Integrity Publishers, Brentwood, Tennessee.

Coppola, Francio Ford (1972). <u>The Godfather</u>. Paramount Pictures, Hollywood, California.

Eggerichs, Emerson (2004). <u>Love & Respect</u>. Integrity Publishers, Nashville, Tennessee.

Elliott, Elisabeth (1986). <u>Through Gates of Splendor</u>. Tyndale House Publishers, Wheaton, Illinois.

Gray, John (1992). <u>Men are from Mars and Women are from Venus</u>. HarperCollins, New York.

Harley, Willard F., Jr. (2001). <u>His Needs, Her Needs</u>. Revell Publishers, Grand Rapids, Michigan

Harley, Willard F., Jr. (2002). <u>Love Busters</u>. Revell Publishers, Grand Rapids, Michigan.

Hart, Archibald, and Morris, Sharon Hart (2003). <u>Safe Haven Marriage</u>. W Publishing Company, Nashville, Tennessee.

Kenyon, E. W. (1969). <u>The Blood Covenant</u>. Kenyon's Gospel Publishing Society. Lynwood, Washington.

Landau, Sidney I (1997). <u>The New International Webster's Concise Dictionary of the English Language</u>. Trident Press International, Naples, Florida

Lemmel, Helen H. (1922). "Turn Your Eyes Upon Jesus." Song.

Markman, Howard, Stanley, Scott, and Blumberg, Susan (1994). <u>Fighting for Your Marriage</u>. Jossey-Bass, San Francisco, California.

McDowell, Josh (1972). <u>Evidence That Demands A Verdict Vol I.</u> Campus Crusade for Christ, Inc., U.S.A.

McDowell, Josh (1975). <u>Evidence That Demands A Verdict Vol II.</u> Campus Crusade for Christ, Inc., U.S.A.

McGee, Robert S., Springle, Pat, and Joiner, Susan (1990). <u>Overcoming Chemical Dependency.</u> RAPHA Publishing/Word, Inc., Houston and Dallas, Texas.

McGee, Robert S. (1990). <u>The Search for Significance</u>. Rapha Publishing, Houston, Texas.

Morris, Charles G. (1973). <u>Psychology, An Introduction</u>. Prentice Hall, Upper Saddle River, New Jersey.

Muller, George (1984). <u>The Autobiography of George Muller</u>. Whitaker House, New Kensington, Pennsylvania

Mumford, Bob (1971). <u>Take Another Look At Guidance</u>. Logos International. Plainfield, New Jersey.

Mumford, Bob (undated). "The Nature and Spirit of Obedience." Audio tape series.

Nee Watchman (1957). <u>Sit, Walk, Stand</u>. Richard Clay (The Chaucer Press), Ltd, Bungay, Suffolk, Great Britain.

Nee, Watchman (1972). <u>Spiritual Authority</u>. Christian Fellowship Publishers, Inc., New York.

Nee, Watchman (1968). <u>The Spiritual Man.</u>Vol. 1-3. Christian Fellowship Publishers, Inc., New York.

Pierce, Larry (1996). <u>The Online Bible for Windows</u>. Larry Pierce, Winterbourne, Ontario.

Reiner, Troy D. (2005). <u>Faith Therapy. Using Faith to Resolve Deeply Rooted Problems</u>. Pleasant Word, Enumclaw, Washington.

Reiner, Troy D. (2005). <u>Revelations that Set You Free. The Biblical Roadmap for Psychological And Spiritual Growth</u>. Pleasant Word, Enumclaw, Washington.

Reiner, Troy D. (2005). <u>Transformation! How Simple Bible Stories Provide In-depth Answers for Life's Most Difficult Problems.</u> Pleasant Word, Enumclaw, Washington.

Ries, Raul and Gilbert, Lela (1986). "Fury to Freedom." Harvest House Publishers, Eugene, Oregon.

Slemming, C. W. (1974). <u>Made According to Pattern.</u> Christian Literature Crusade, Fort Washington, Pennsylvania.

Smalley, Gary (1988). <u>Hidden Keys of a Loving Lasting Marriage</u>. Zondervan Publishing, Grand Rapids, Michigan.

Smith, Ed M. (1996). <u>Beyond Tolerable Recovery.</u> Family Care Ministers, Campbellsville, Kentucky.

Smith, Hannah Whithall (1983). <u>The Christian's Secret of a Happy Life</u>. Whitaker House, New Kensington Pennsylvania.

Springle, Pat (1993). <u>Conquering Codependency.</u> Lifeway Press, Nashville, Tennessee.

Tan, Paul Lee (1979). <u>Encyclopedia of 7,700 Illustrations</u>. Assurance Publishers, Rockville, Maryland.

Vine, W. E. (1985). <u>An Expository Dictionary of Biblical Words.</u> Thomas Nelson Publishers, Nashville, Tennessee.

CPSIA information can be obtained
at www.ICGtesting.com
Printed in the USA
BVHW061220190221
600367BV00011B/789